REUNION

Written & Colored by

Otis Frampton

Illustrated by

Sergio Quijada

A Viper Comics Trade Paperback Original

Published by Viper Comics
9400 N. MacArthur Blvd., Suite 124-215
Irving, TX 75063
USA

First edition: May 2007
ISBN10: 0-9777883-9-3
ISBN13: 978-0-9777883-9-2

Written and colored by Otis Frampton
Illustrated by Sergio Quijada
Lettering and chapter illustrations by Otis Frampton

™

Jessie Garza president & publisher
Jim Resnowski editor-in-chief & creative director
Jason M. Burns assistant publisher

VIPER COMICS   WWW.VIPERCOMICS.COM | EST. 2001

The Story So Far...

ODDLY NORMAL IS A 10-YEAR OLD GIRL WITH THE MOST UNFORTUNATE NAME AND THE LUCK TO GO WITH IT.

THE PRODUCT OF A UNIQUE MIXED-MARRIAGE (HER MOTHER IS A WITCH AND HER FATHER IS HUMAN), ODDLY HAS GROWN UP BETWEEN CULTURES AND SHE IS THE PROVERBIAL OUTSIDER.

ON HER 10TH BIRTHDAY, HER PARENTS MYSTERIOUSLY DISAPPEARED AND SHE WAS LEFT IN THE CARE OF HER GREAT AUNT, A CITIZEN OF A FANTASTICAL PLACE CALLED "FIGNATION."

DURING HER TIME IN FIGNATION, ODDLY HAS FINALLY MADE SOME FRIENDS AS WELL AS SOME NEW ENEMIES. SHE HAS ALSO COME INTO POSSESSION OF A CREATURE NAMED "OOPIE." THIS ARTIFICIAL LIFE-FORM HAS NOT ONLY BECOME ODDLY'S PET, BUT HER CONSTANT COMPANION . . .

Chapter 1

Hero Worship

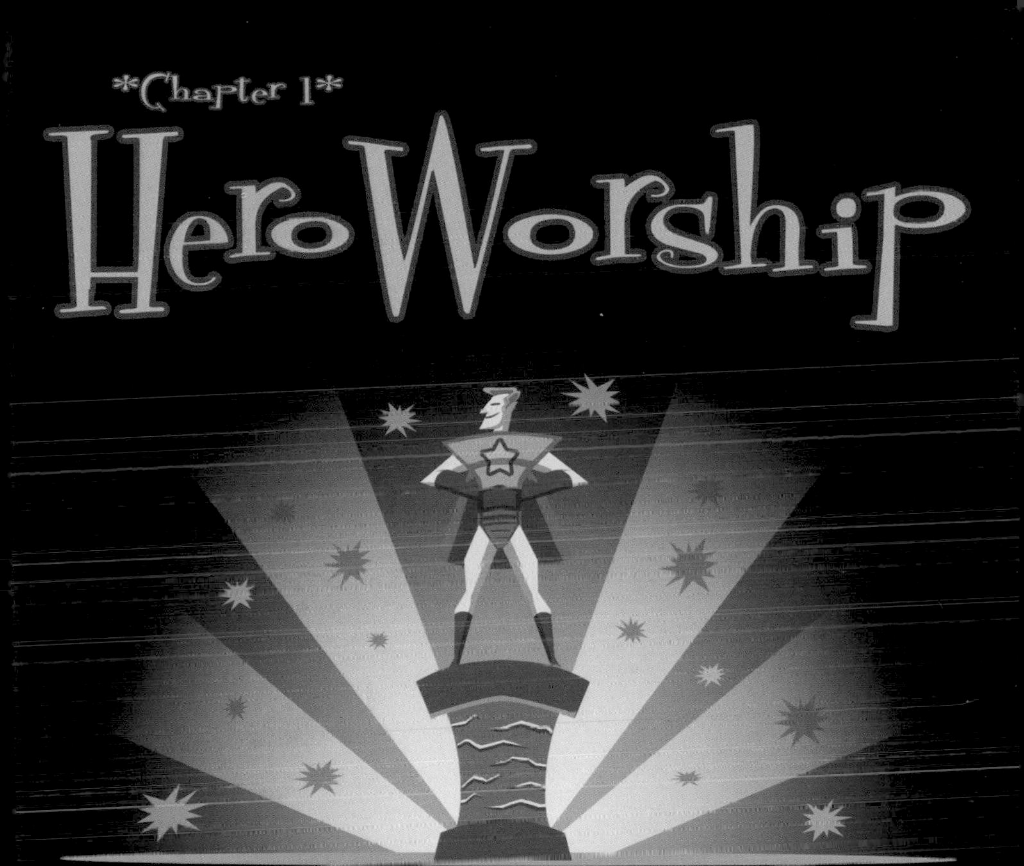

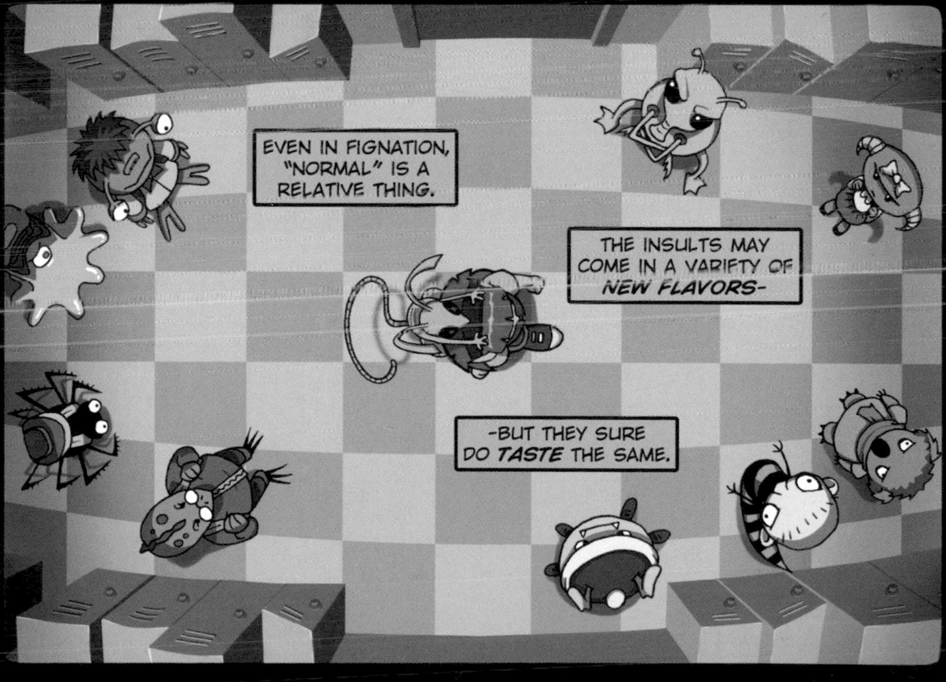
EVEN IN FIGNATION, "NORMAL" IS A RELATIVE THING.
THE INSULTS MAY COME IN A VARIFTY OF NEW FLAVORS-
-BUT THEY SURE DO TASTE THE SAME.

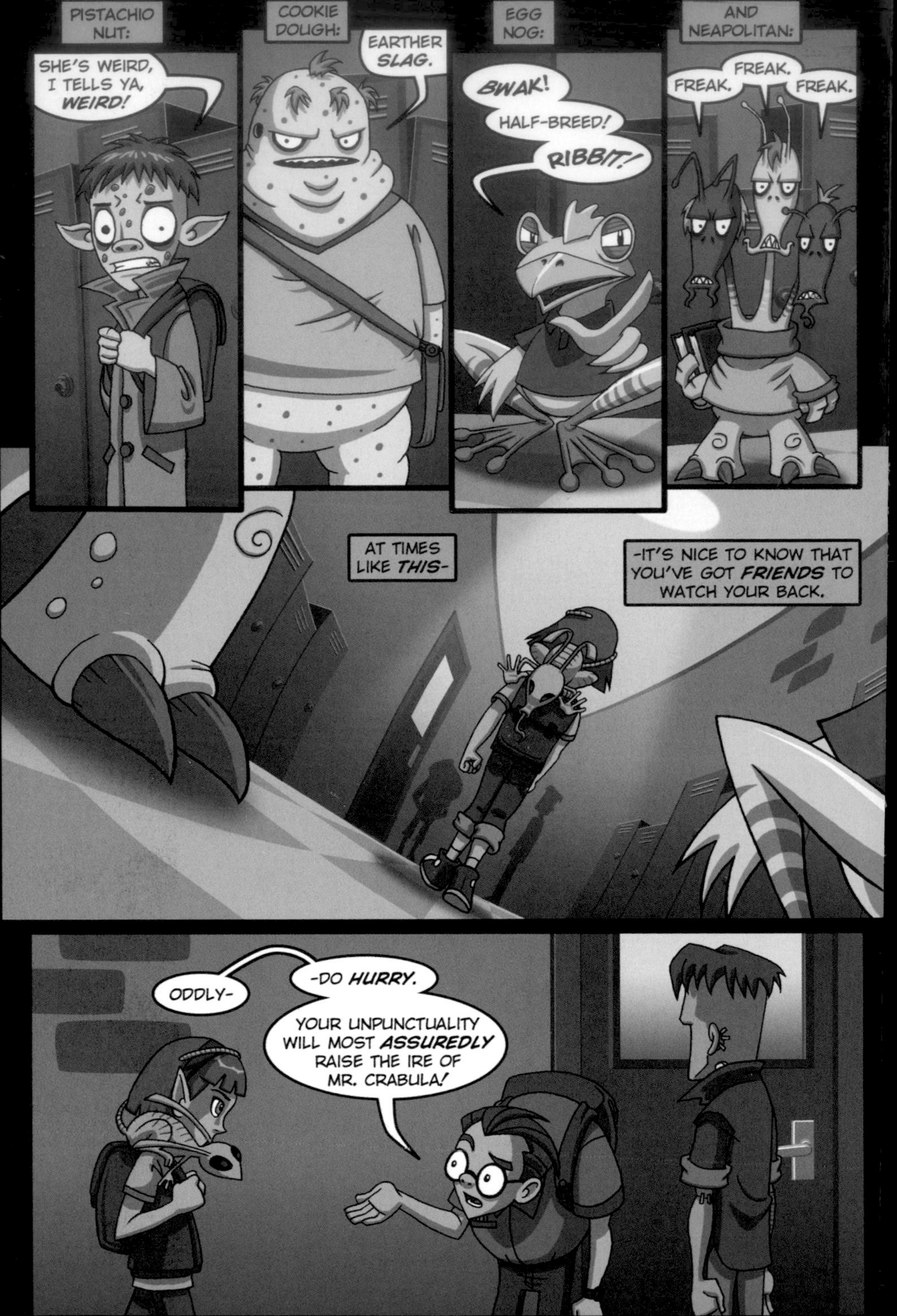
PISTACHIO NUT:
SHE'S WEIRD, I TELLS YA, WEIRD!
COOKIE DOUGH:
EARTHER SLAG.
EGG NOG:
BWAK!
HALF-BREED!
RIBBIT!
AND NEAPOLITAN:
FREAK.
FREAK.
FREAK.
AT TIMES LIKE THIS-
-IT'S NICE TO KNOW THAT YOU'VE GOT FRIENDS TO WATCH YOUR BACK.
ODDLY-
-DO HURRY.
YOUR UNPUNCTUALITY WILL MOST ASSUREDLY RAISE THE IRE OF MR. CRABULA!

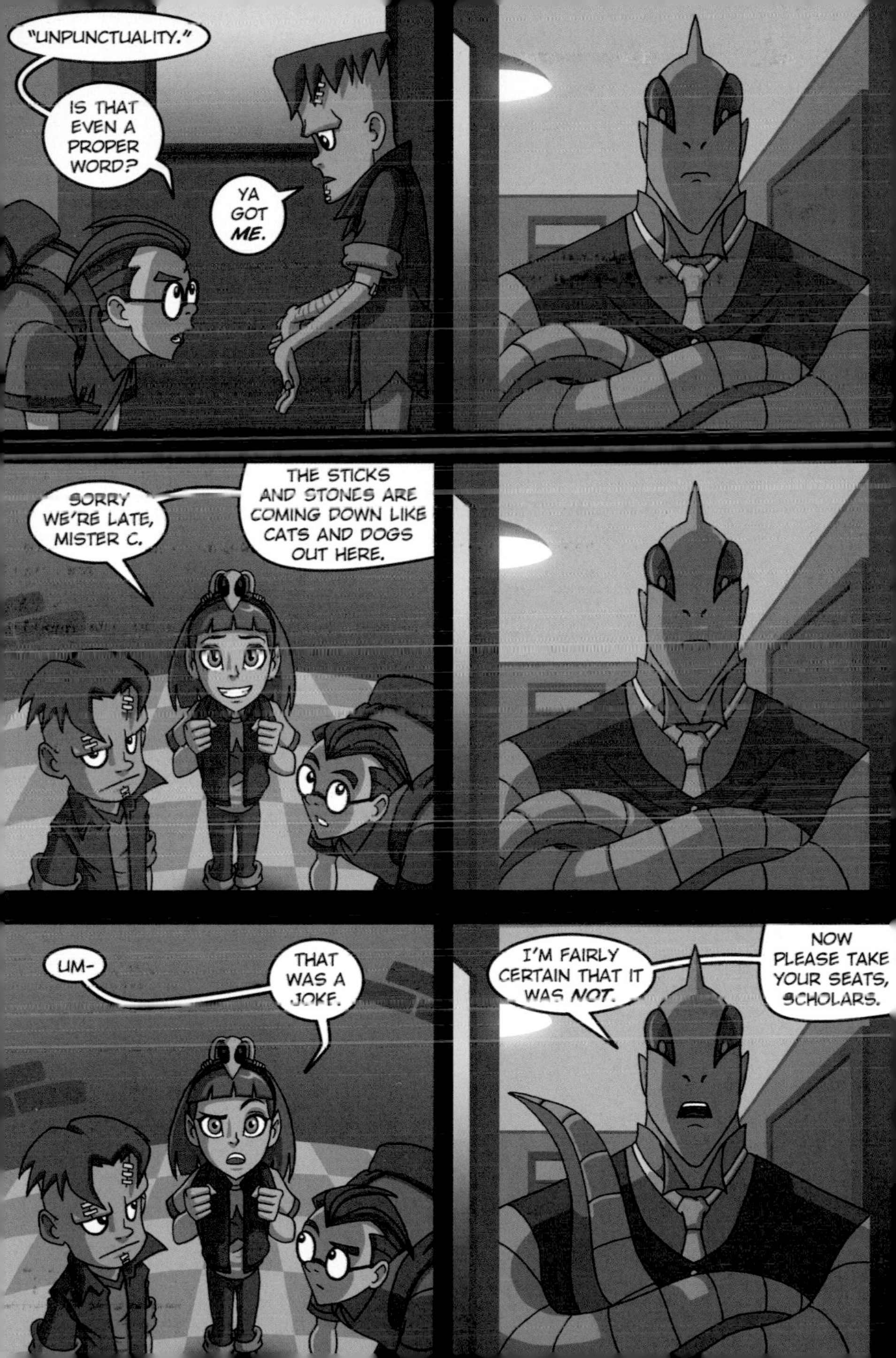
"UNPUNCTUALITY."
IS THAT EVEN A PROPER WORD?
YA GOT ME.
SORRY WE'RE LATE, MISTER C.
THE STICKS AND STONES ARE COMING DOWN LIKE CATS AND DOGS OUT HERE.
UM-
THAT WAS A JOKE.
I'M FAIRLY CERTAIN THAT IT WAS NOT.
NOW PLEASE TAKE YOUR SEATS, SCHOLARS.

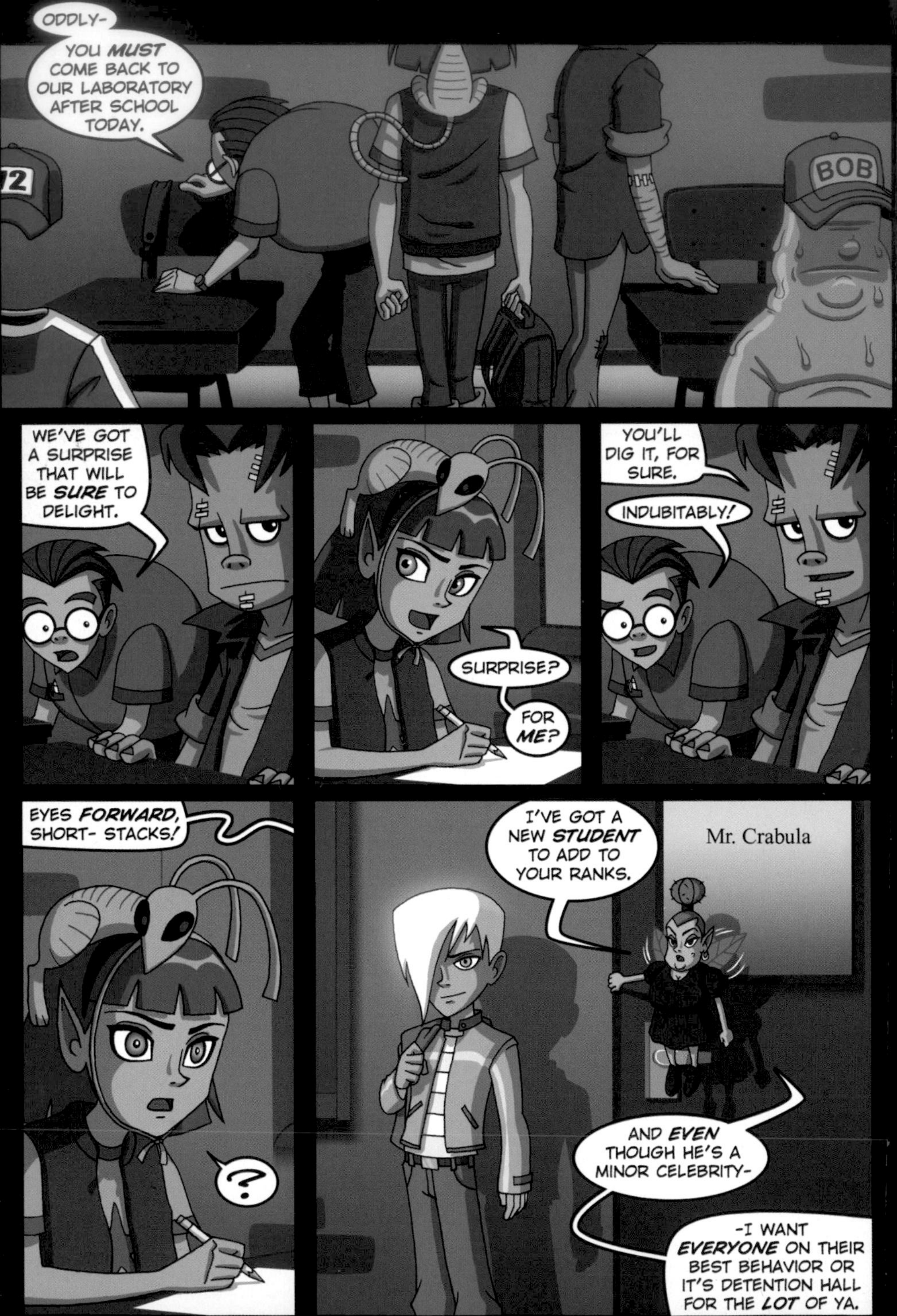
ODDLY-
YOU MUST COME BACK TO OUR LABORATORY AFTER SCHOOL TODAY.
72
BOB
WE'VE GOT A SURPRISE THAT WILL BE SURE TO DELIGHT.
SURPRISE?
FOR ME?
YOU'LL DIG IT, FOR SURE.
INDUBITABLY!
EYES FORWARD, SHORT- STACKS!
?
I'VE GOT A NEW STUDENT TO ADD TO YOUR RANKS.
Mr. Crabula
AND EVEN THOUGH HE'S A MINOR CELEBRITY-
-I WANT EVERYONE ON THEIR BEST BEHAVIOR OR IT'S DETENTION HALL FOR THE LOT OF YA.

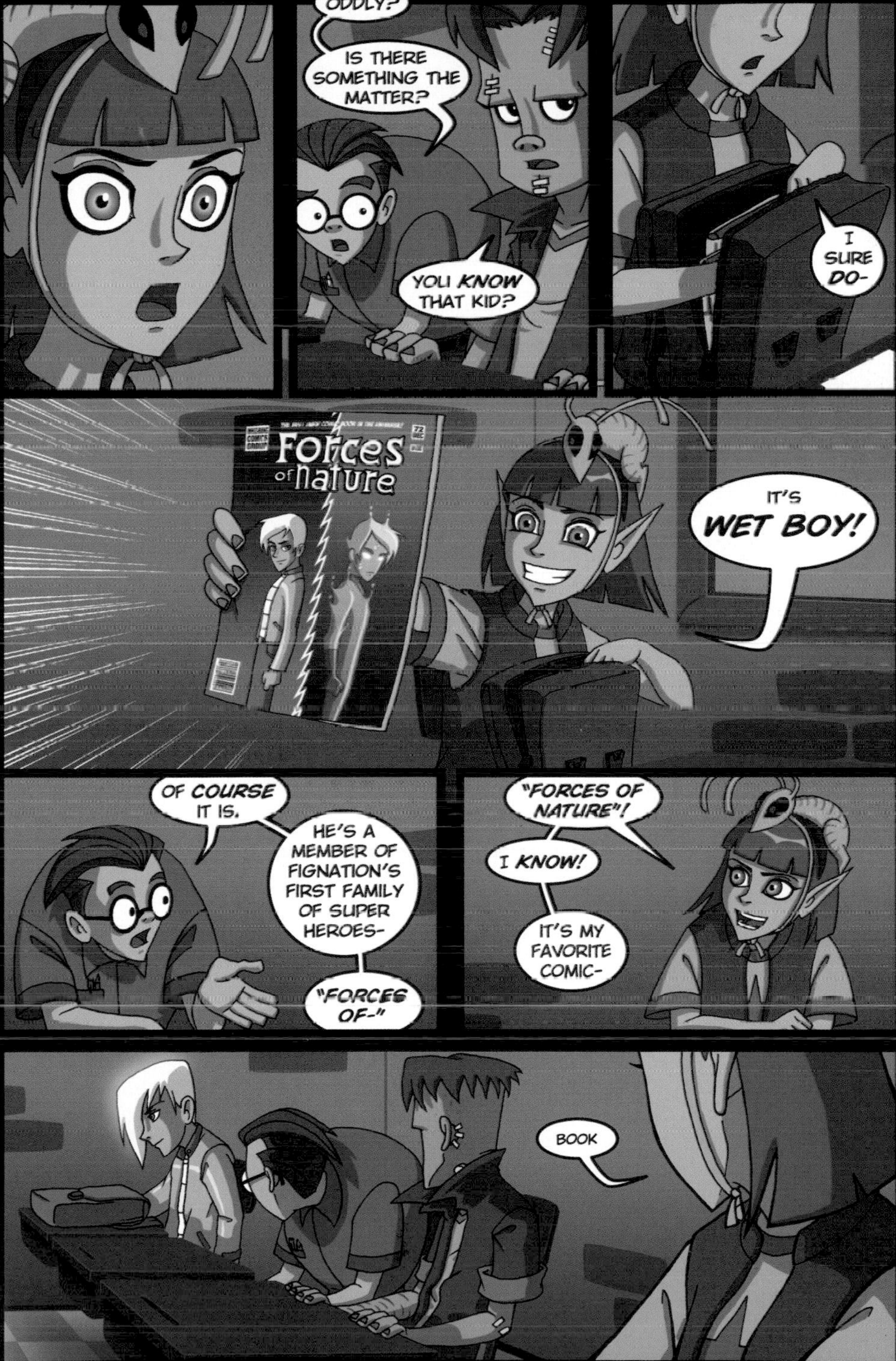
ODDLY?
IS THERE SOMETHING THE MATTER?
YOU KNOW THAT KID?
I SURE DO-
Forces of Nature
IT'S WET BOY!
OF COURSE IT IS.
HE'S A MEMBER OF FIGNATION'S FIRST FAMILY OF SUPER HEROES-
"FORCES OF-"
"FORCES OF NATURE"!
I KNOW!
IT'S MY FAVORITE COMIC-
BOOK

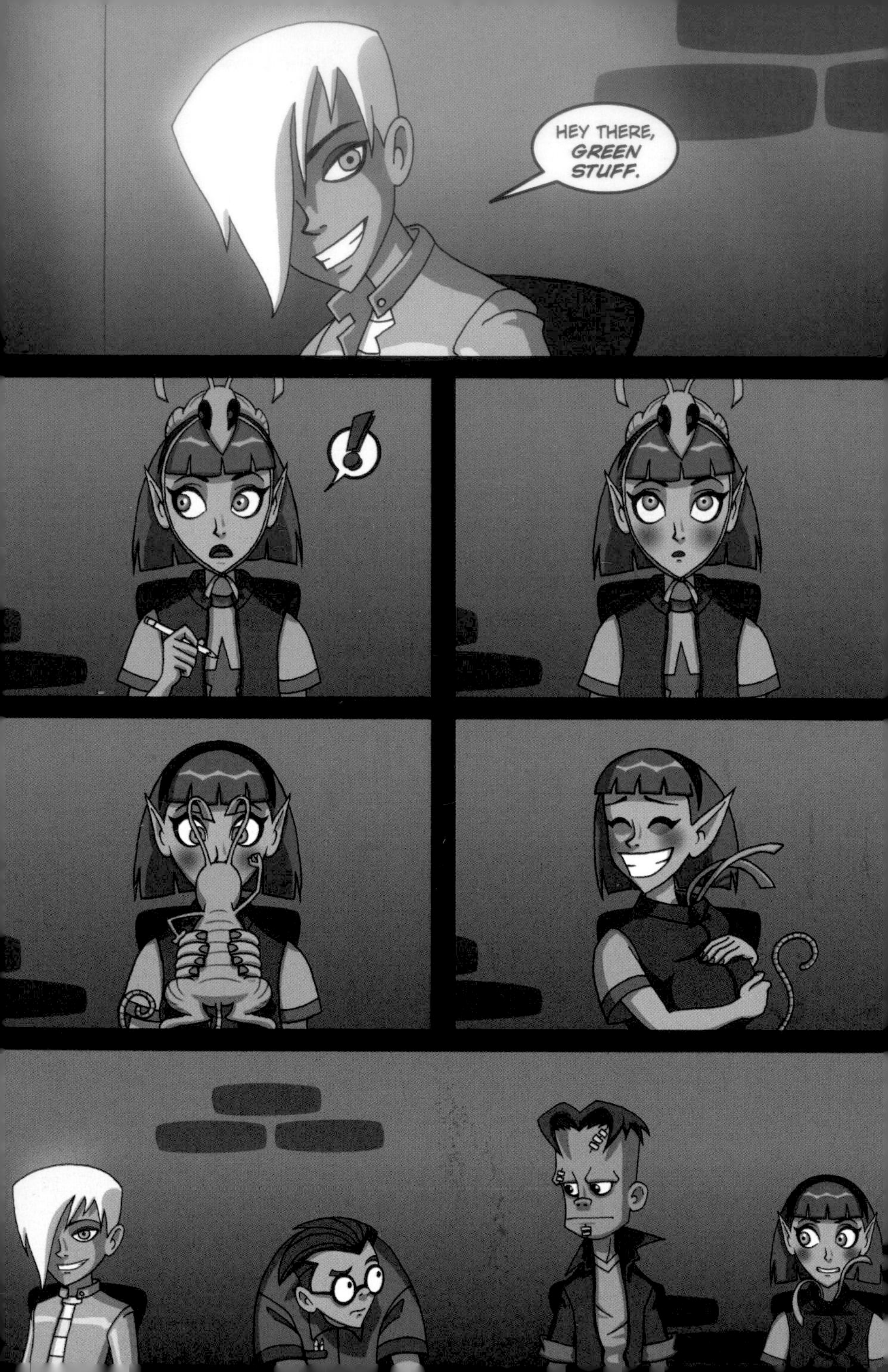
HEY THERE,
GREEN
STUFF.
!

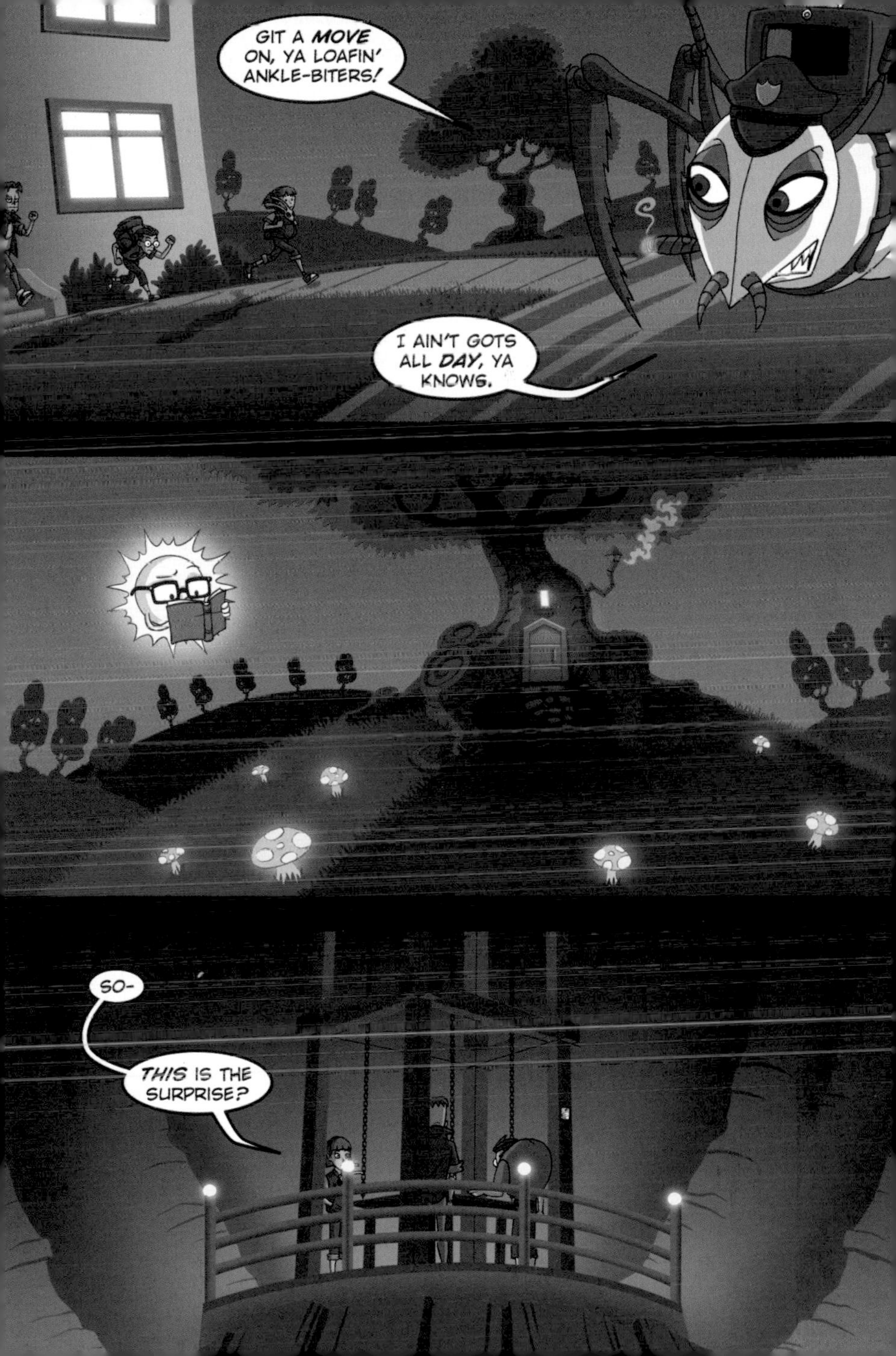
GIT A *MOVE* ON, YA LOAFIN' ANKLE-BITERS!
I AIN'T GOTS ALL *DAY*, YA KNOWS.
SO-
THIS IS THE SURPRISE?

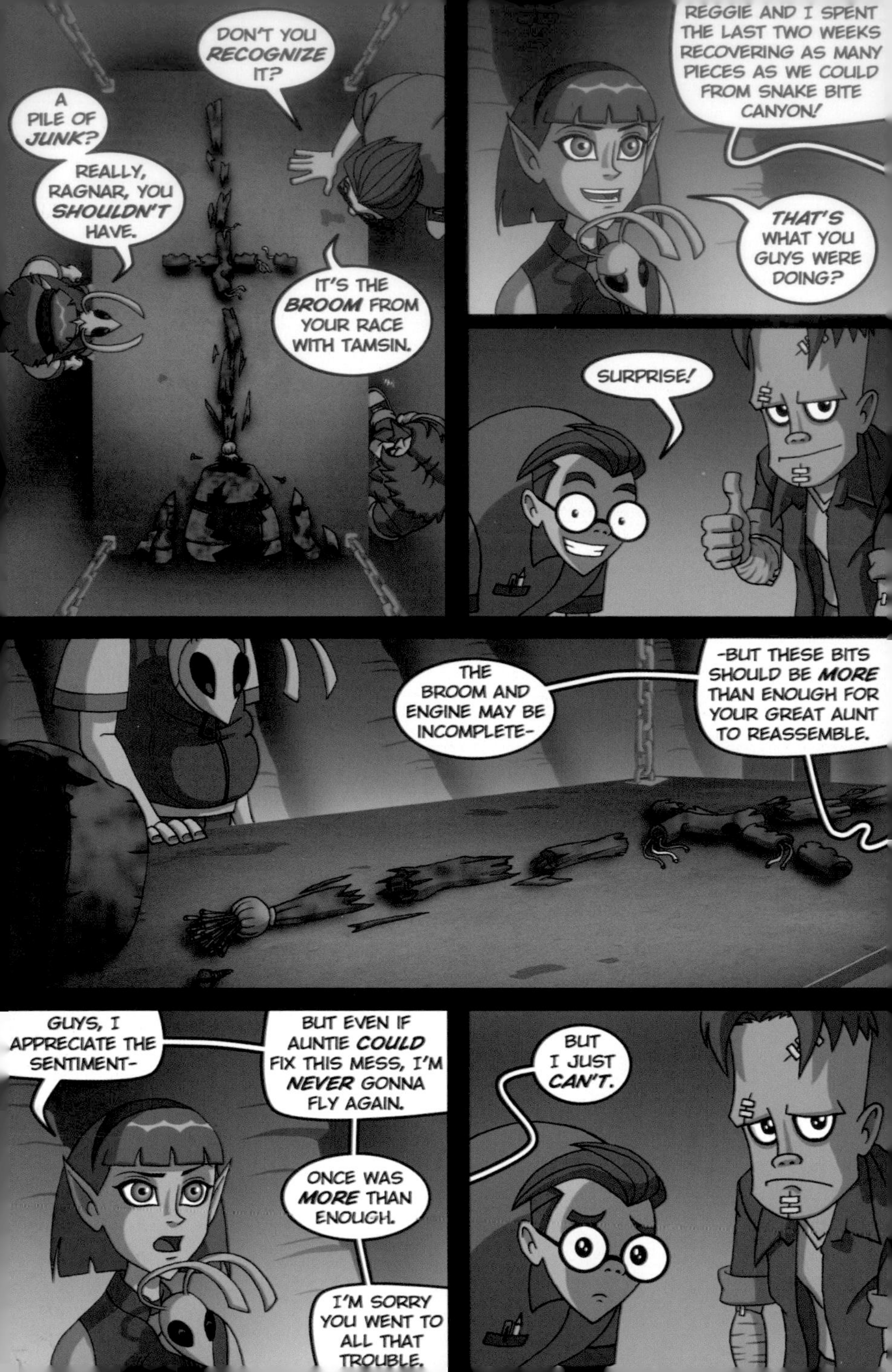
A PILE OF JUNK?
DON'T YOU RECOGNIZE IT?
REALLY, RAGNAR, YOU SHOULDN'T HAVE.
IT'S THE BROOM FROM YOUR RACE WITH TAMSIN.
REGGIE AND I SPENT THE LAST TWO WEEKS RECOVERING AS MANY PIECES AS WE COULD FROM SNAKE BITE CANYON!
THAT'S WHAT YOU GUYS WERE DOING?
SURPRISE!
THE BROOM AND ENGINE MAY BE INCOMPLETE-
-BUT THESE BITS SHOULD BE MORE THAN ENOUGH FOR YOUR GREAT AUNT TO REASSEMBLE.
GUYS, I APPRECIATE THE SENTIMENT-
BUT EVEN IF AUNTIE COULD FIX THIS MESS, I'M NEVER GONNA FLY AGAIN.
ONCE WAS MORE THAN ENOUGH.
I'M SORRY YOU WENT TO ALL THAT TROUBLE.
BUT I JUST CAN'T.

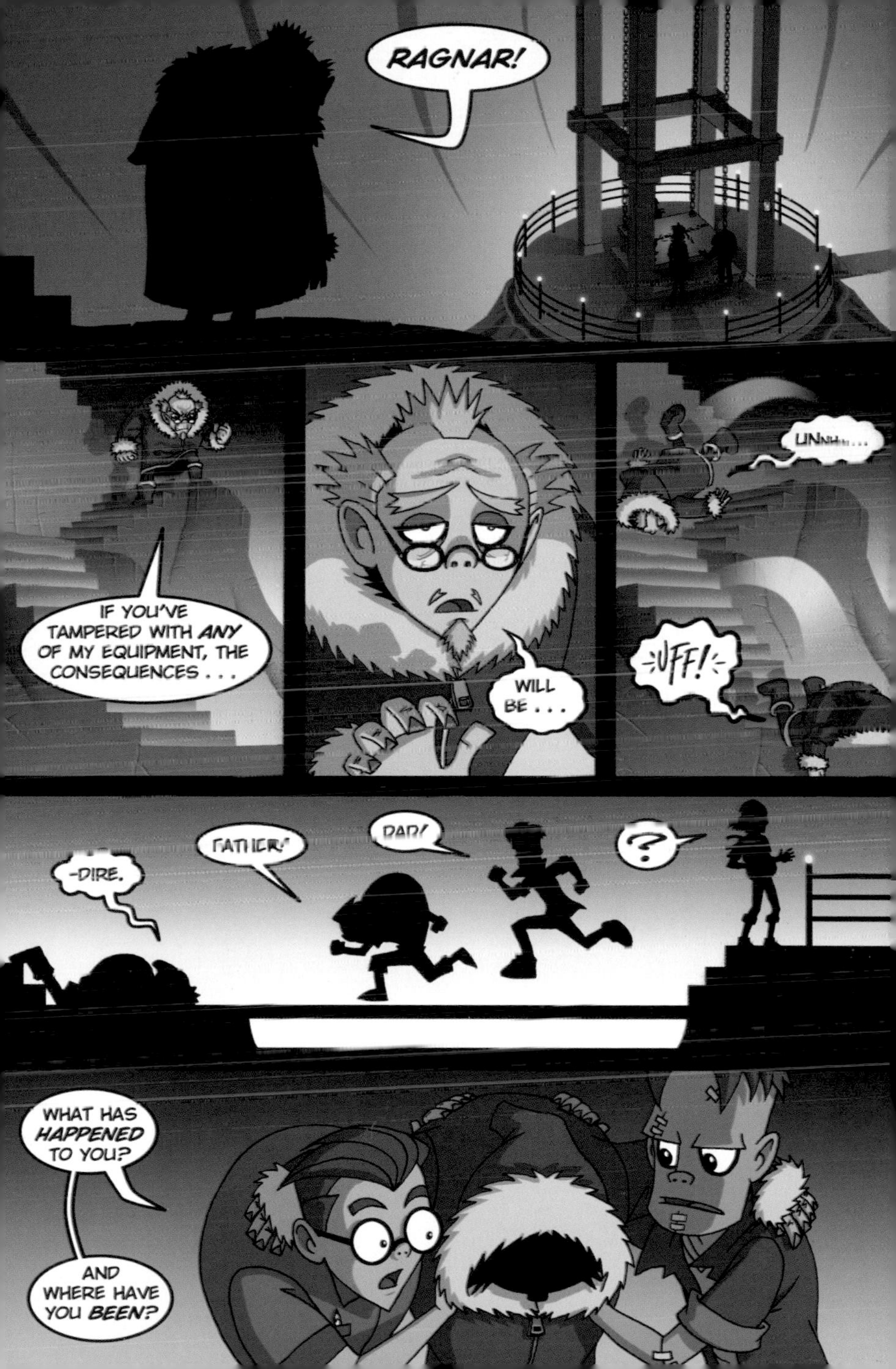
RAGNAR!
IF YOU'VE TAMPERED WITH ANY OF MY EQUIPMENT, THE CONSEQUENCES . . .
WILL BE . . .
UNNH....
UFF!
-DIRE.
FATHER!
DAD!
?
WHAT HAS HAPPENED TO YOU?
AND WHERE HAVE YOU BEEN?

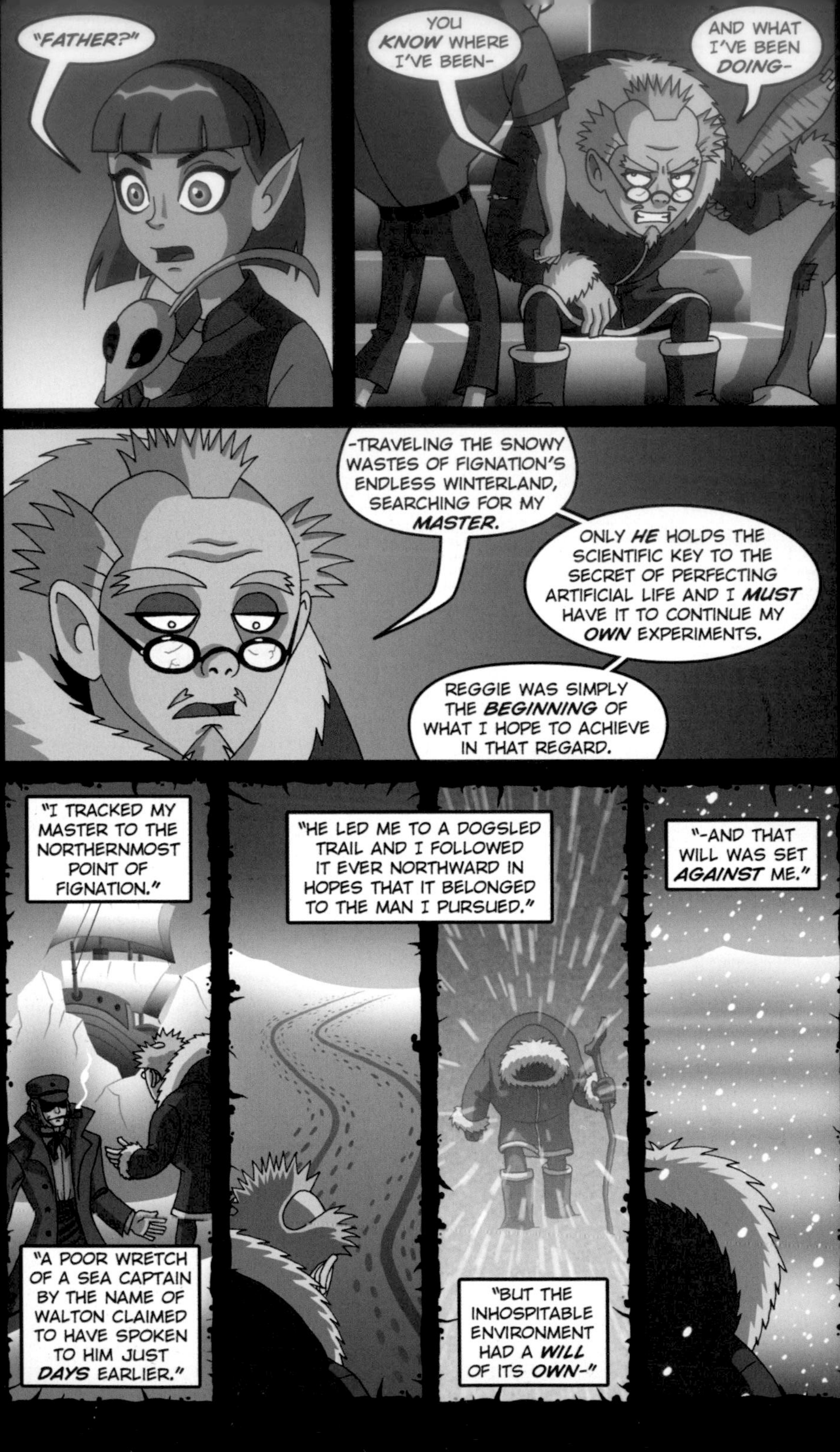
"FATHER?"
YOU KNOW WHERE I'VE BEEN-
AND WHAT I'VE BEEN DOING-
-TRAVELING THE SNOWY WASTES OF FIGNATION'S ENDLESS WINTERLAND, SEARCHING FOR MY MASTER.
ONLY HE HOLDS THE SCIENTIFIC KEY TO THE SECRET OF PERFECTING ARTIFICIAL LIFE AND I MUST HAVE IT TO CONTINUE MY OWN EXPERIMENTS.
REGGIE WAS SIMPLY THE BEGINNING OF WHAT I HOPE TO ACHIEVE IN THAT REGARD.
"I TRACKED MY MASTER TO THE NORTHERNMOST POINT OF FIGNATION."
"A POOR WRETCH OF A SEA CAPTAIN BY THE NAME OF WALTON CLAIMED TO HAVE SPOKEN TO HIM JUST DAYS EARLIER."
"HE LED ME TO A DOGSLED TRAIL AND I FOLLOWED IT EVER NORTHWARD IN HOPES THAT IT BELONGED TO THE MAN I PURSUED."
"BUT THE INHOSPITABLE ENVIRONMENT HAD A WILL OF ITS OWN-"
"-AND THAT WILL WAS SET AGAINST ME."

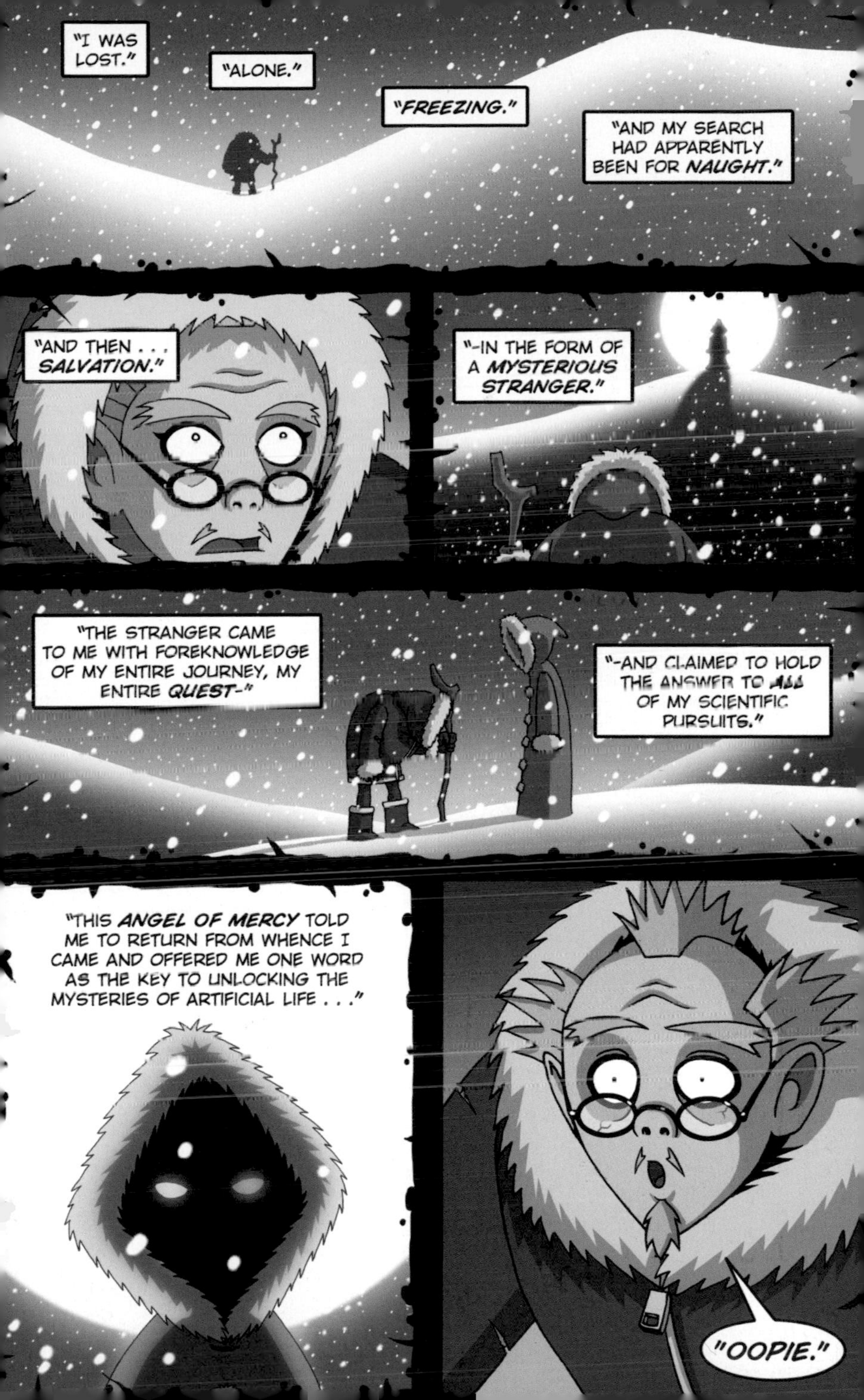
"I WAS LOST."
"ALONE."
"FREEZING."
"AND MY SEARCH HAD APPARENTLY BEEN FOR NAUGHT."
"AND THEN . . . SALVATION."
"-IN THE FORM OF A MYSTERIOUS STRANGER."
"THE STRANGER CAME TO ME WITH FOREKNOWLEDGE OF MY ENTIRE JOURNEY, MY ENTIRE QUEST-"
"-AND CLAIMED TO HOLD THE ANSWER TO
OF MY SCIENTIFIC PURSUITS."
"THIS ANGEL OF MERCY TOLD ME TO RETURN FROM WHENCE I CAME AND OFFERED ME ONE WORD AS THE KEY TO UNLOCKING THE MYSTERIES OF ARTIFICIAL LIFE . . ."
"OOPIE."

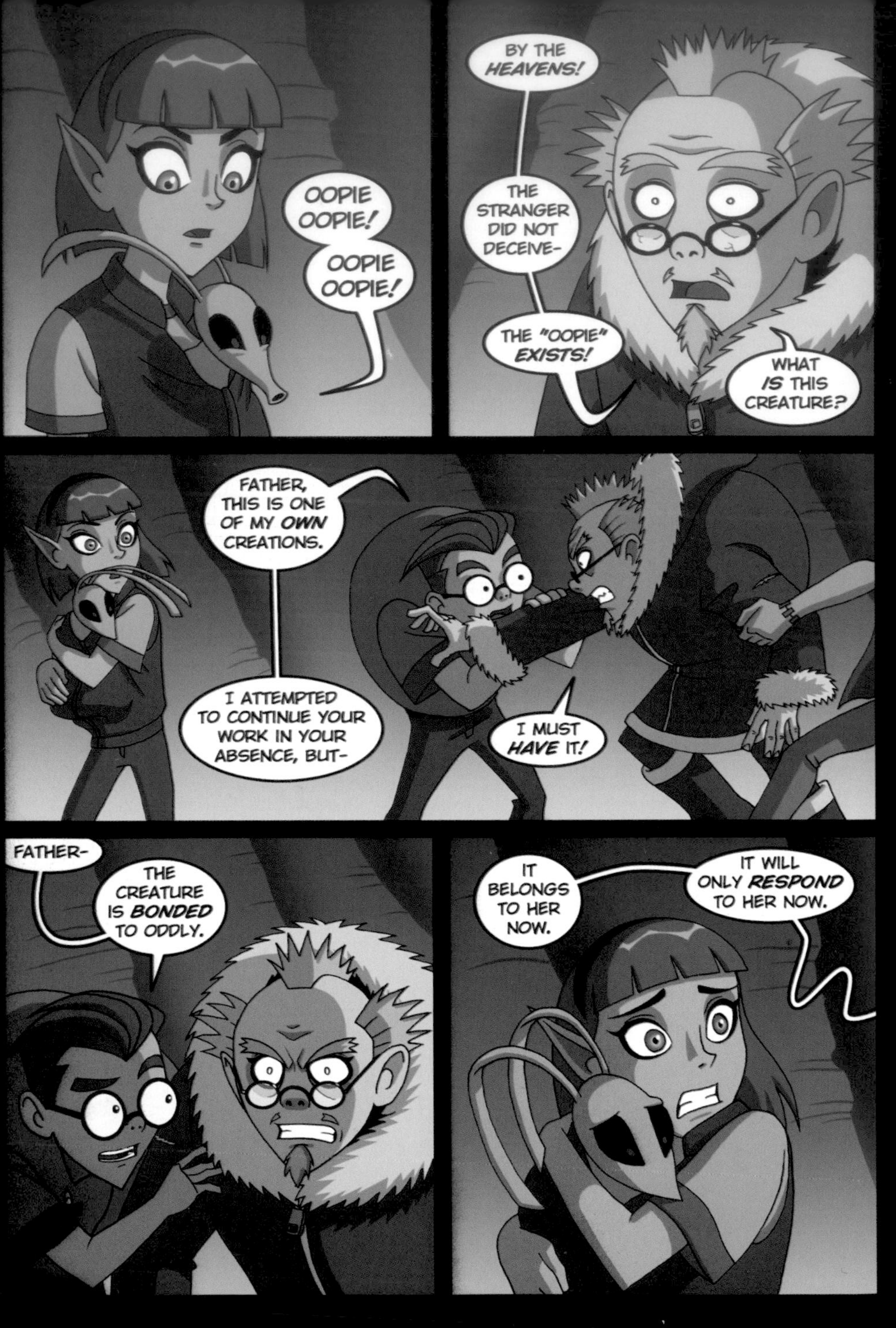
OOPIE OOPIE!
OOPIE OOPIE!
BY THE HEAVENS!
THE STRANGER DID NOT DECEIVE-
THE "OOPIE" EXISTS!
WHAT IS THIS CREATURE?
FATHER, THIS IS ONE OF MY OWN CREATIONS.
I ATTEMPTED TO CONTINUE YOUR WORK IN YOUR ABSENCE, BUT-
I MUST HAVE IT!
FATHER-
THE CREATURE IS BONDED TO ODDLY.
IT BELONGS TO HER NOW.
IT WILL ONLY RESPOND TO HER NOW.

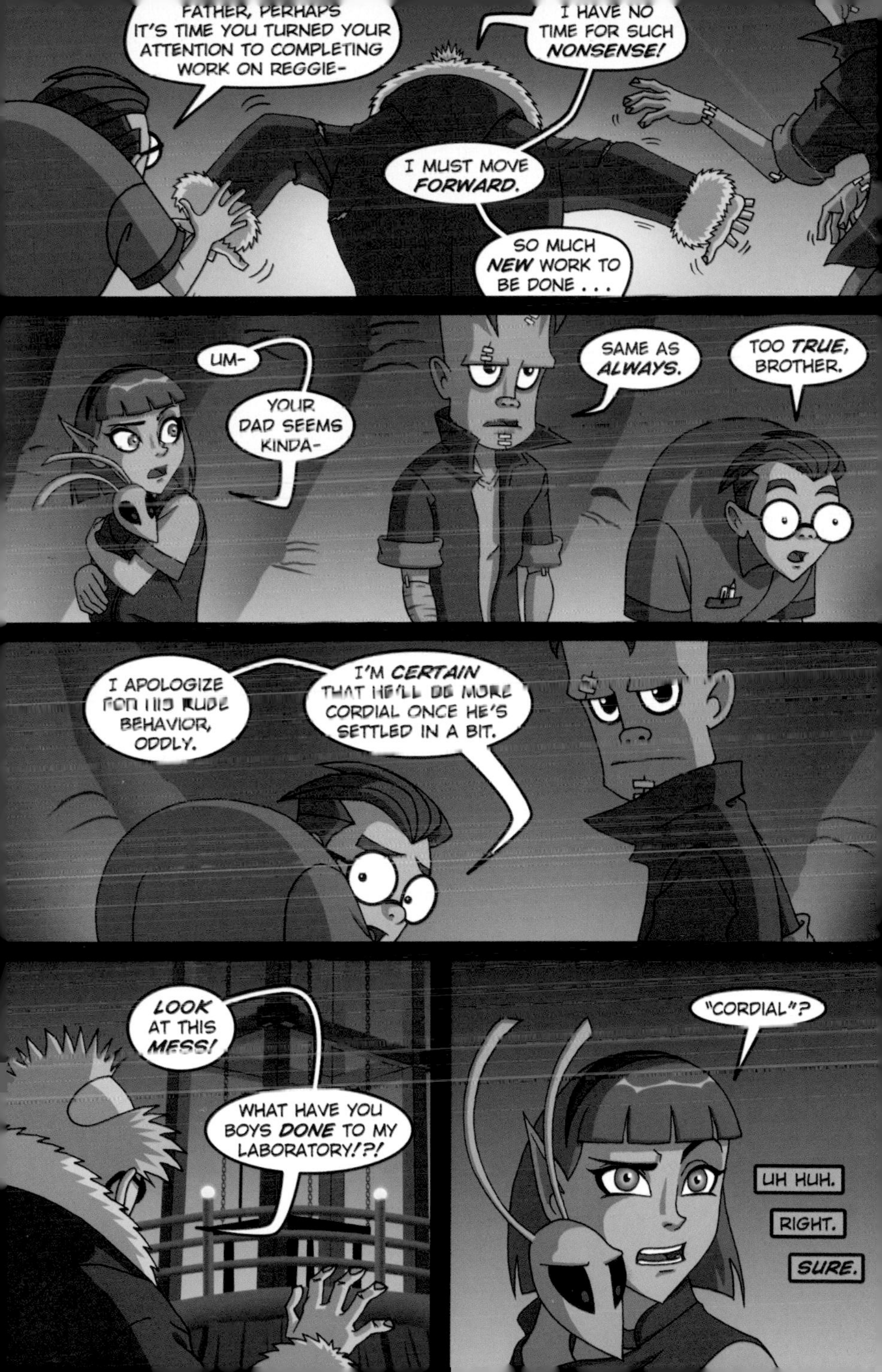
FATHER, PERHAPS IT'S TIME YOU TURNED YOUR ATTENTION TO COMPLETING WORK ON REGGIE-
I HAVE NO TIME FOR SUCH NONSENSE!
I MUST MOVE FORWARD.
SO MUCH NEW WORK TO BE DONE . . .
UM-
YOUR DAD SEEMS KINDA-
SAME AS ALWAYS.
TOO TRUE, BROTHER.
I APOLOGIZE FOR HIS RUDE BEHAVIOR, ODDLY.
I'M CERTAIN THAT HE'LL BE MORE CORDIAL ONCE HE'S SETTLED IN A BIT.
LOOK AT THIS MESS!
WHAT HAVE YOU BOYS DONE TO MY LABORATORY!?!
"CORDIAL"?
UH HUH.
RIGHT.
SURE.

Chapter 2

Familiar Faces

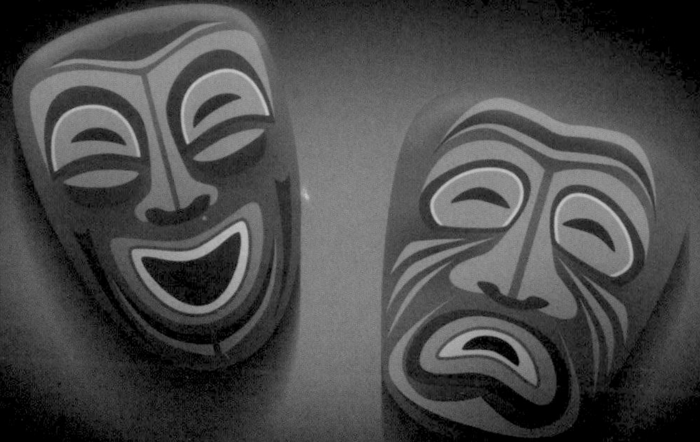

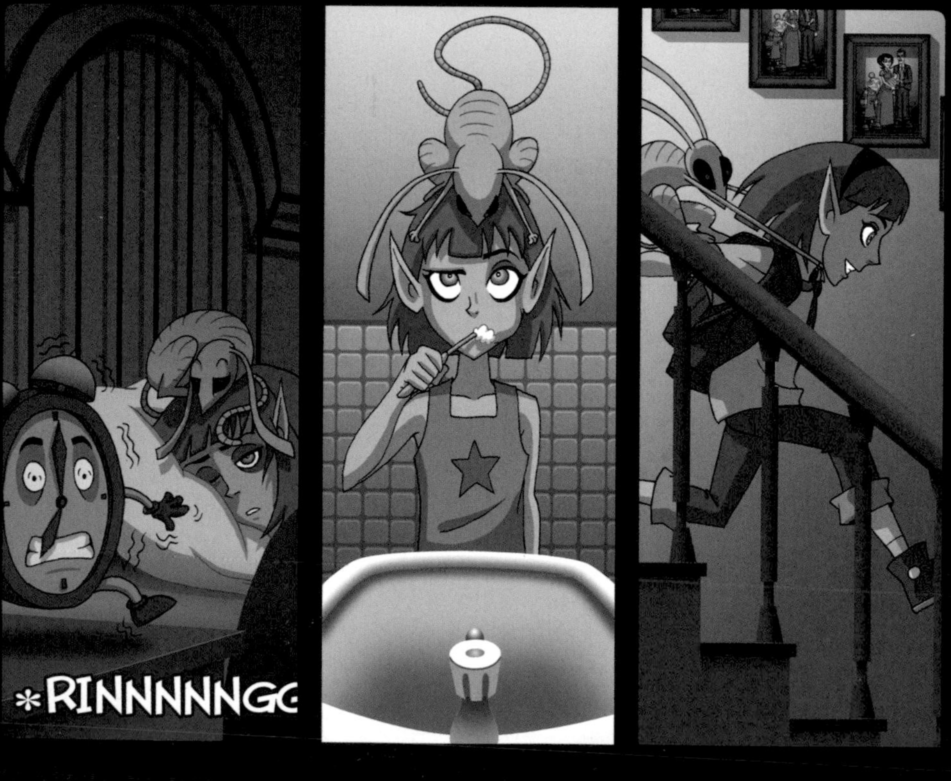
*RINNNNNGG

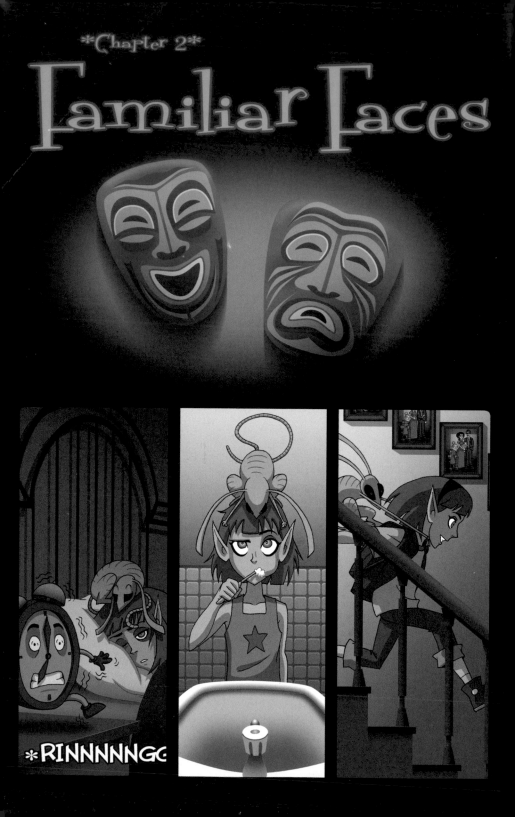

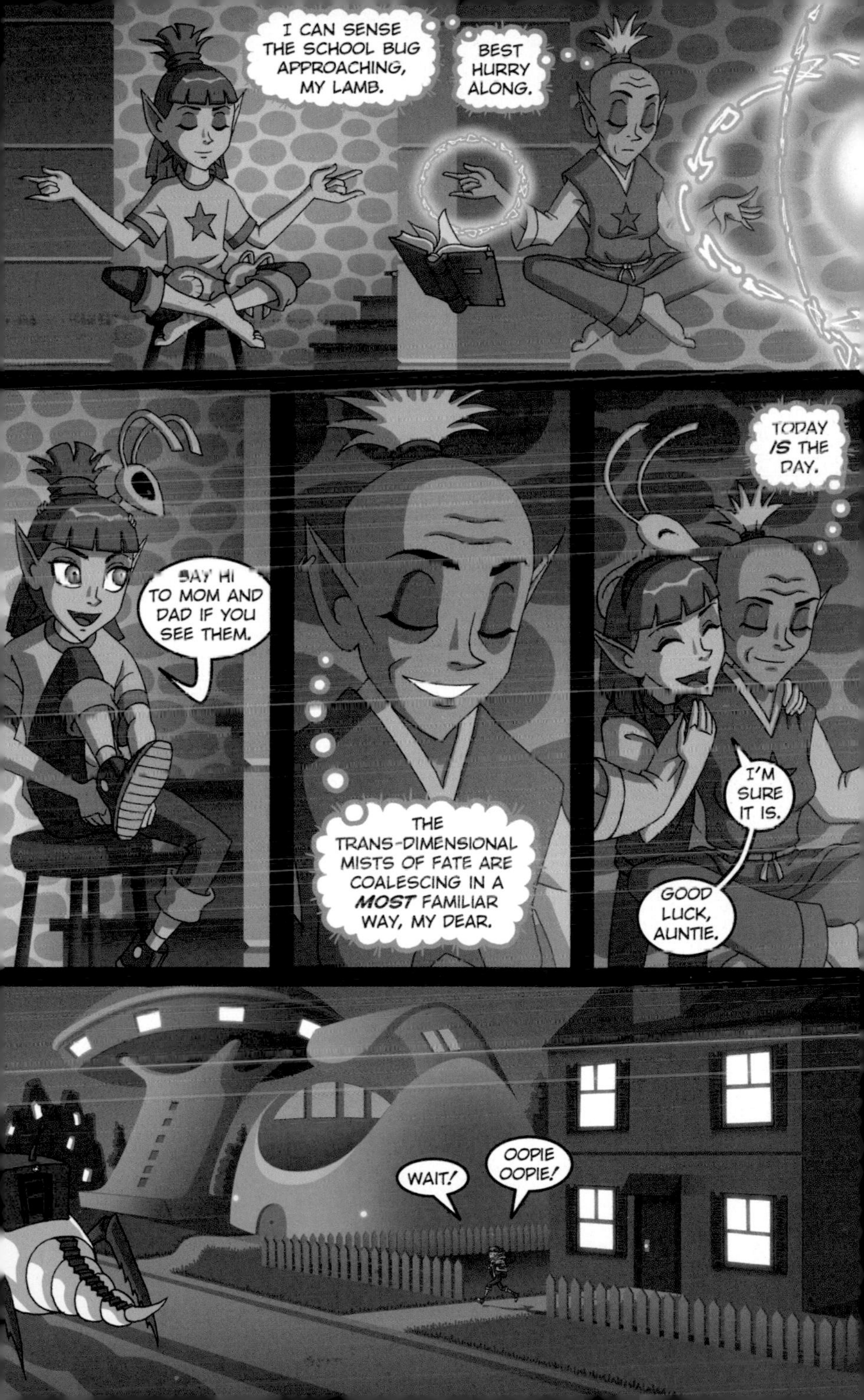
I CAN SENSE THE SCHOOL BUG APPROACHING, MY LAMB.
BEST HURRY ALONG.
SAY HI TO MOM AND DAD IF YOU SEE THEM.
THE TRANS-DIMENSIONAL MISTS OF FATE ARE COALESCING IN A MOST FAMILIAR WAY, MY DEAR.
TODAY IS THE DAY.
I'M SURE IT IS.
GOOD LUCK, AUNTIE.
WAIT!
OOPIE OOPIE!

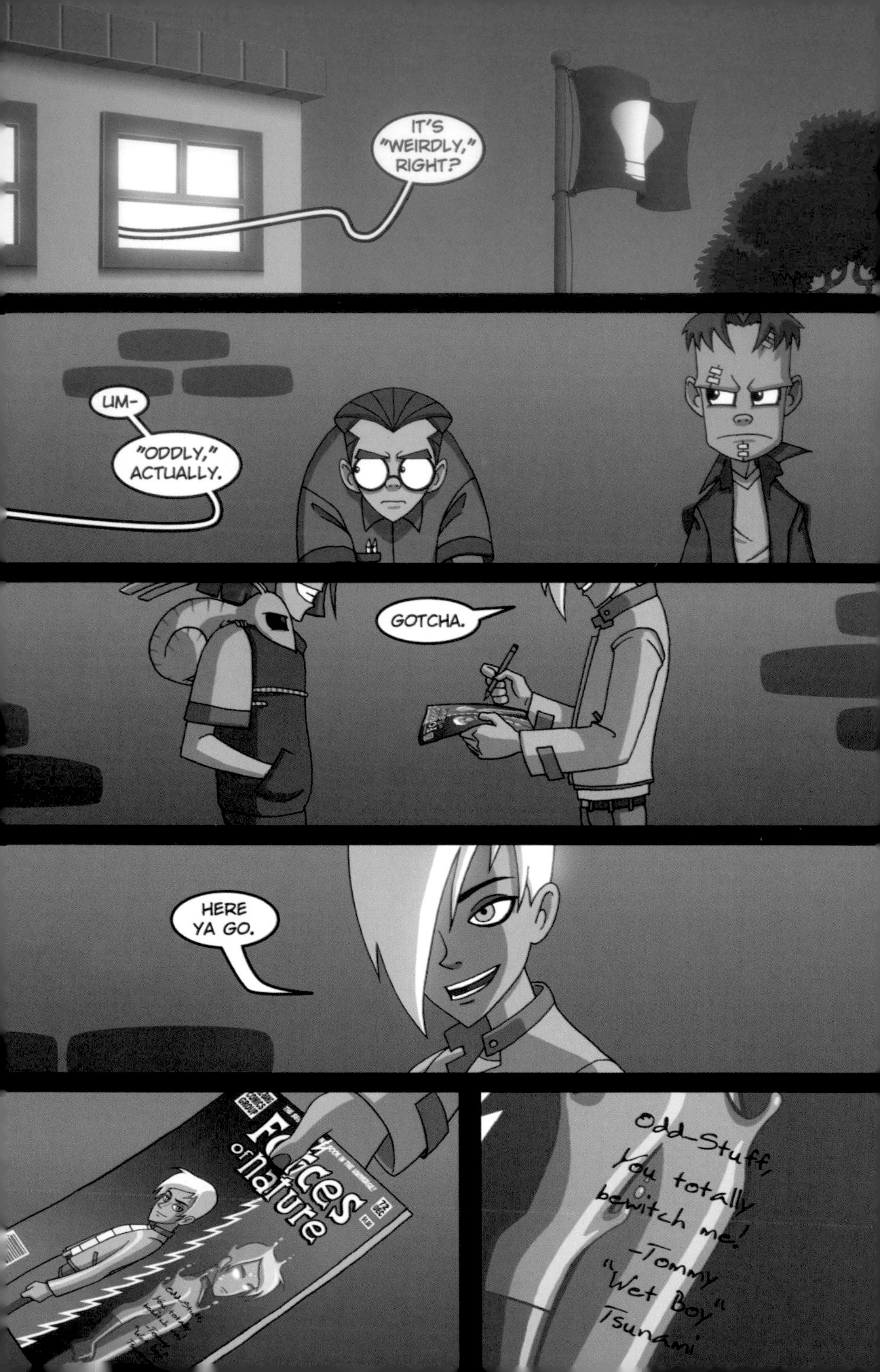
IT'S "WEIRDLY," RIGHT?
UM-
"ODDLY," ACTUALLY.
GOTCHA.
HERE YA GO.
Forces of Nature
Odd-Stuff, You totally bewitch me! -Tommy "Wet Boy" Tsunami

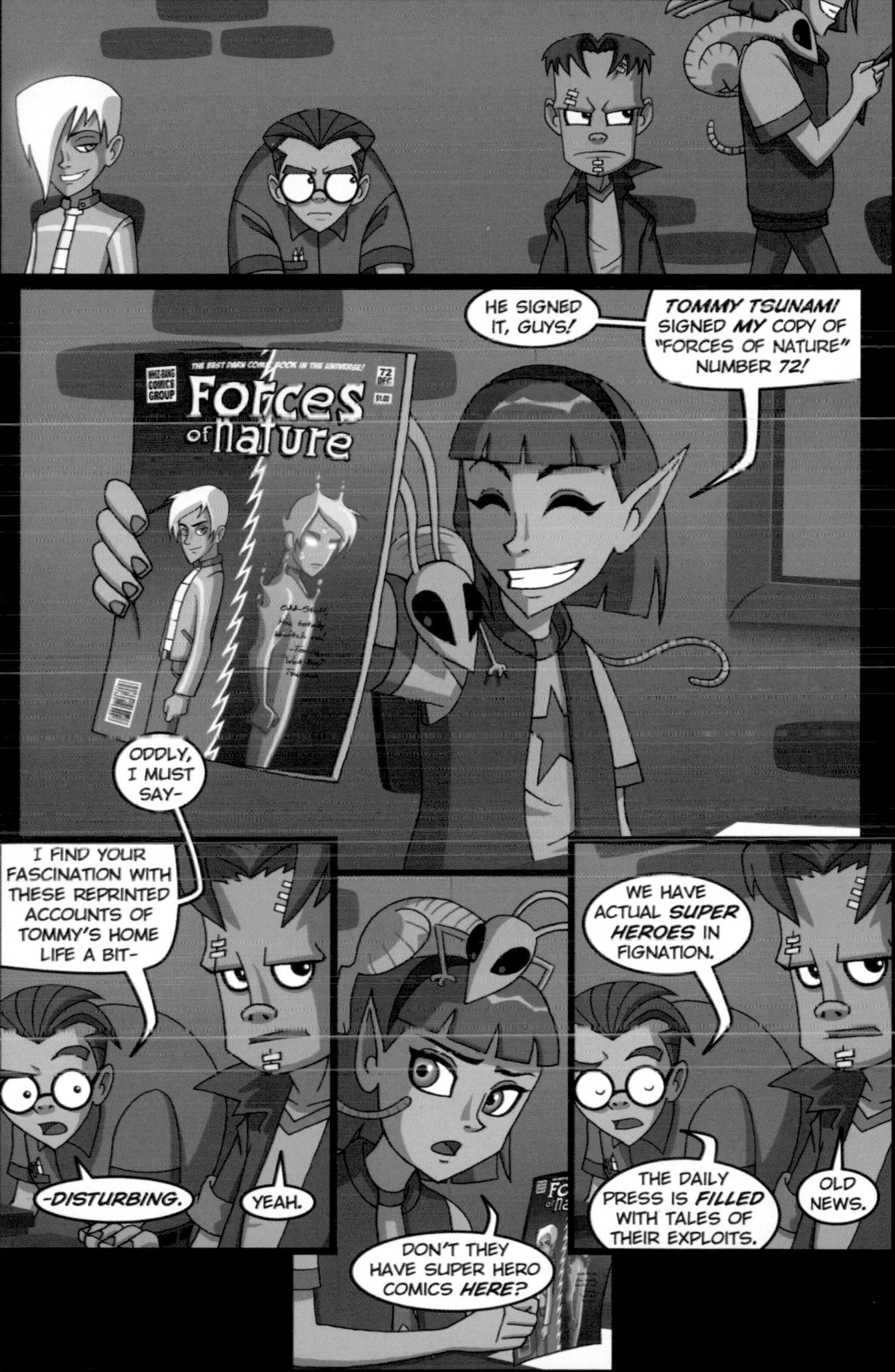
HE SIGNED IT, GUYS!
TOMMY TSUNAMI SIGNED MY COPY OF "FORCES OF NATURE" NUMBER 72!
THE BEST DARN COMIC BOOK IN THE UNIVERSE!
WHIZ-BANG COMICS GROUP
Forces of Nature
72
ODDLY, I MUST SAY-
I FIND YOUR FASCINATION WITH THESE REPRINTED ACCOUNTS OF TOMMY'S HOME LIFE A BIT-
-DISTURBING.
YEAH.
DON'T THEY HAVE SUPER HERO COMICS HERE?
WE HAVE ACTUAL SUPER HEROES IN FIGNATION.
THE DAILY PRESS IS FILLED WITH TALES OF THEIR EXPLOITS.
OLD NEWS.

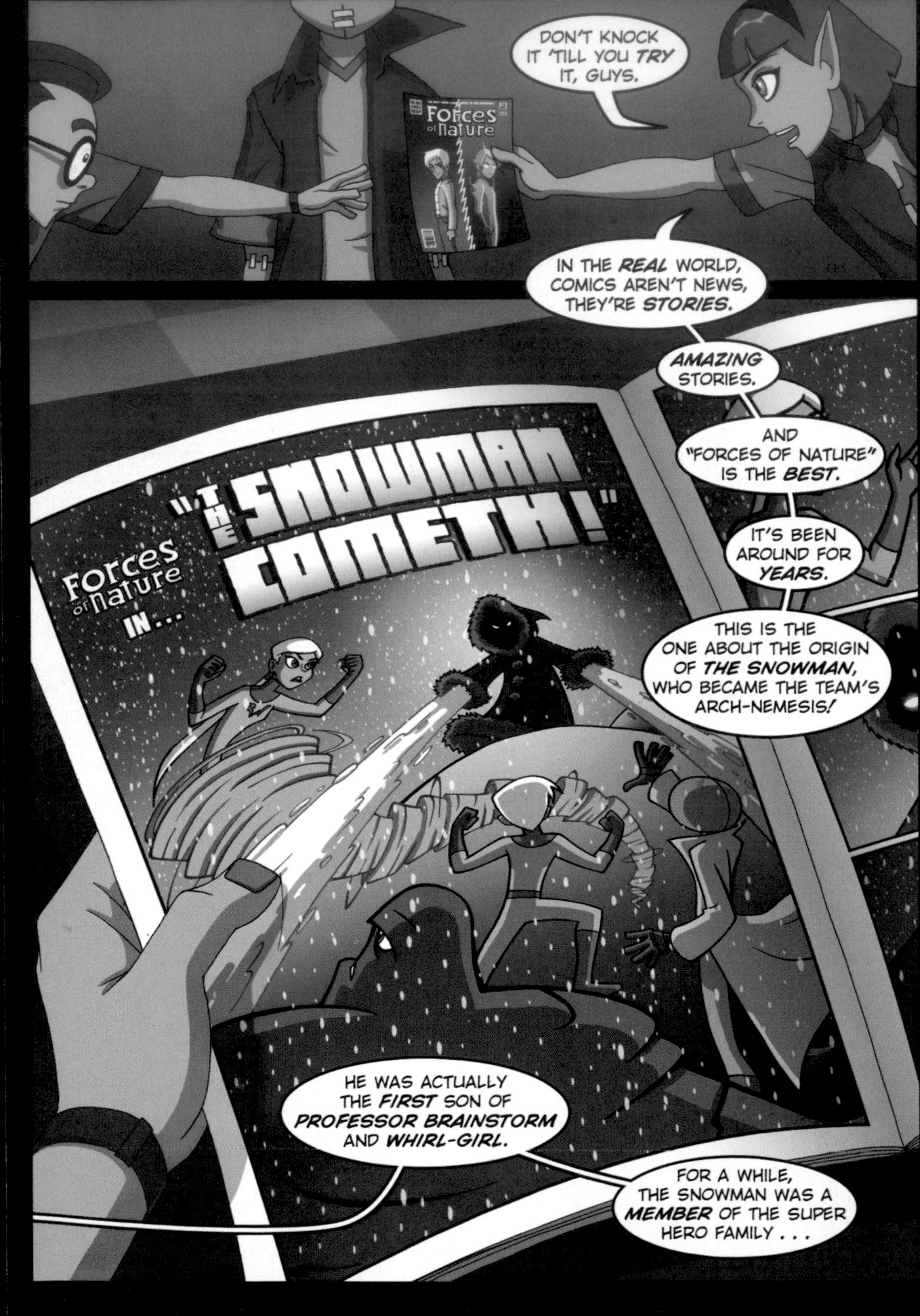

DON'T KNOCK IT 'TILL YOU TRY IT, GUYS.
Forces of Nature
IN THE REAL WORLD, COMICS AREN'T NEWS, THEY'RE STORIES.
AMAZING STORIES.
AND "FORCES OF NATURE" IS THE BEST.
IT'S BEEN AROUND FOR YEARS.
THIS IS THE ONE ABOUT THE ORIGIN OF THE SNOWMAN, WHO BECAME THE TEAM'S ARCH-NEMESIS!
Forces of Nature IN...
"THE SNOWMAN COMETH!"
HE WAS ACTUALLY THE FIRST SON OF PROFESSOR BRAINSTORM AND WHIRL-GIRL.
FOR A WHILE, THE SNOWMAN WAS A MEMBER OF THE SUPER HERO FAMILY . . .

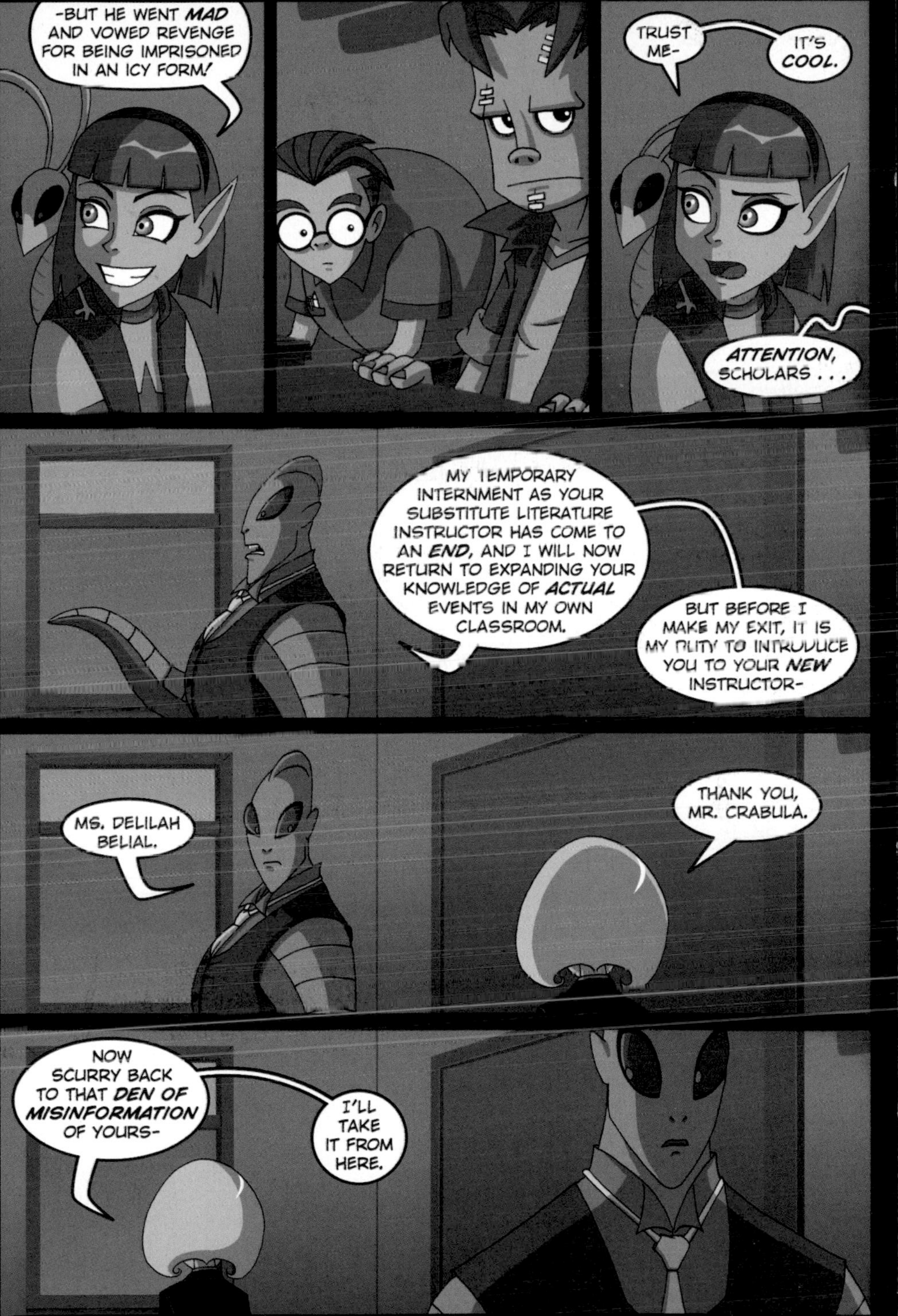
-BUT HE WENT MAD AND VOWED REVENGE FOR BEING IMPRISONED IN AN ICY FORM!
TRUST ME-
IT'S COOL.
ATTENTION, SCHOLARS . . .
MY TEMPORARY INTERNMENT AS YOUR SUBSTITUTE LITERATURE INSTRUCTOR HAS COME TO AN END, AND I WILL NOW RETURN TO EXPANDING YOUR KNOWLEDGE OF ACTUAL EVENTS IN MY OWN CLASSROOM.
BUT BEFORE I MAKE MY EXIT, IT IS MY DUTY TO INTRODUCE YOU TO YOUR NEW INSTRUCTOR-
MS. DELILAH BELIAL.
THANK YOU, MR. CRABULA.
NOW SCURRY BACK TO THAT DEN OF MISINFORMATION OF YOURS-
I'LL TAKE IT FROM HERE.

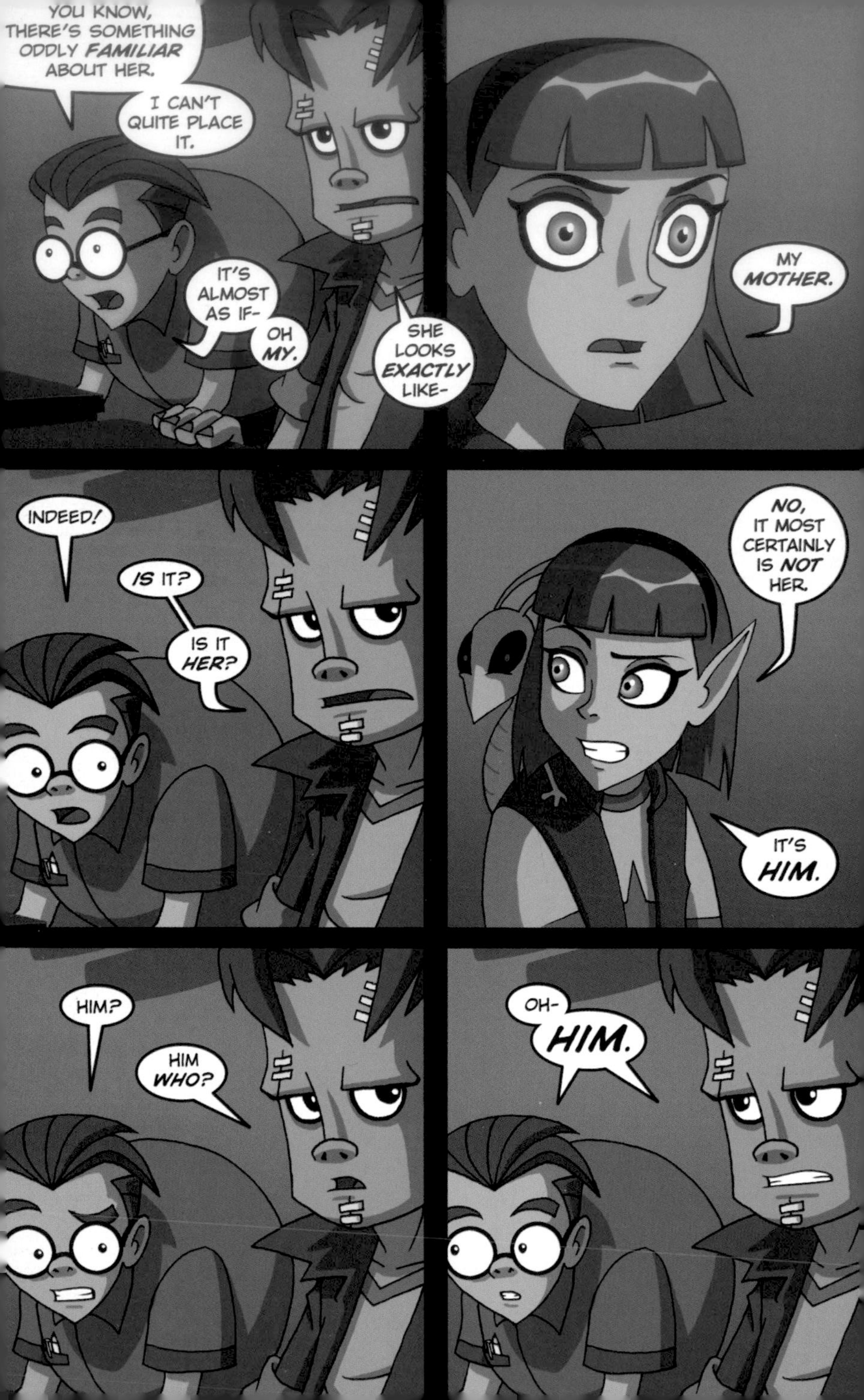

YOU KNOW, THERE'S SOMETHING ODDLY FAMILIAR ABOUT HER.
I CAN'T QUITE PLACE IT.
IT'S ALMOST AS IF-
OH MY.
SHE LOOKS EXACTLY LIKE-
MY MOTHER.
INDEED!
IS IT?
IS IT HER?
NO, IT MOST CERTAINLY IS NOT HER.
IT'S HIM.
HIM?
HIM WHO?
OH-
HIM.

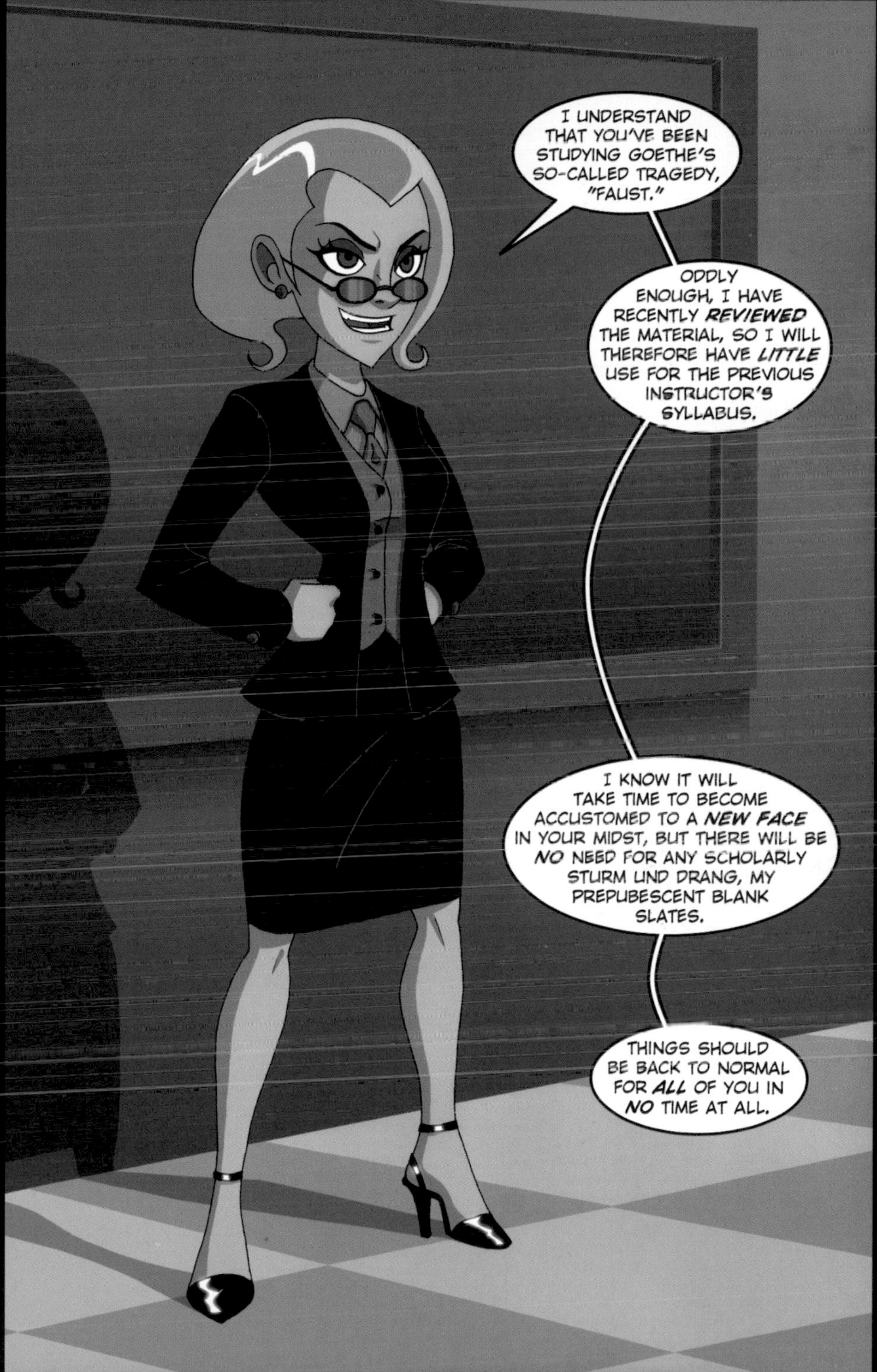
I UNDERSTAND THAT YOU'VE BEEN STUDYING GOETHE'S SO-CALLED TRAGEDY, "FAUST."
ODDLY ENOUGH, I HAVE RECENTLY *REVIEWED* THE MATERIAL, SO I WILL THEREFORE HAVE *LITTLE* USE FOR THE PREVIOUS INSTRUCTOR'S SYLLABUS.
I KNOW IT WILL TAKE TIME TO BECOME ACCUSTOMED TO A *NEW FACE* IN YOUR MIDST, BUT THERE WILL BE *NO* NEED FOR ANY SCHOLARLY STURM UND DRANG, MY PREPUBESCENT BLANK SLATES.
THINGS SHOULD BE BACK TO NORMAL FOR *ALL* OF YOU IN *NO* TIME AT ALL.

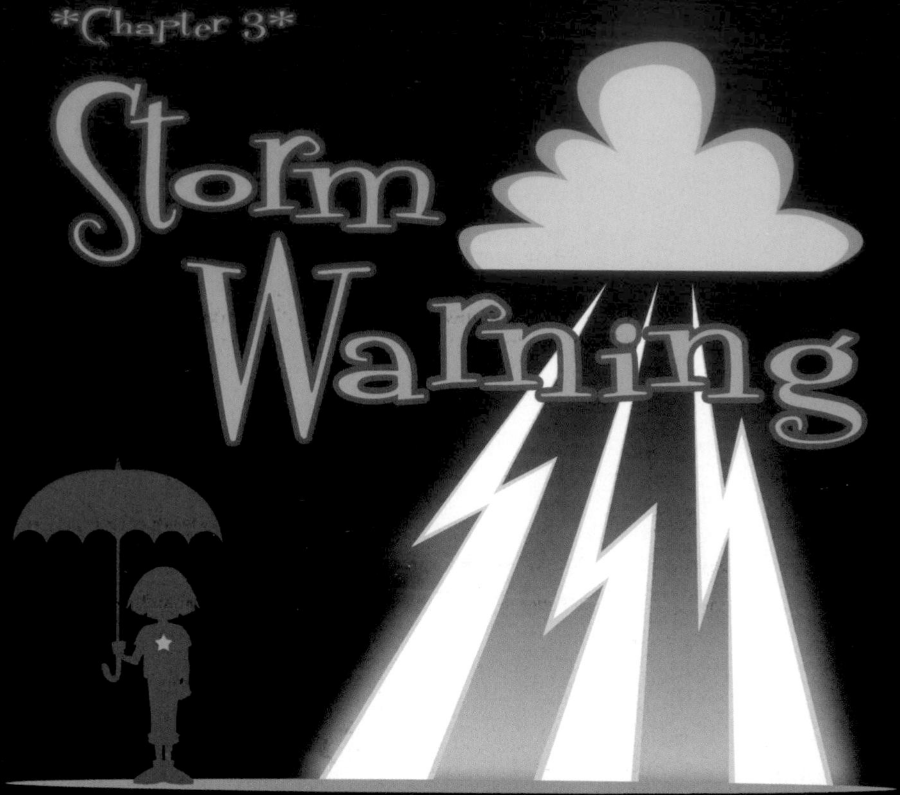
Chapter 3
Storm Warning

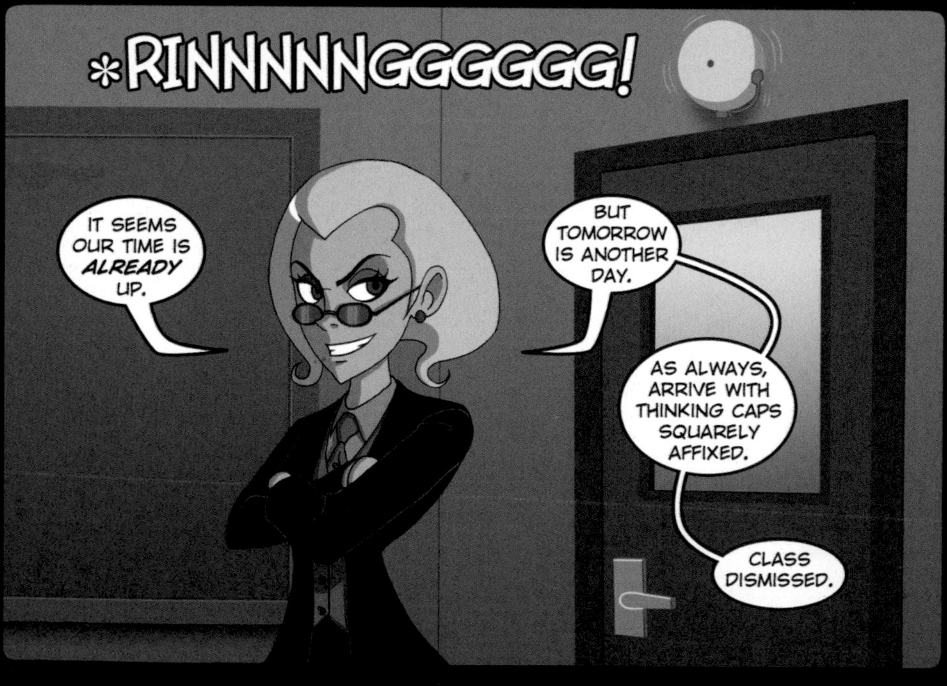
*RINNNNNGGGGGG!
IT SEEMS OUR TIME IS *ALREADY* UP.
BUT TOMORROW IS ANOTHER DAY.
AS ALWAYS, ARRIVE WITH THINKING CAPS SQUARELY AFFIXED.
CLASS DISMISSED.

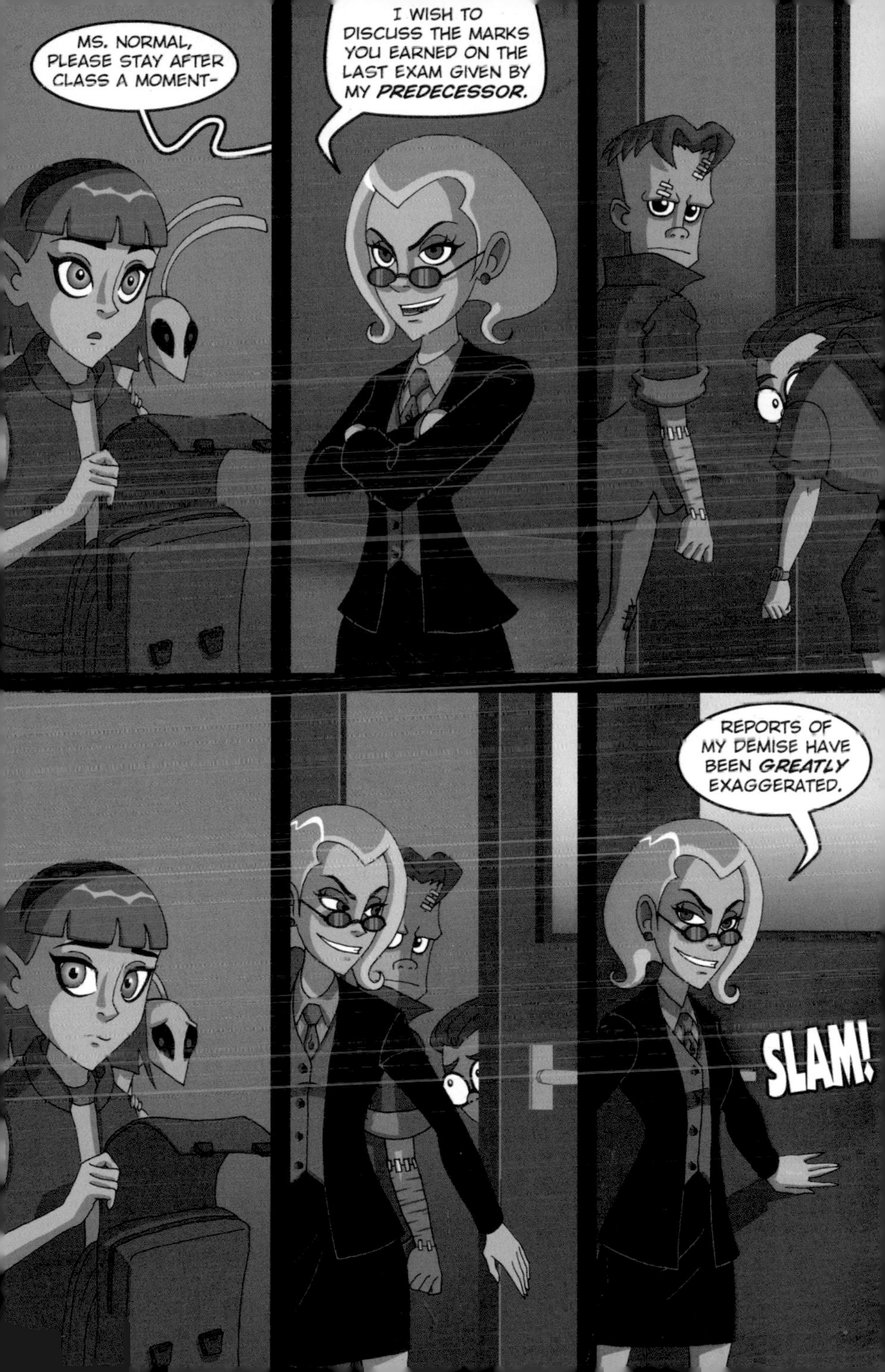
MS. NORMAL, PLEASE STAY AFTER CLASS A MOMENT-
I WISH TO DISCUSS THE MARKS YOU EARNED ON THE LAST EXAM GIVEN BY MY *PREDECESSOR.*
REPORTS OF MY DEMISE HAVE BEEN *GREATLY* EXAGGERATED.
SLAM!

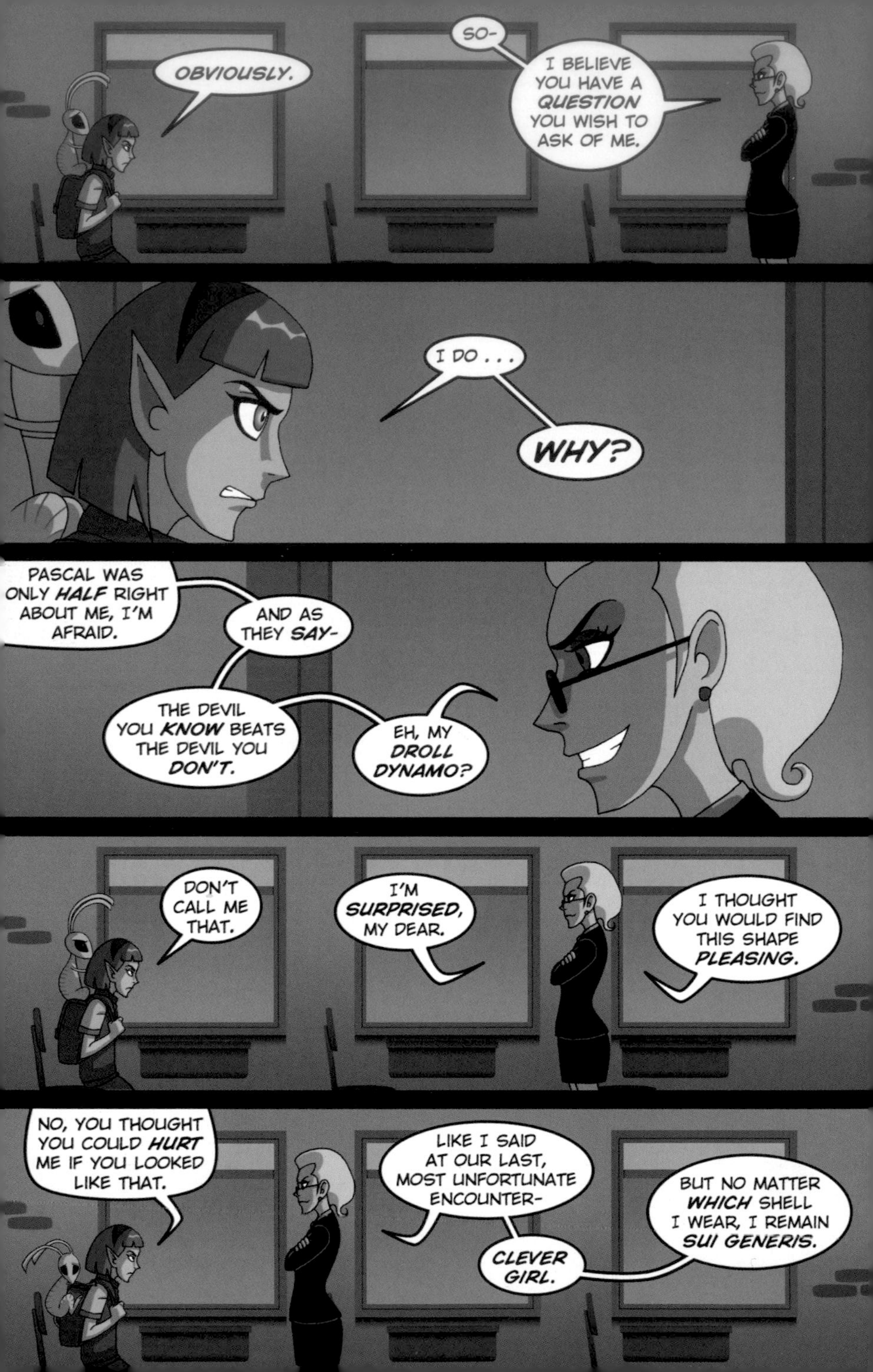
OBVIOUSLY.
SO-
I BELIEVE YOU HAVE A QUESTION YOU WISH TO ASK OF ME.
I DO . . .
WHY?
PASCAL WAS ONLY HALF RIGHT ABOUT ME, I'M AFRAID.
AND AS THEY SAY-
THE DEVIL YOU KNOW BEATS THE DEVIL YOU DON'T.
EH, MY DROLL DYNAMO?
DON'T CALL ME THAT.
I'M SURPRISED, MY DEAR.
I THOUGHT YOU WOULD FIND THIS SHAPE PLEASING.
NO, YOU THOUGHT YOU COULD HURT ME IF YOU LOOKED LIKE THAT.
LIKE I SAID AT OUR LAST, MOST UNFORTUNATE ENCOUNTER-
CLEVER GIRL.
BUT NO MATTER WHICH SHELL I WEAR, I REMAIN SUI GENERIS.

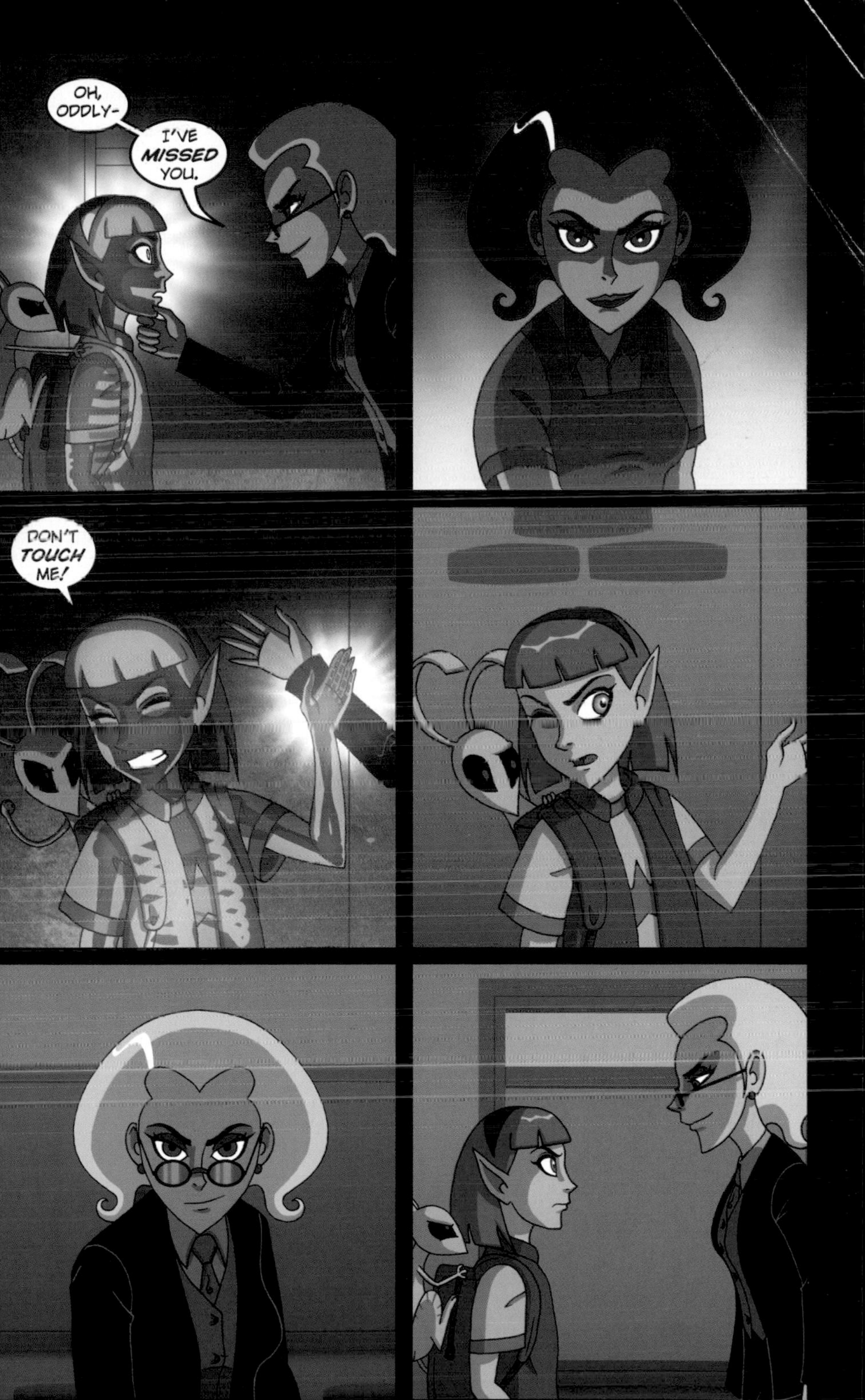
OH, ODDLY-
I'VE MISSED YOU.
DON'T TOUCH ME!

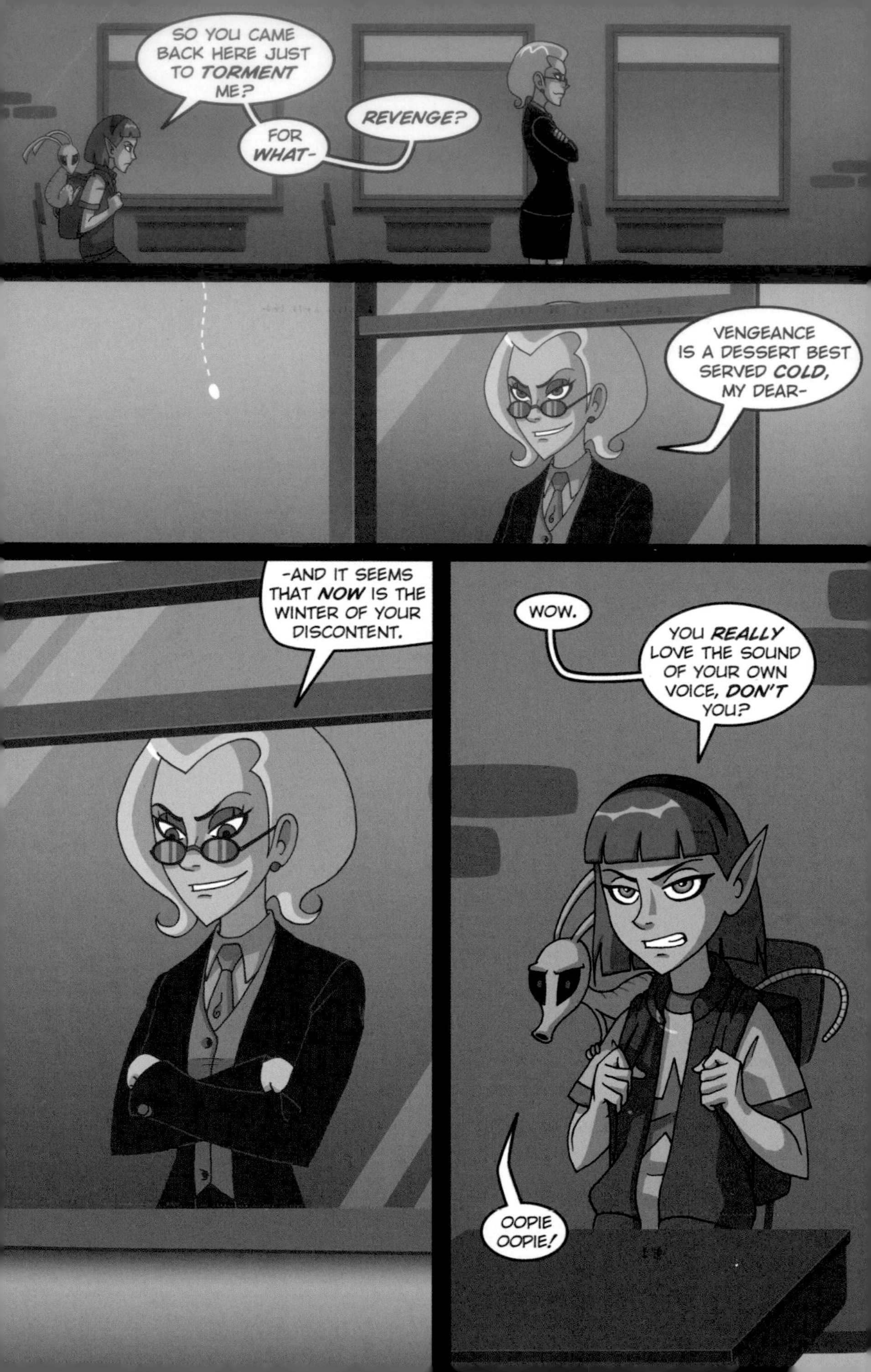
SO YOU CAME BACK HERE JUST TO TORMENT ME?
FOR WHAT-
REVENGE?
VENGEANCE IS A DESSERT BEST SERVED COLD, MY DEAR-
-AND IT SEEMS THAT NOW IS THE WINTER OF YOUR DISCONTENT.
WOW.
YOU REALLY LOVE THE SOUND OF YOUR OWN VOICE, DON'T YOU?
OOPIE OOPIE!

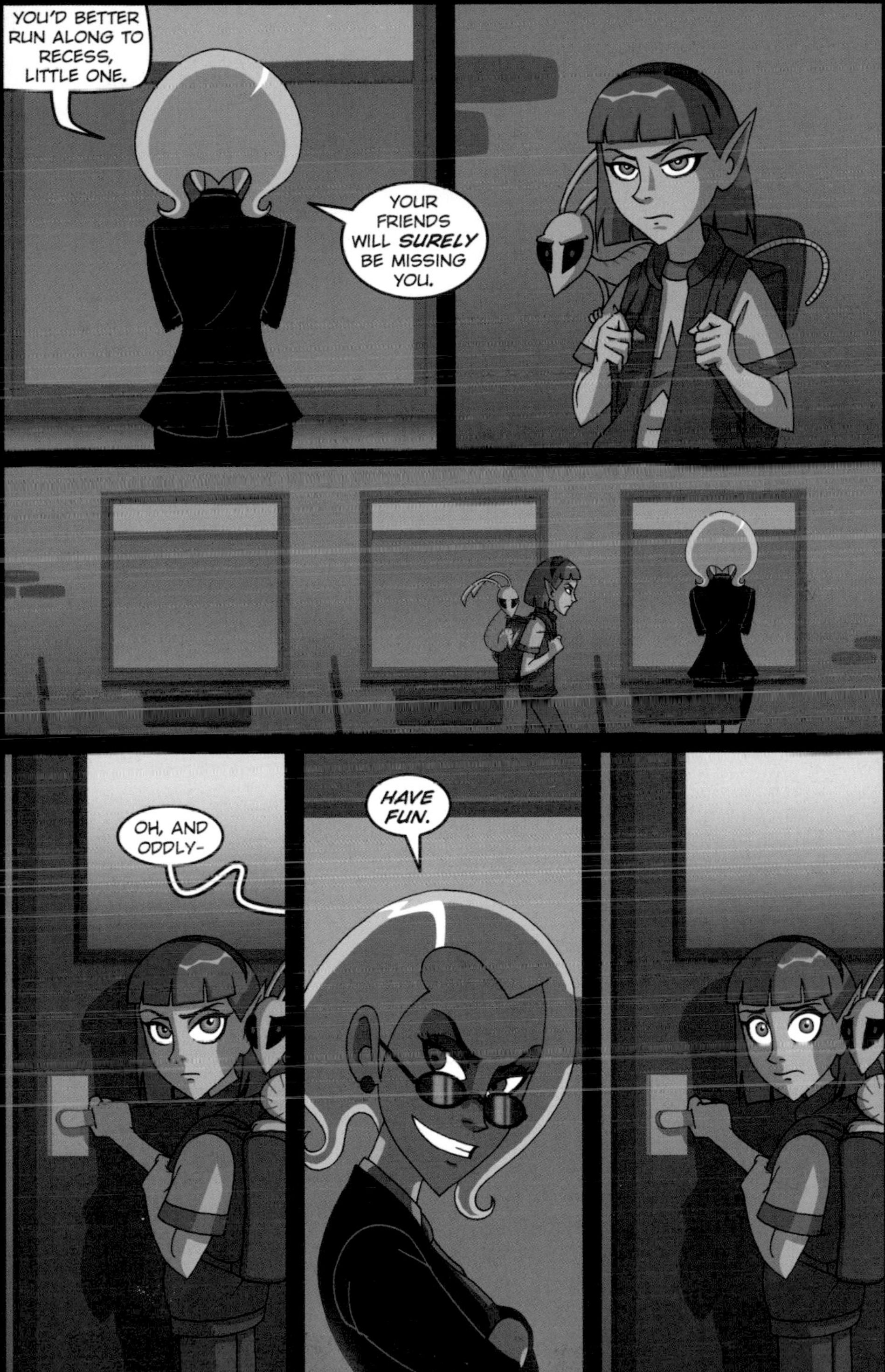
YOU'D BETTER RUN ALONG TO RECESS, LITTLE ONE.
YOUR FRIENDS WILL SURELY BE MISSING YOU.
OH, AND ODDLY-
HAVE FUN.

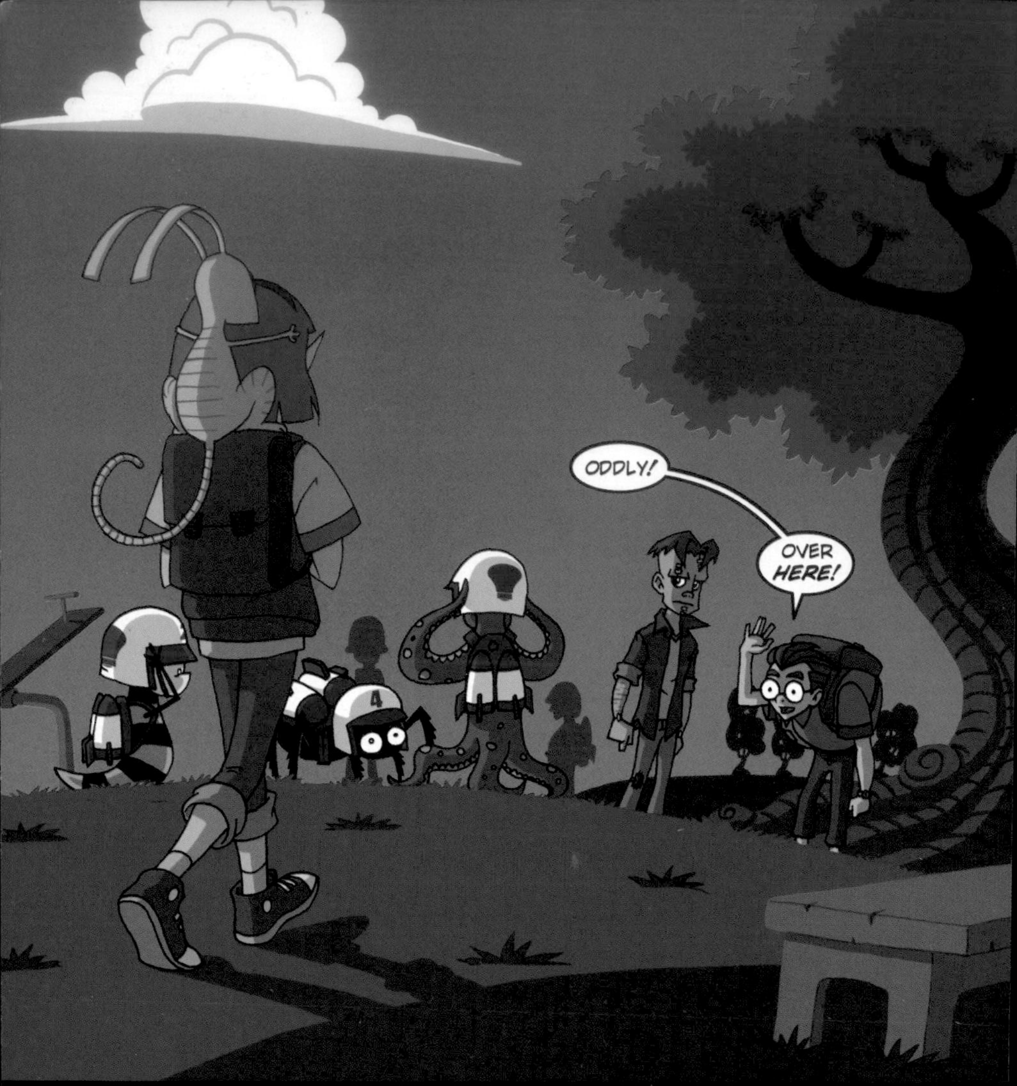
ODDLY!
OVER HERE!

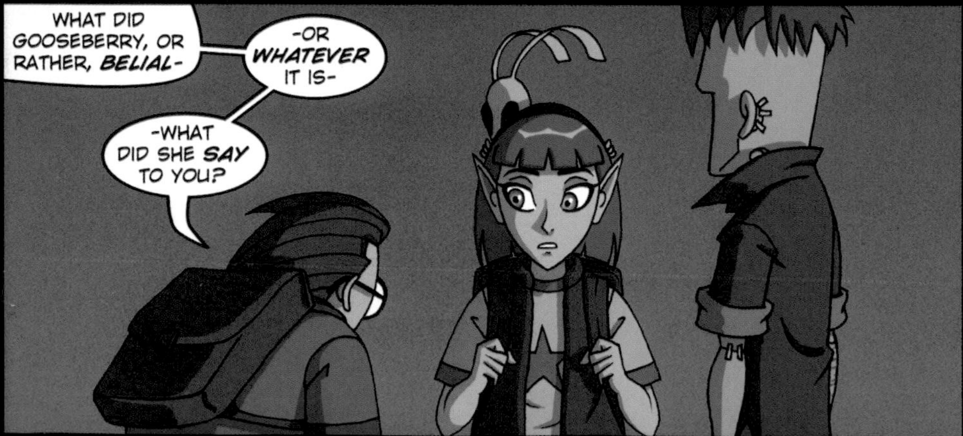
WHAT DID GOOSEBERRY, OR RATHER, BELIAL-
-OR WHATEVER IT IS-
-WHAT DID SHE SAY TO YOU?

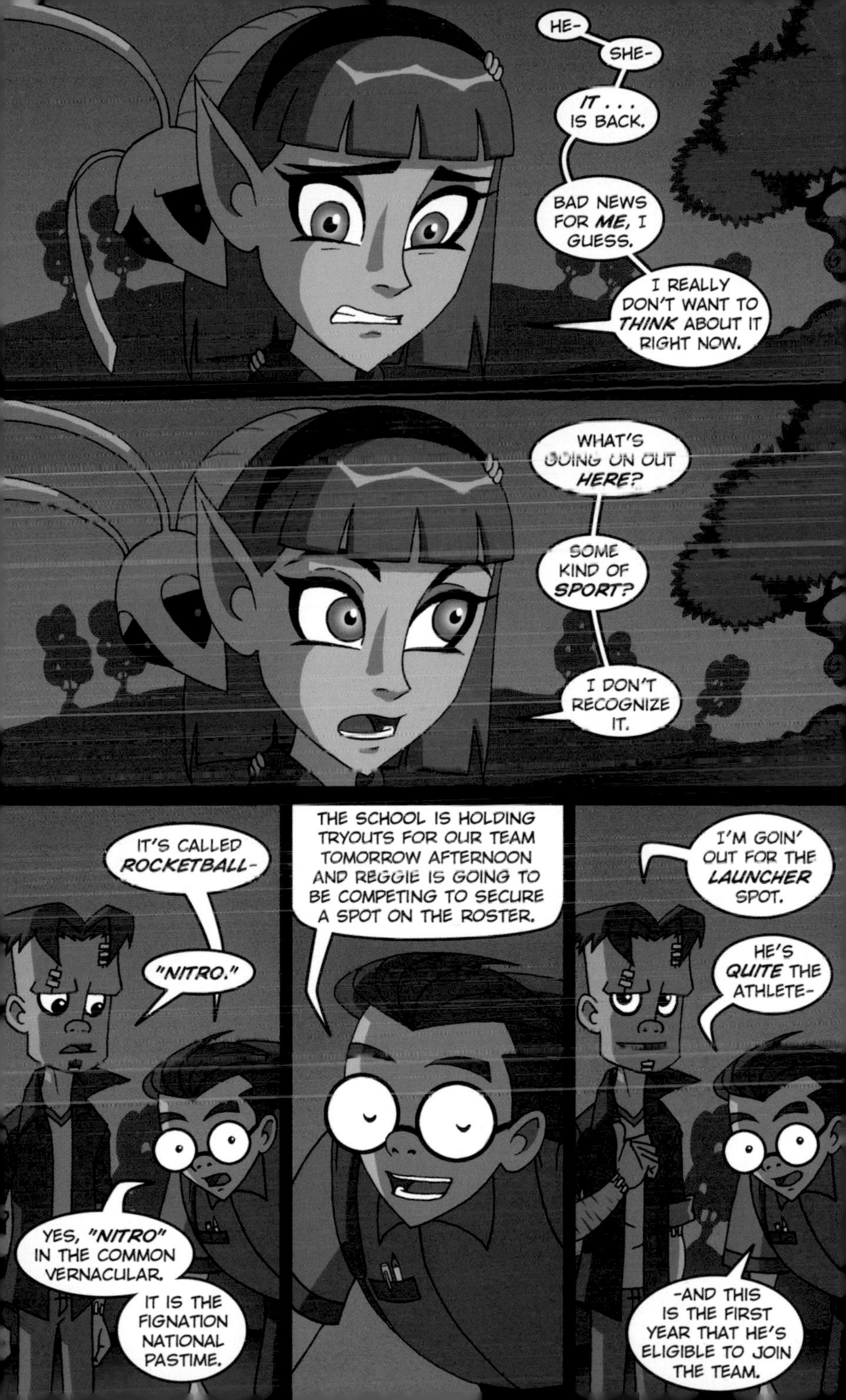
HE-
SHE-
IT . . . IS BACK.
BAD NEWS FOR ME, I GUESS.
I REALLY DON'T WANT TO THINK ABOUT IT RIGHT NOW.
WHAT'S GOING ON OUT HERE?
SOME KIND OF SPORT?
I DON'T RECOGNIZE IT.
IT'S CALLED ROCKETBALL-
"NITRO."
YES, "NITRO" IN THE COMMON VERNACULAR.
IT IS THE FIGNATION NATIONAL PASTIME.
THE SCHOOL IS HOLDING TRYOUTS FOR OUR TEAM TOMORROW AFTERNOON AND REGGIE IS GOING TO BE COMPETING TO SECURE A SPOT ON THE ROSTER.
I'M GOIN' OUT FOR THE LAUNCHER SPOT.
HE'S QUITE THE ATHLETE-
-AND THIS IS THE FIRST YEAR THAT HE'S ELIGIBLE TO JOIN THE TEAM.

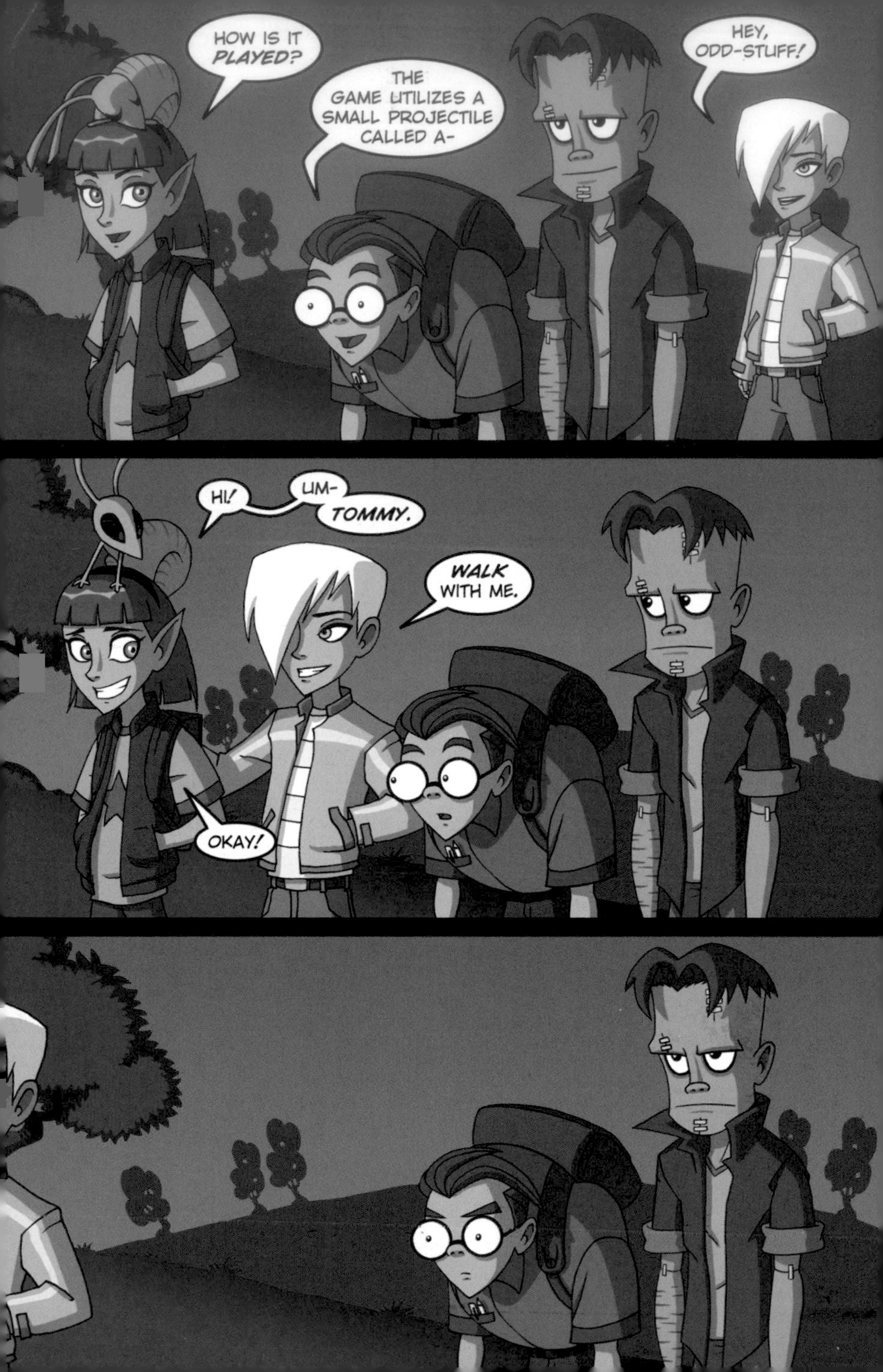
HOW IS IT PLAYED?
THE GAME UTILIZES A SMALL PROJECTILE CALLED A-
HEY, ODD-STUFF!
HI!
UM- TOMMY.
WALK WITH ME.
OKAY!

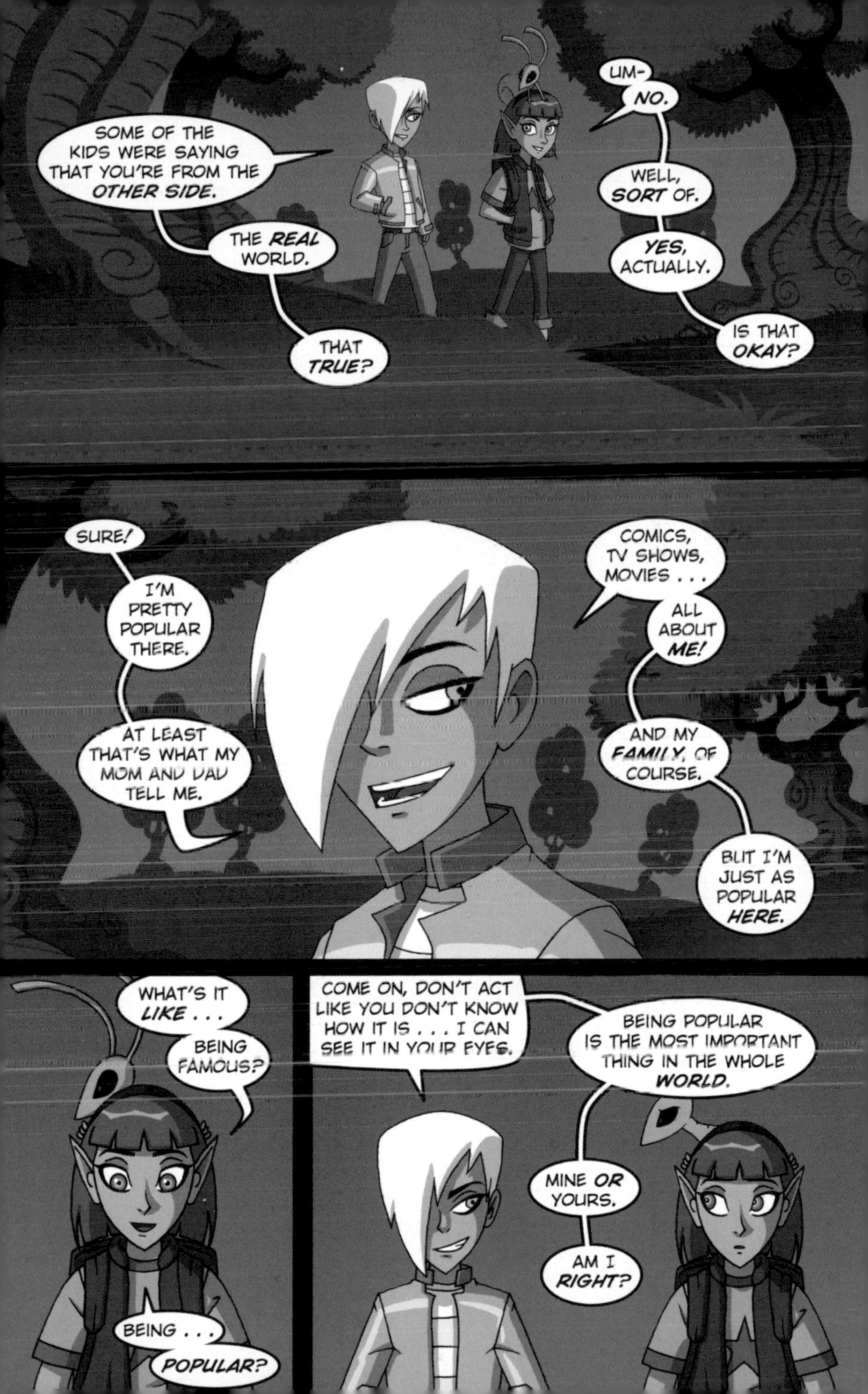
SOME OF THE KIDS WERE SAYING THAT YOU'RE FROM THE *OTHER SIDE.*
THE *REAL* WORLD.
THAT *TRUE?*
UM-
NO.
WELL, *SORT* OF.
YES, ACTUALLY.
IS THAT *OKAY?*
SURE!
I'M PRETTY POPULAR THERE.
AT LEAST THAT'S WHAT MY MOM AND DAD TELL ME.
COMICS, TV SHOWS, MOVIES . . .
ALL ABOUT *ME!*
AND MY *FAMILY,* OF COURSE.
BUT I'M JUST AS POPULAR *HERE.*
WHAT'S IT *LIKE . . .*
BEING FAMOUS?
BEING . . .
POPULAR?
COME ON, DON'T ACT LIKE YOU DON'T KNOW HOW IT IS . . . I CAN SEE IT IN YOUR EYES.
BEING POPULAR IS THE MOST IMPORTANT THING IN THE WHOLE *WORLD.*
MINE *OR* YOURS.
AM I *RIGHT?*

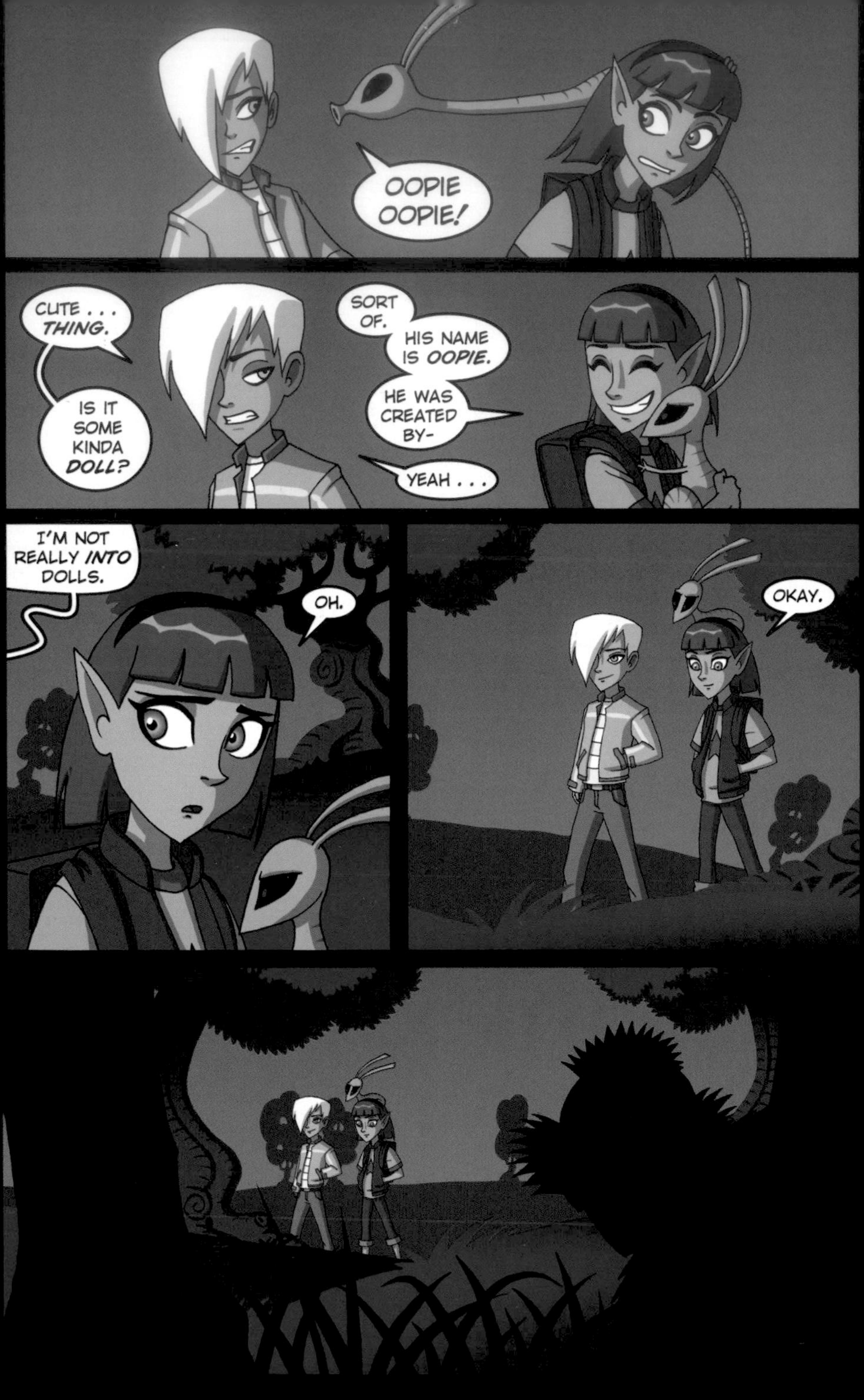
OOPIE OOPIE!
CUTE . . . THING.
IS IT SOME KINDA DOLL?
SORT OF.
HIS NAME IS OOPIE.
HE WAS CREATED BY-
YEAH . . .
I'M NOT REALLY INTO DOLLS.
OH.
OKAY.

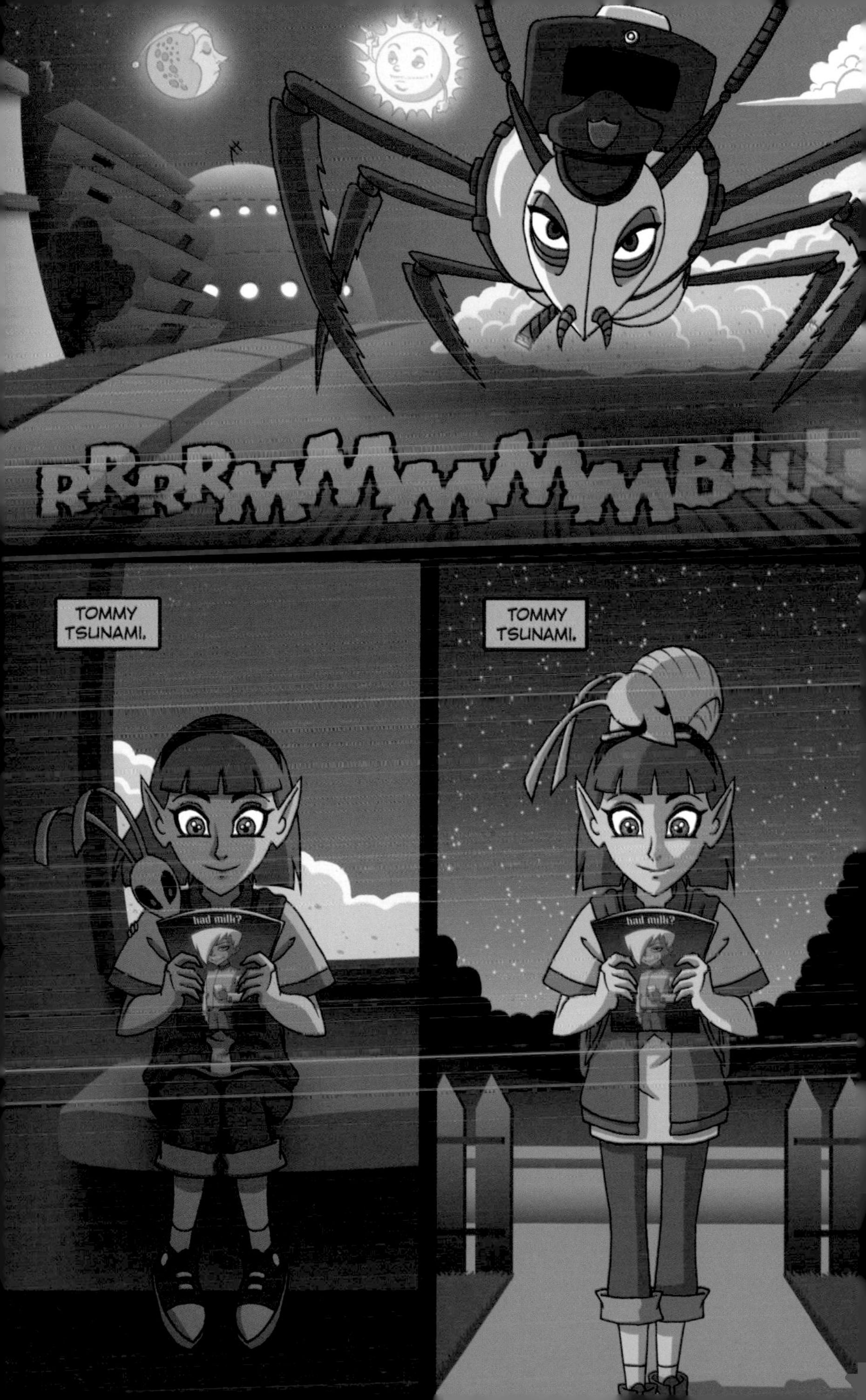
RRRRMMMMMMMBLL
TOMMY TSUNAMI.
had milk?
TOMMY TSUNAMI.
had milk?

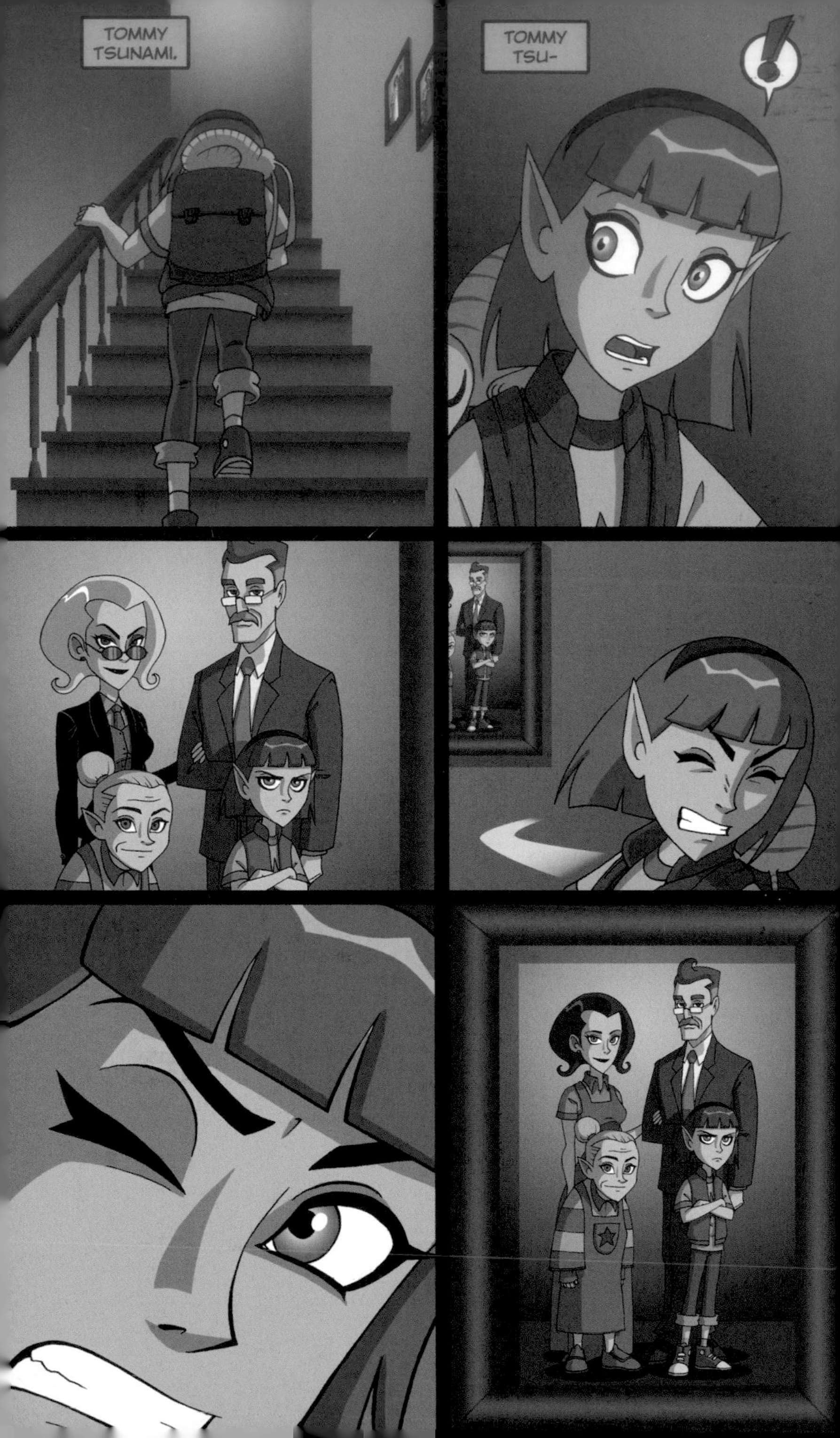
TOMMY TSUNAMI.
TOMMY TSU-
!

Chapter 4

A Change In The Weather

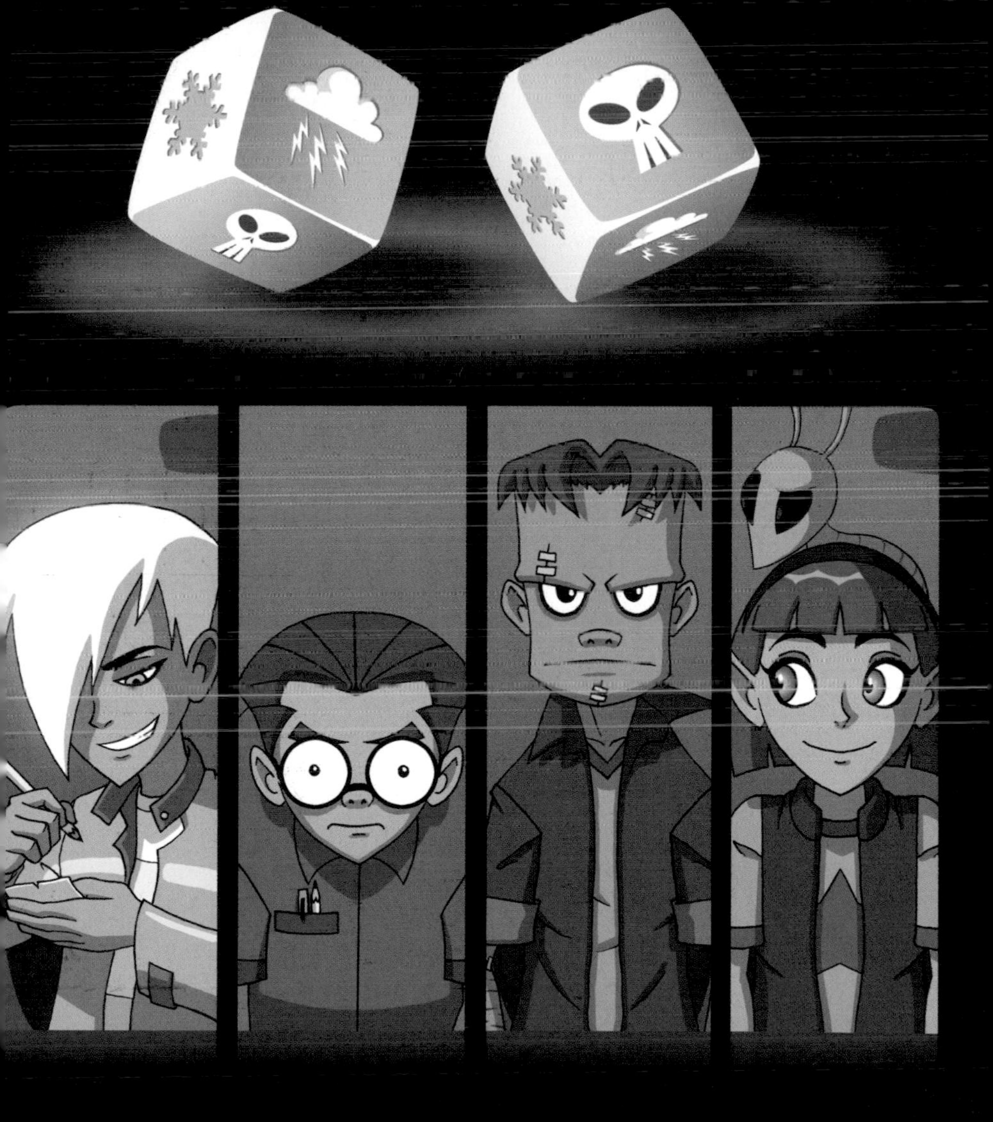

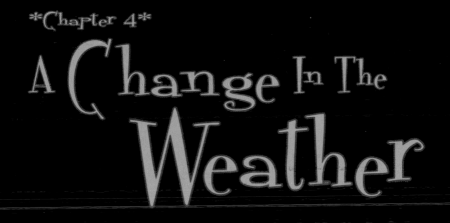

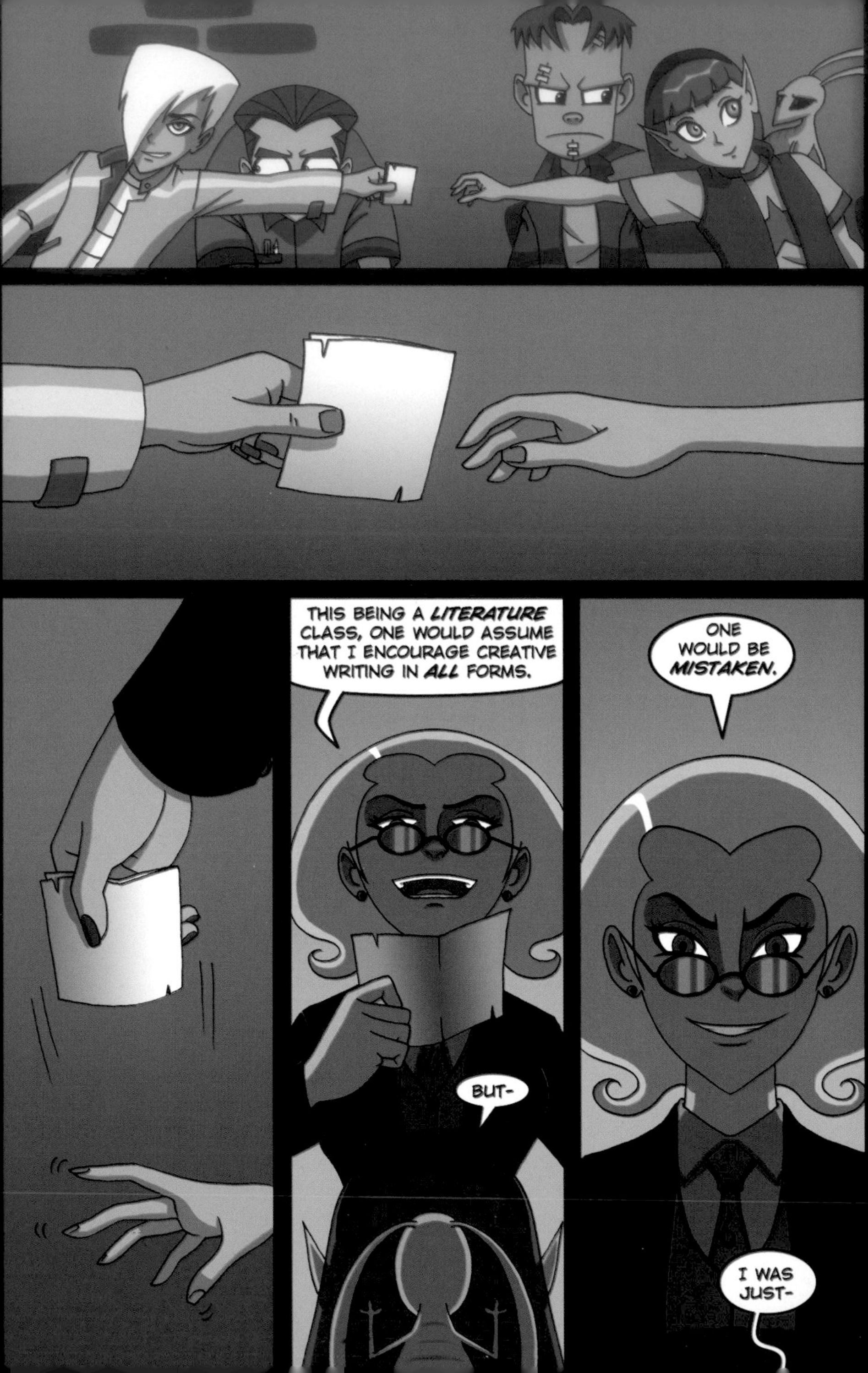
THIS BEING A LITERATURE CLASS, ONE WOULD ASSUME THAT I ENCOURAGE CREATIVE WRITING IN ALL FORMS.
BUT-
ONE WOULD BE MISTAKEN.
I WAS JUST-

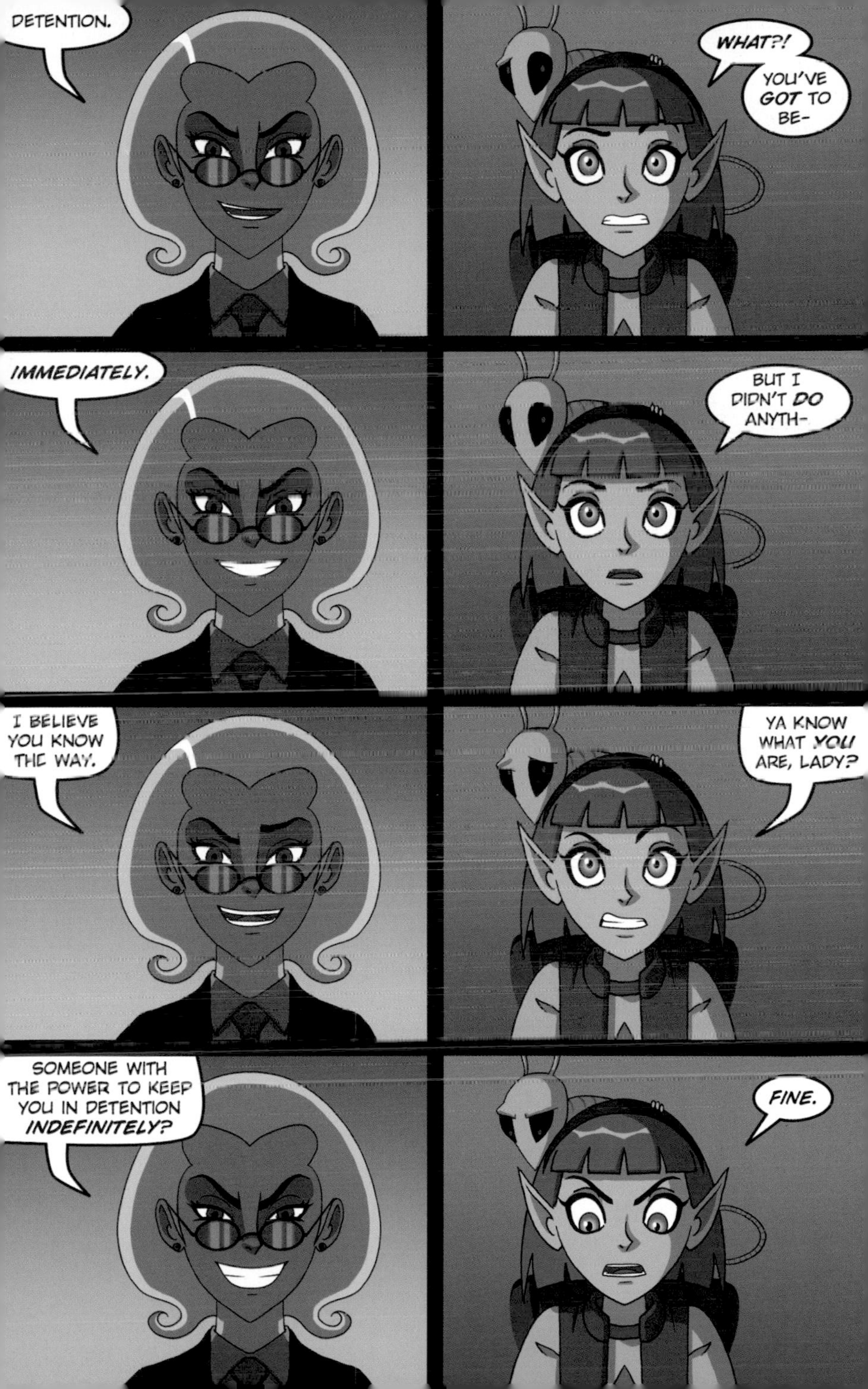
DETENTION.
WHAT?!
YOU'VE GOT TO BE-
IMMEDIATELY.
BUT I DIDN'T DO ANYTH-
I BELIEVE YOU KNOW THE WAY.
YA KNOW WHAT YOU ARE, LADY?
SOMEONE WITH THE POWER TO KEEP YOU IN DETENTION INDEFINITELY?
FINE.

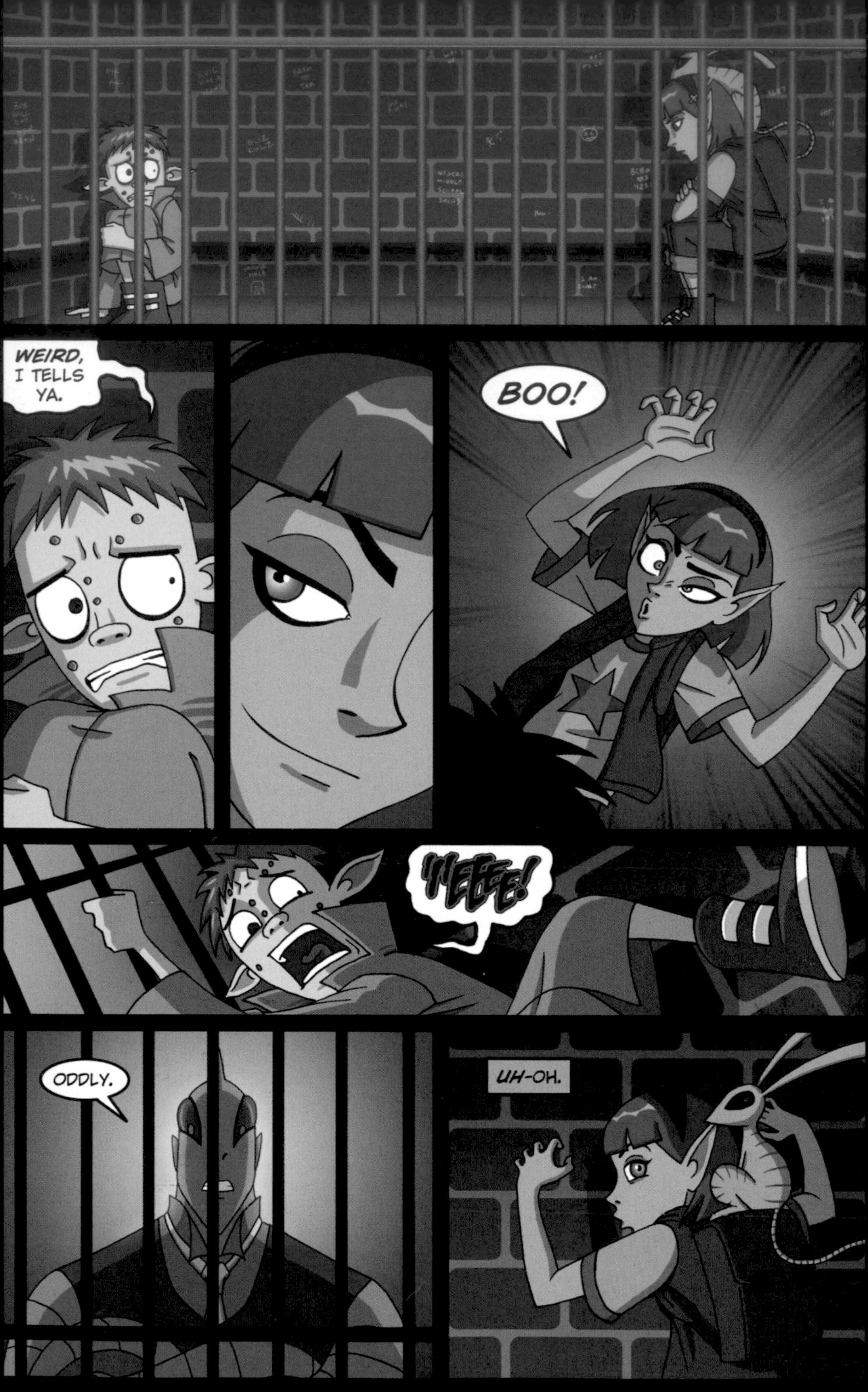
WEIRD, I TELLS YA.
BOO!
IIEEEEE!
ODDLY.
UH-OH.

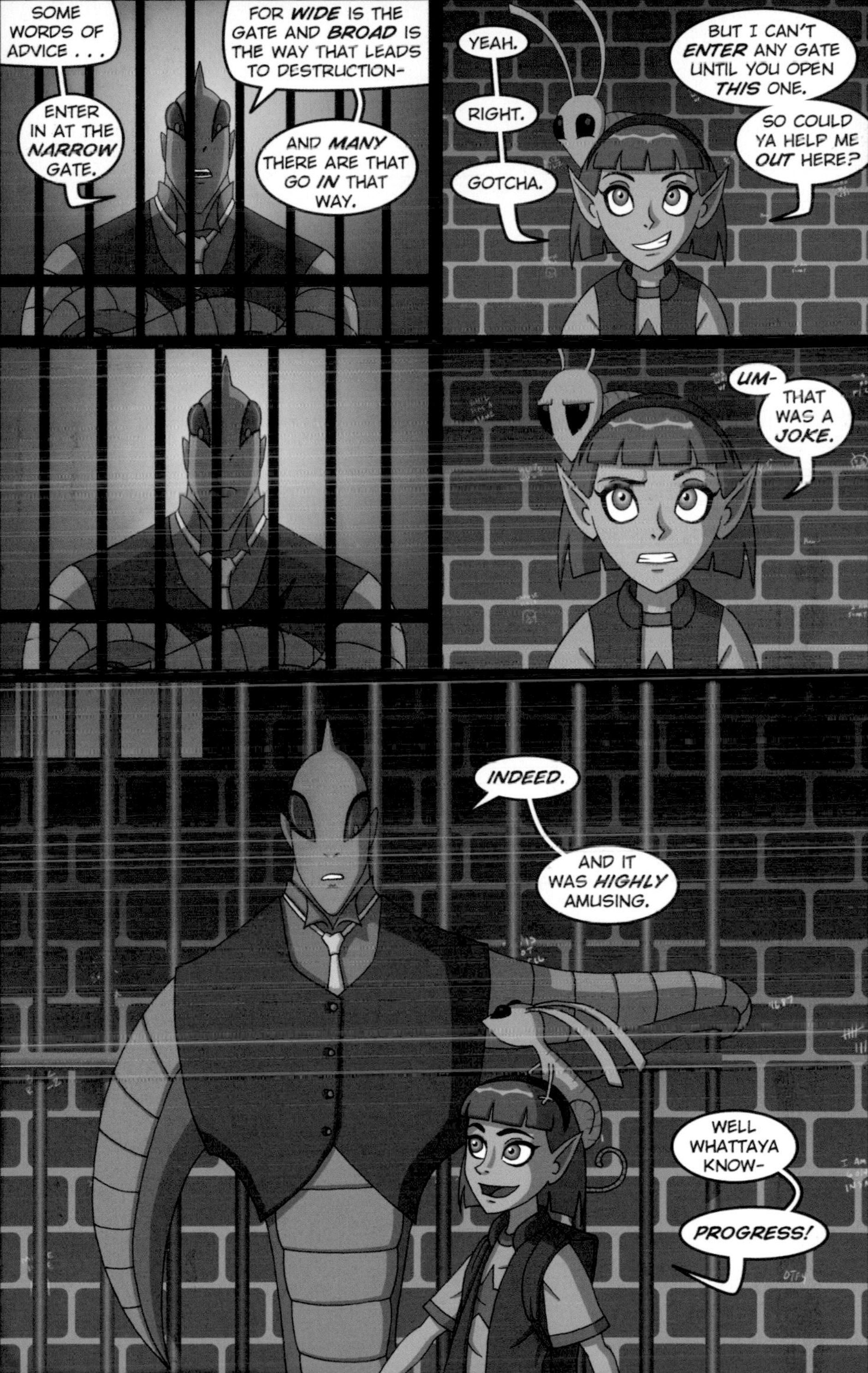
SOME WORDS OF ADVICE . . .
ENTER IN AT THE *NARROW* GATE.
FOR *WIDE* IS THE GATE AND *BROAD* IS THE WAY THAT LEADS TO DESTRUCTION-
AND *MANY* THERE ARE THAT GO *IN* THAT WAY.
YEAH.
RIGHT.
GOTCHA.
BUT I CAN'T *ENTER* ANY GATE UNTIL YOU OPEN *THIS* ONE.
SO COULD YA HELP ME *OUT* HERE?
UM-
THAT WAS A *JOKE.*
INDEED.
AND IT WAS *HIGHLY* AMUSING.
WELL WHATTAYA KNOW-
PROGRESS!

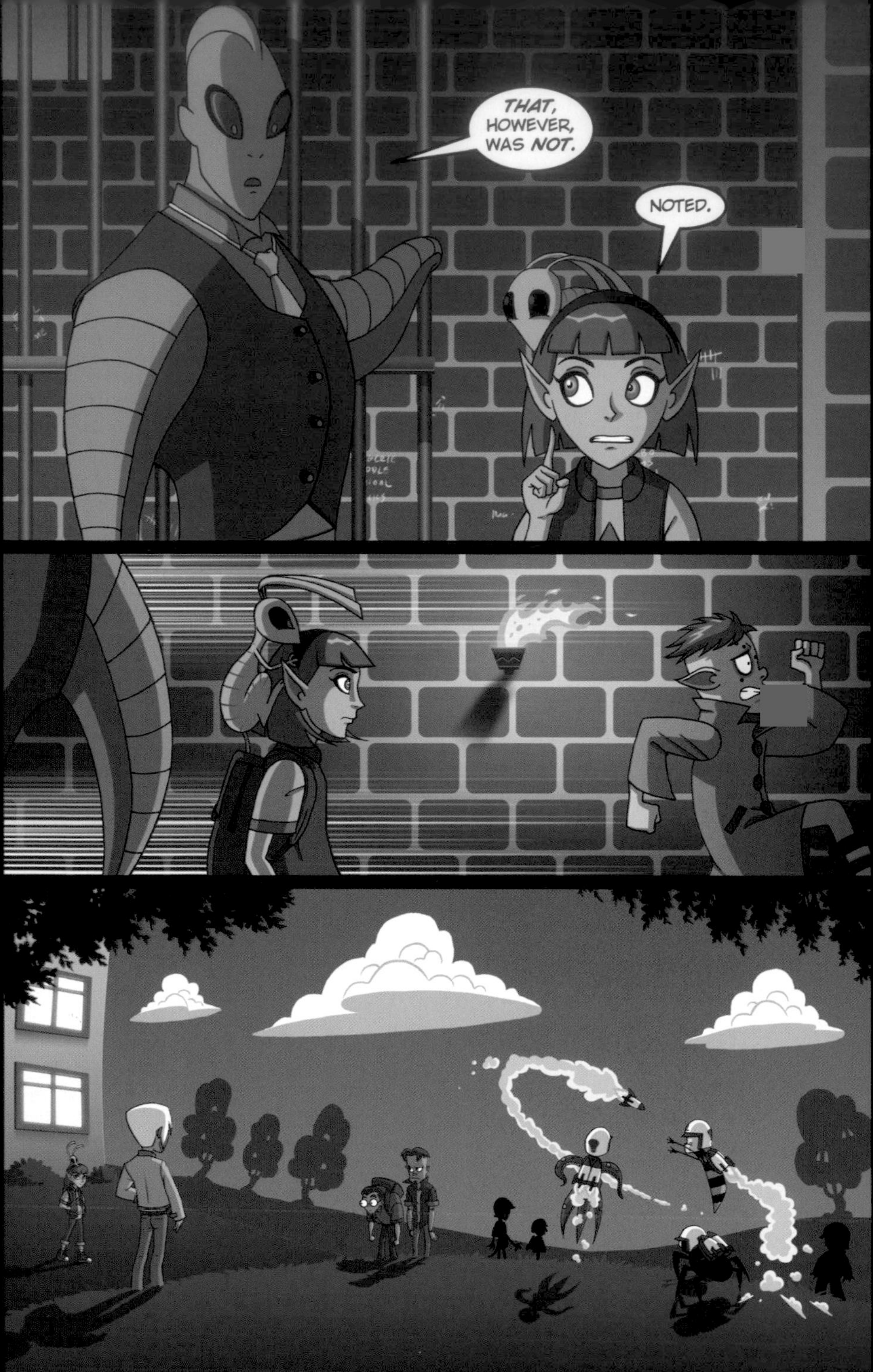
THAT, HOWEVER, WAS NOT.
NOTED.

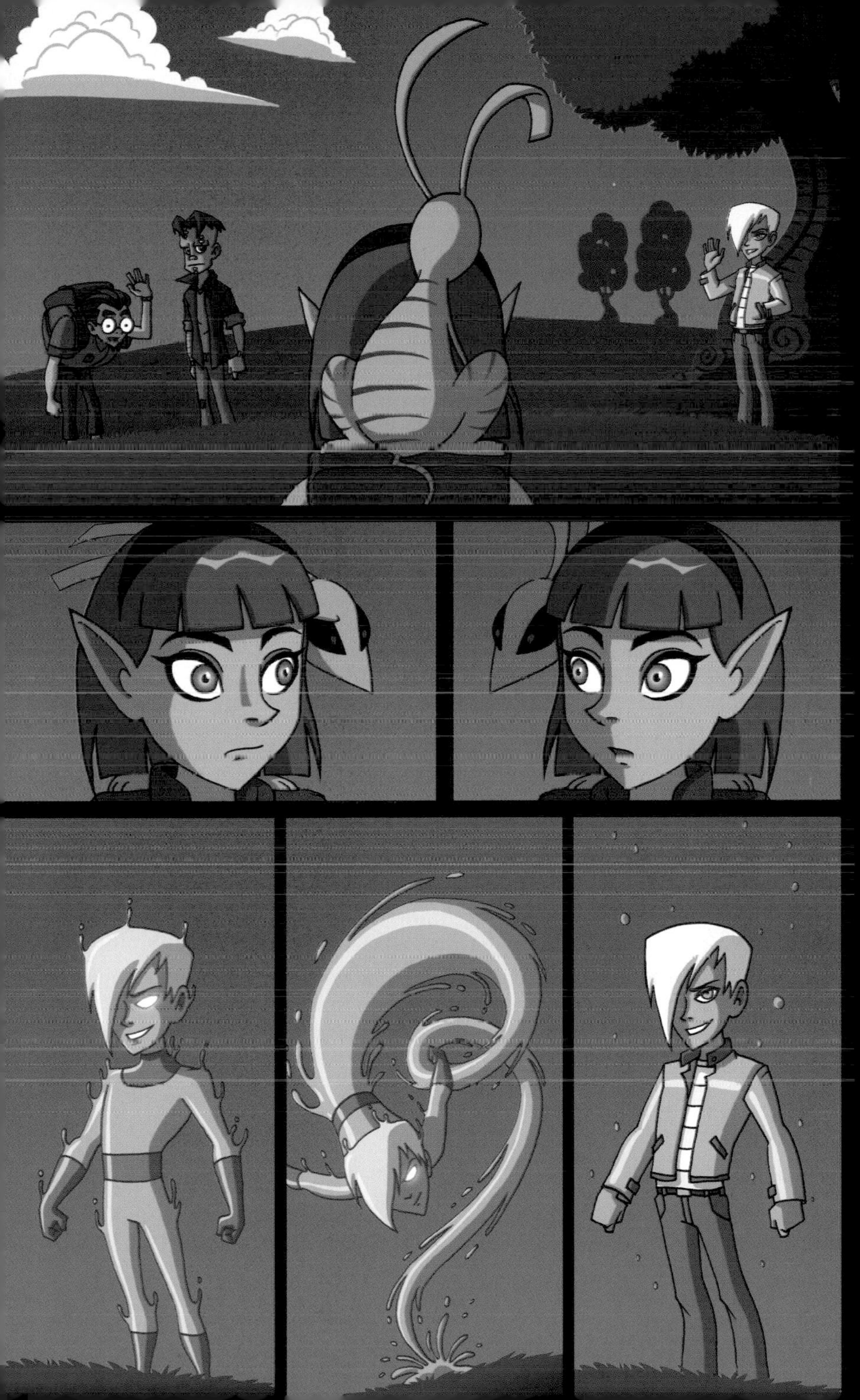

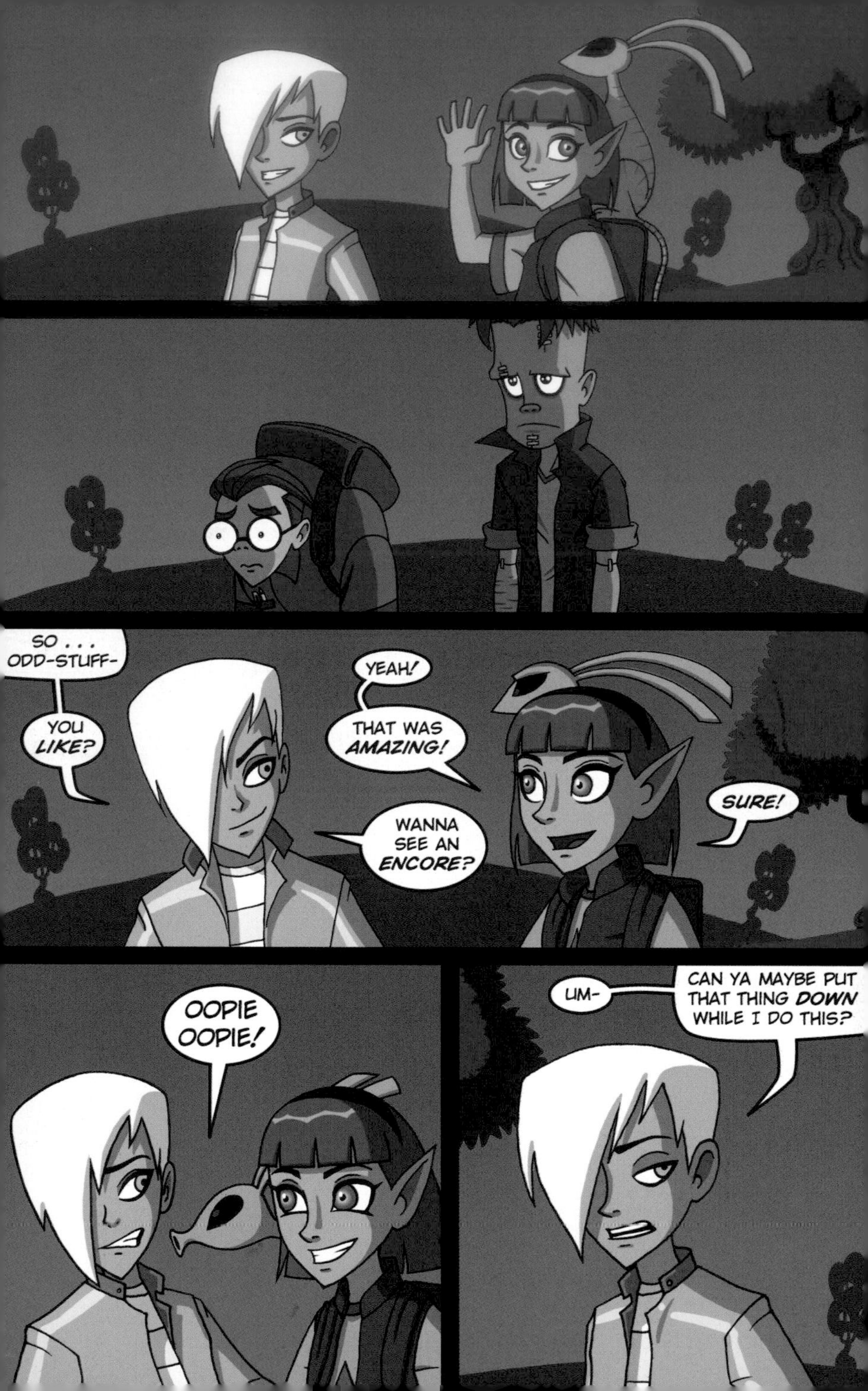
SO . . . ODD-STUFF-
YOU LIKE?
YEAH!
THAT WAS AMAZING!
WANNA SEE AN ENCORE?
SURE!
OOPIE OOPIE!
UM-
CAN YA MAYBE PUT THAT THING DOWN WHILE I DO THIS?

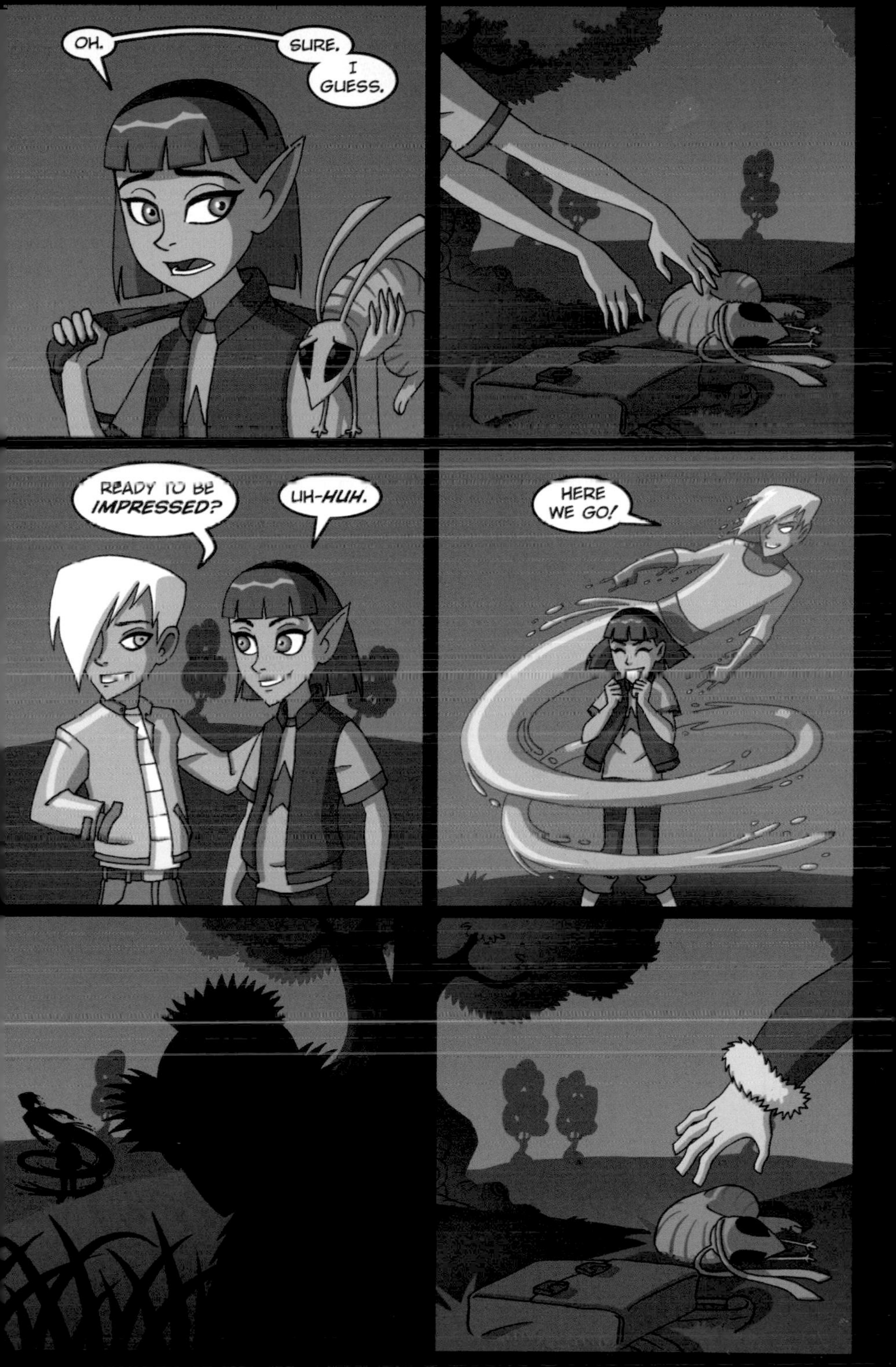
OH.
SURE. I GUESS.
READY TO BE IMPRESSED?
UH-HUH.
HERE WE GO!

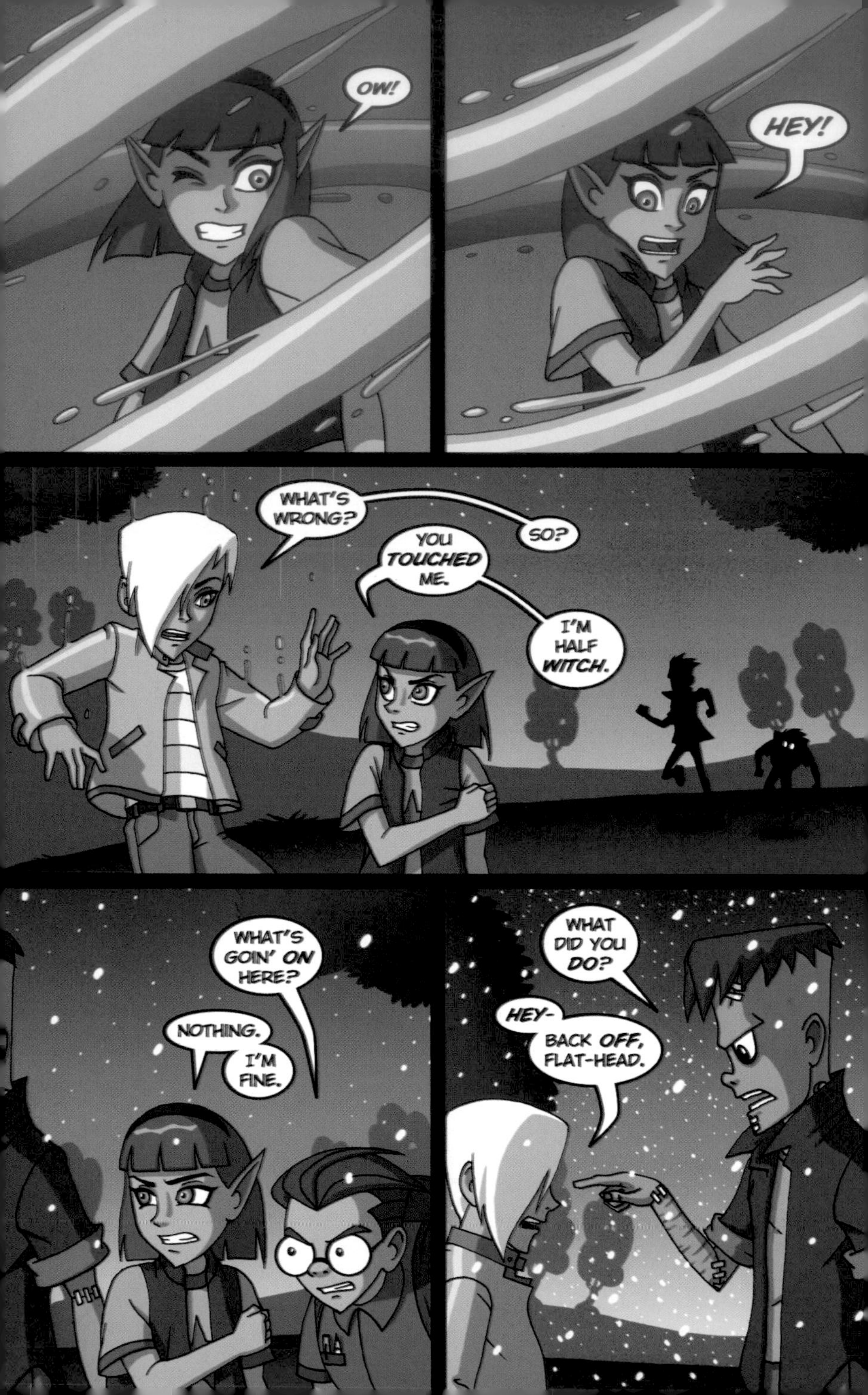
OW!
HEY!
WHAT'S WRONG?
YOU TOUCHED ME.
SO?
I'M HALF WITCH.
WHAT'S GOIN' ON HERE?
NOTHING.
I'M FINE.
WHAT DID YOU DO?
HEY-
BACK OFF, FLAT-HEAD.

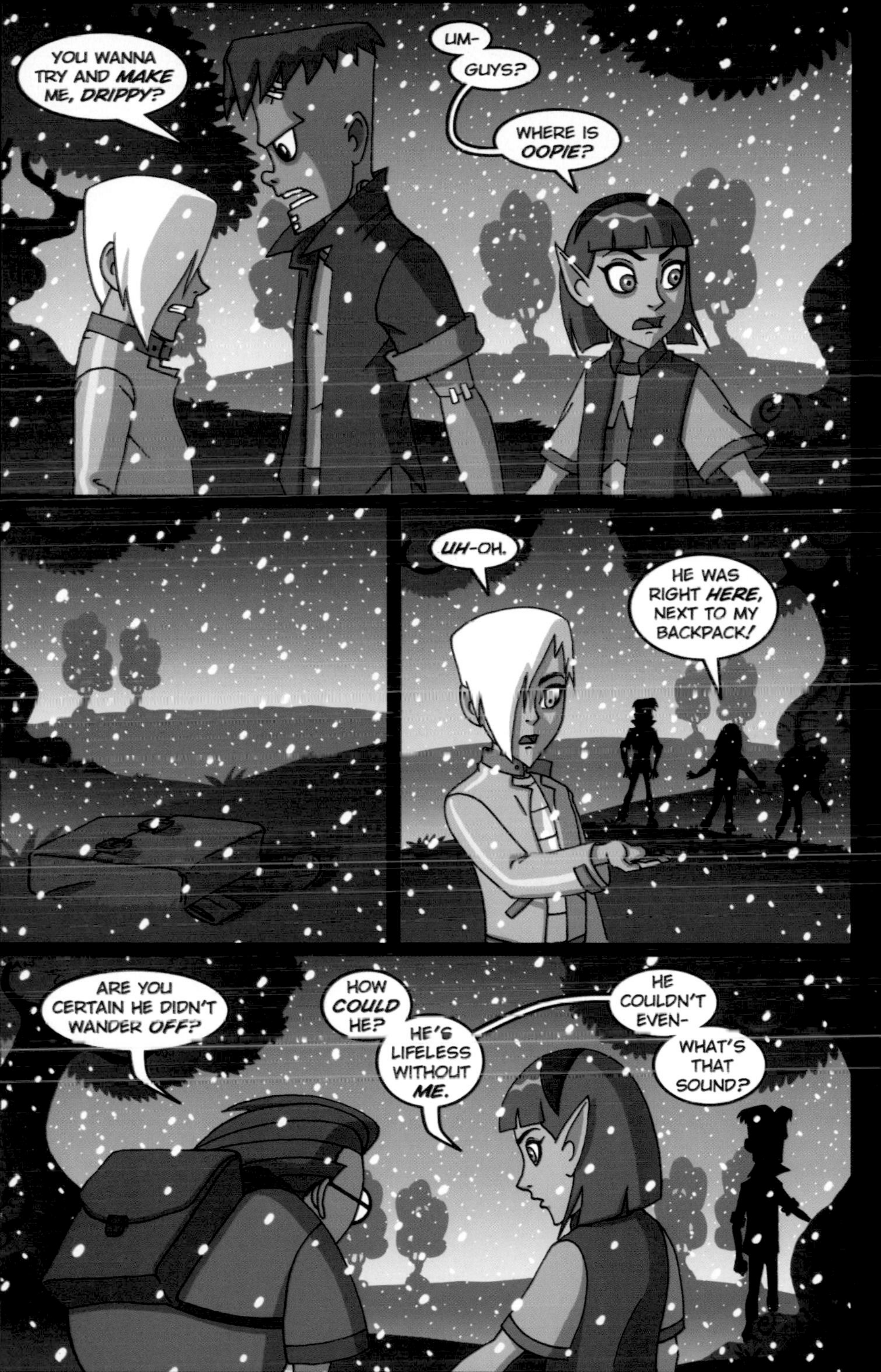
YOU WANNA TRY AND MAKE ME, DRIPPY?
UM-
GUYS?
WHERE IS OOPIE?
UH-OH.
HE WAS RIGHT HERE, NEXT TO MY BACKPACK!
ARE YOU CERTAIN HE DIDN'T WANDER OFF?
HOW COULD HE?
HE'S LIFELESS WITHOUT ME.
HE COULDN'T EVEN-
WHAT'S THAT SOUND?

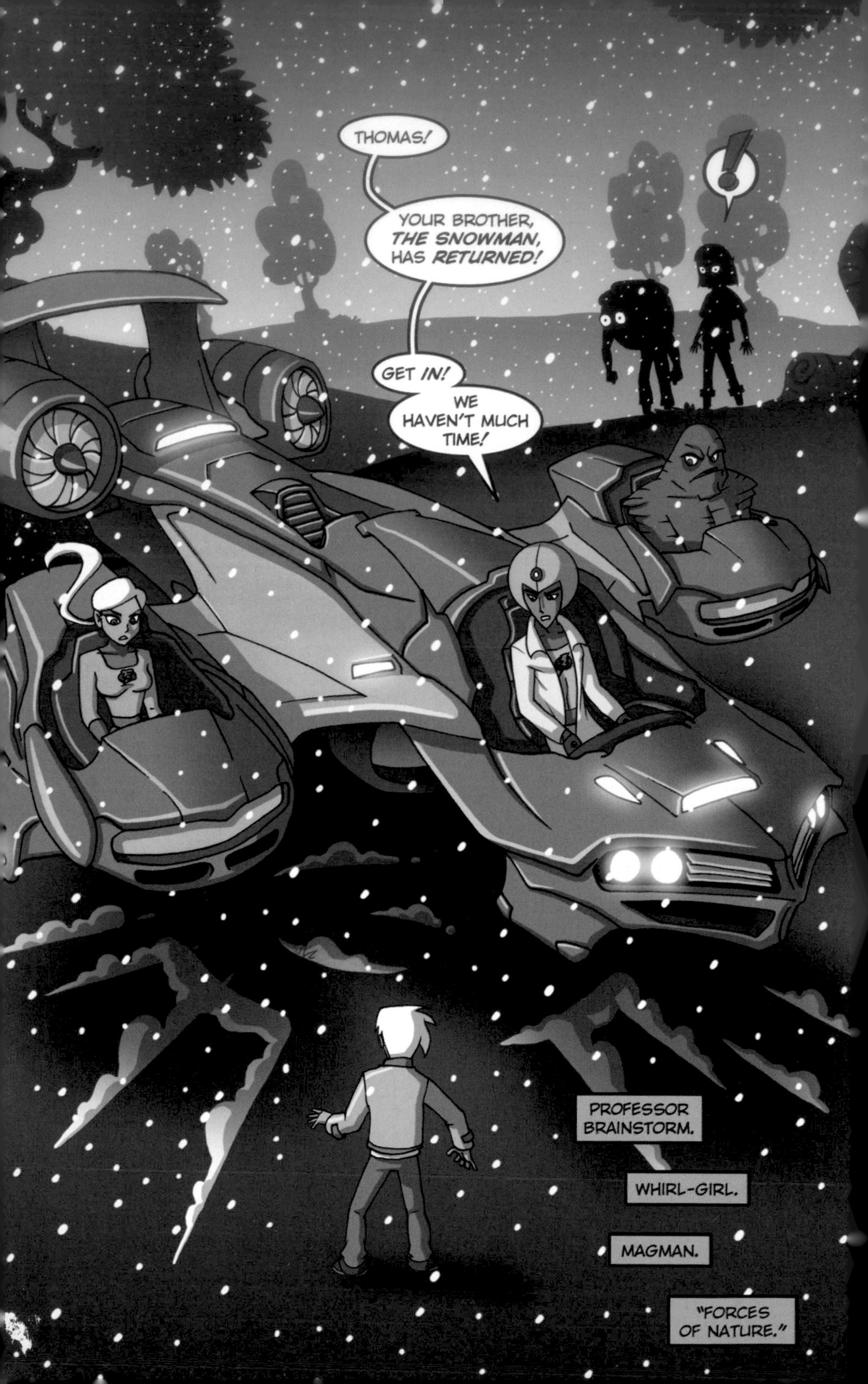
THOMAS!
YOUR BROTHER, THE SNOWMAN, HAS RETURNED!
GET IN!
WE HAVEN'T MUCH TIME!
!
PROFESSOR BRAINSTORM.
WHIRL-GIRL.
MAGMAN.
"FORCES OF NATURE."

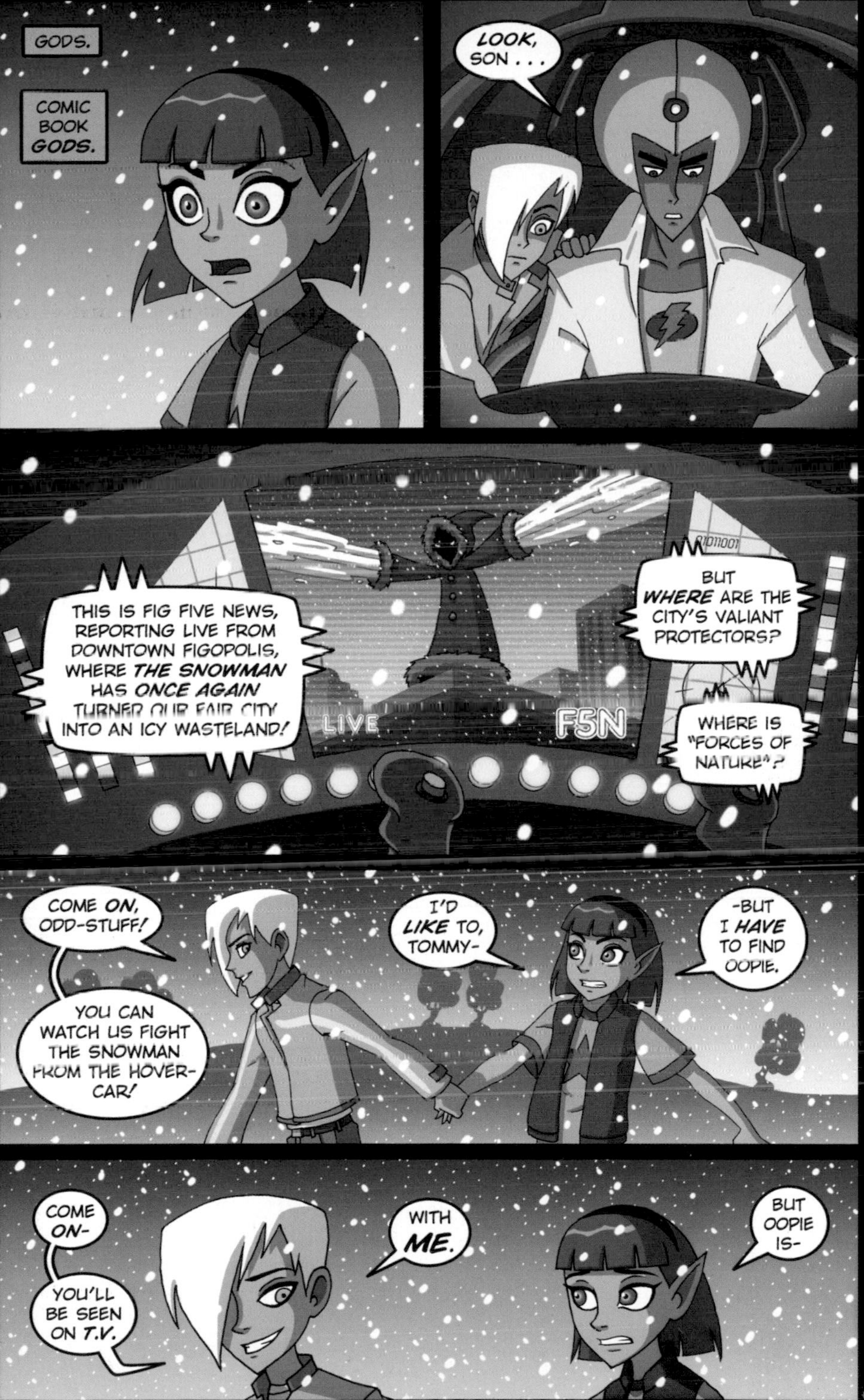

GODS.
COMIC BOOK GODS.
LOOK, SON . . .
THIS IS FIG FIVE NEWS, REPORTING LIVE FROM DOWNTOWN FIGOPOLIS, WHERE THE SNOWMAN HAS ONCE AGAIN TURNED OUR FAIR CITY INTO AN ICY WASTELAND!
LIVE
F5N
BUT WHERE ARE THE CITY'S VALIANT PROTECTORS?
WHERE IS "FORCES OF NATURE"?
COME ON, ODD-STUFF!
YOU CAN WATCH US FIGHT THE SNOWMAN FROM THE HOVER-CAR!
I'D LIKE TO, TOMMY-
-BUT I HAVE TO FIND OOPIE.
COME ON-
YOU'LL BE SEEN ON T.V.
WITH ME.
BUT OOPIE IS-

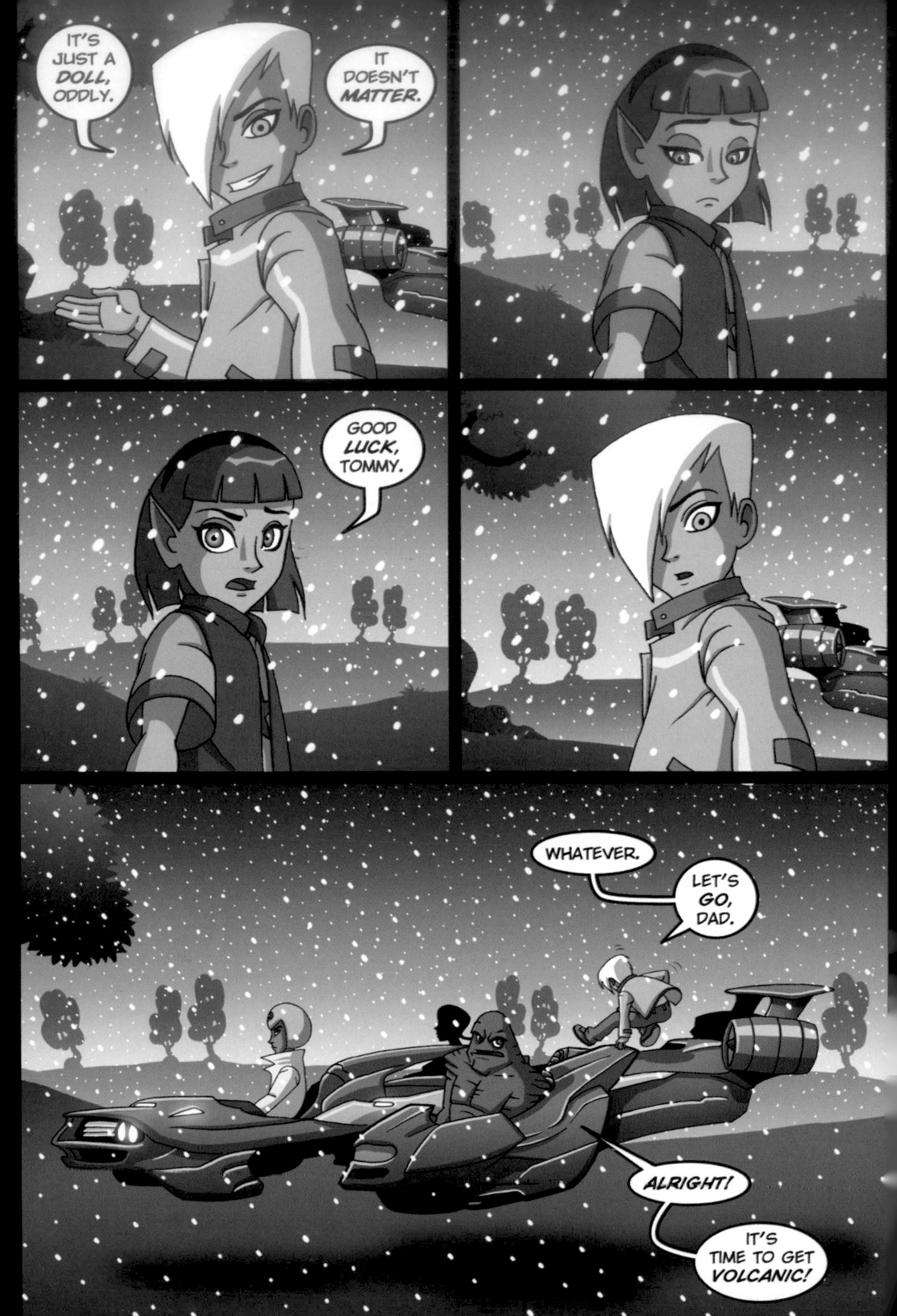
IT'S JUST A DOLL, ODDLY.
IT DOESN'T MATTER.
GOOD LUCK, TOMMY.
WHATEVER.
LET'S GO, DAD.
ALRIGHT!
IT'S TIME TO GET VOLCANIC!

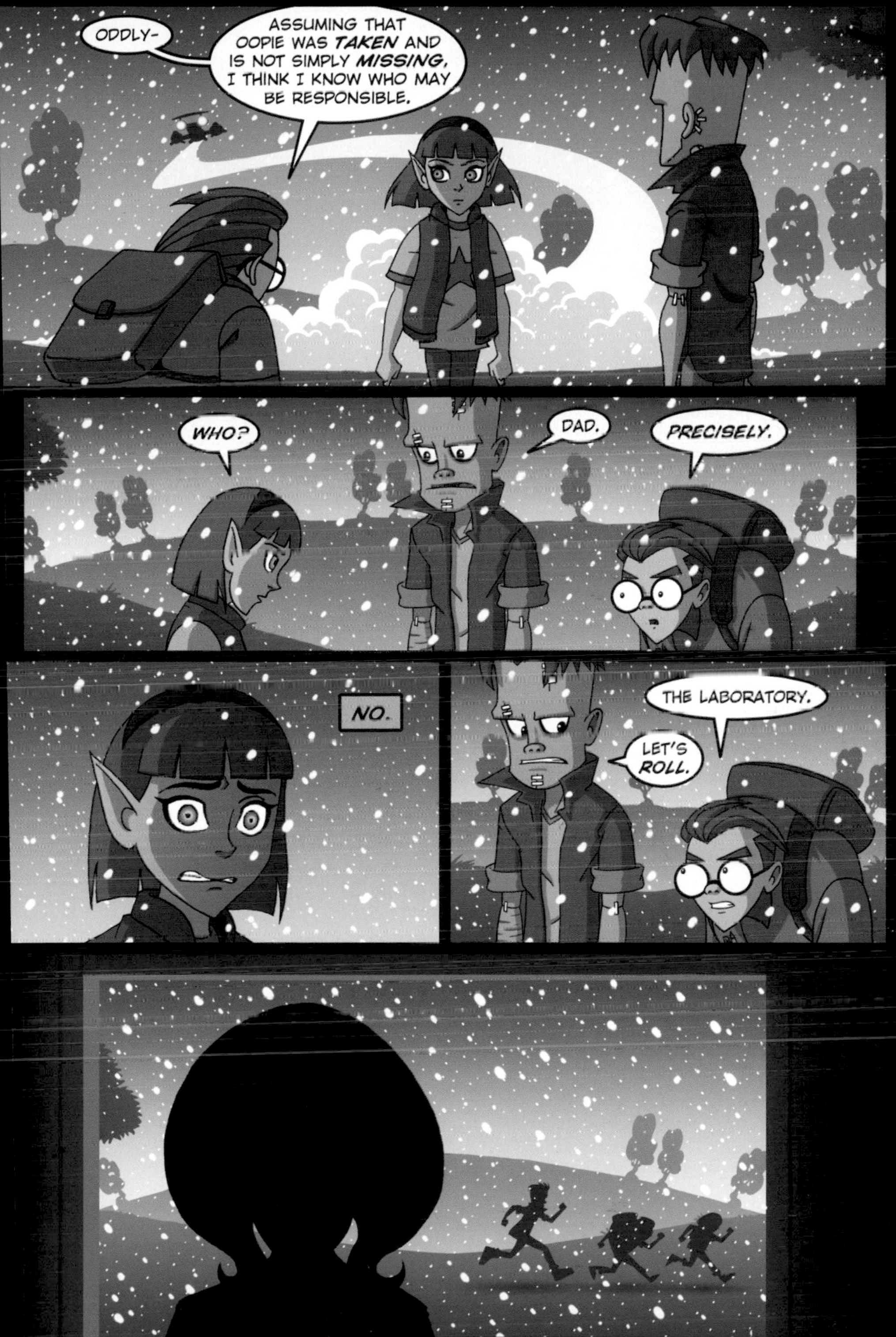
ODDLY-
ASSUMING THAT OOPIE WAS TAKEN AND IS NOT SIMPLY MISSING, I THINK I KNOW WHO MAY BE RESPONSIBLE.
WHO?
DAD.
PRECISELY.
NO.
THE LABORATORY.
LET'S ROLL.

Chapter 5

OOPS

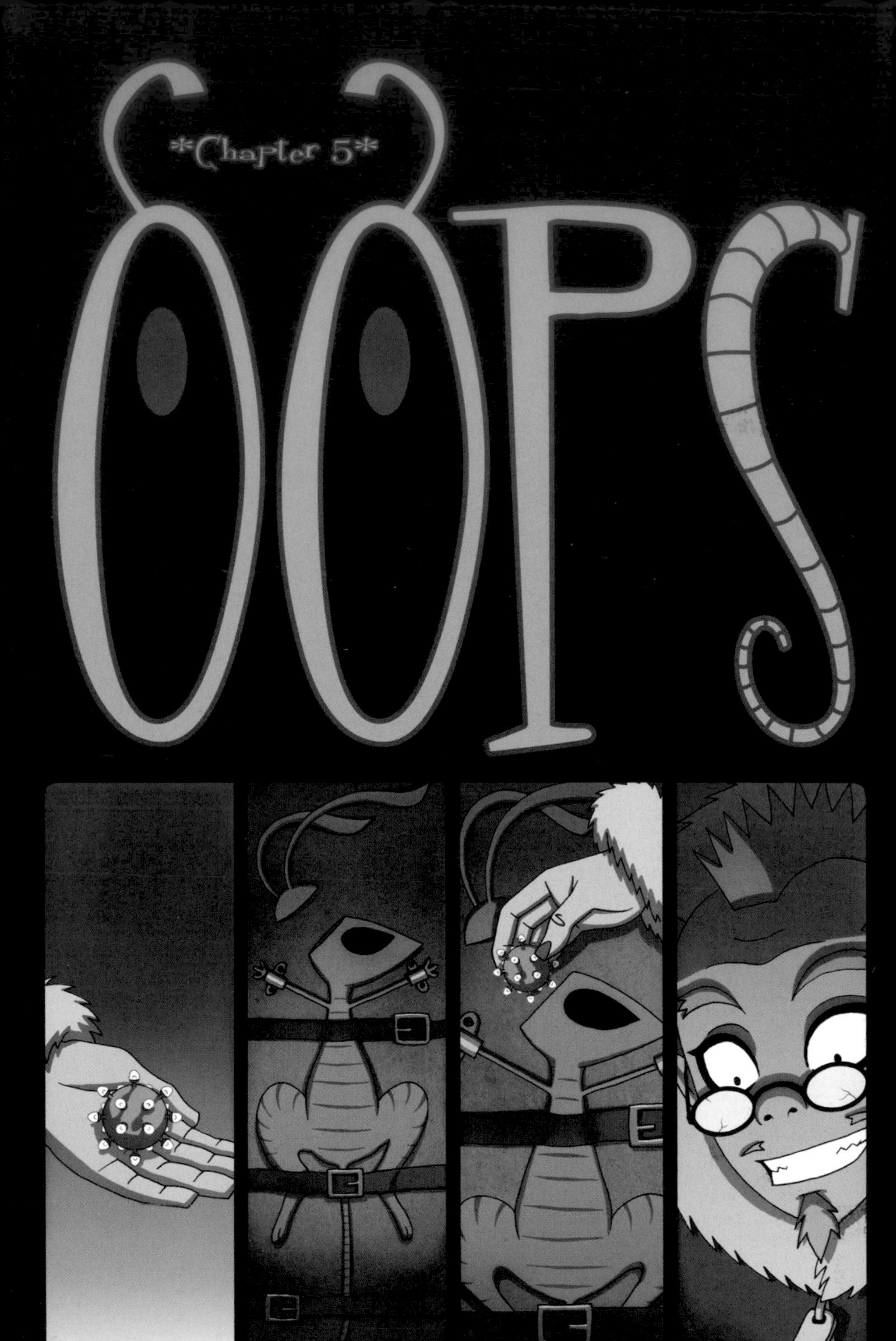

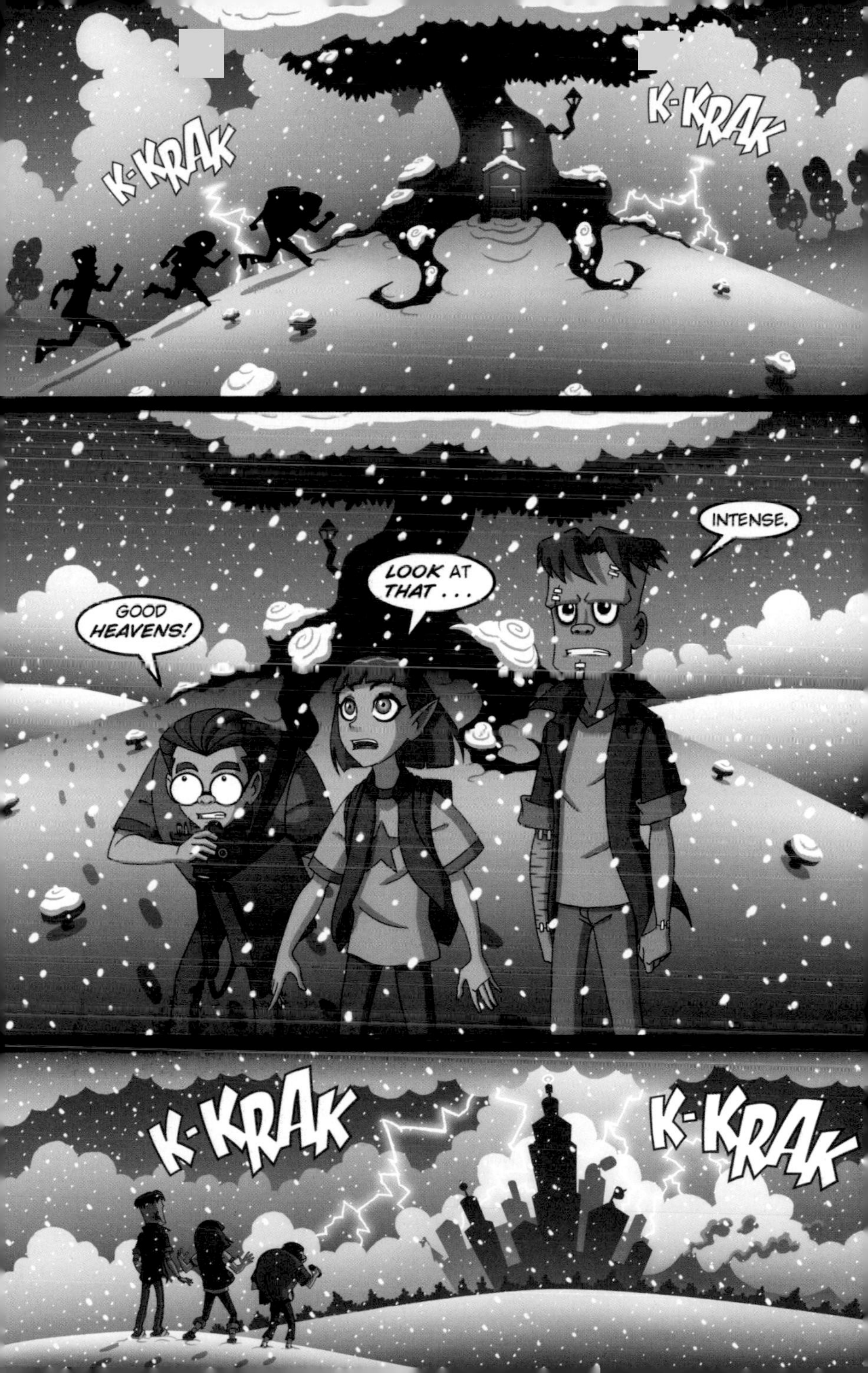
K-KRAK
K-KRAK
GOOD HEAVENS!
LOOK AT THAT . . .
INTENSE.
K-KRAK
K-KRAK

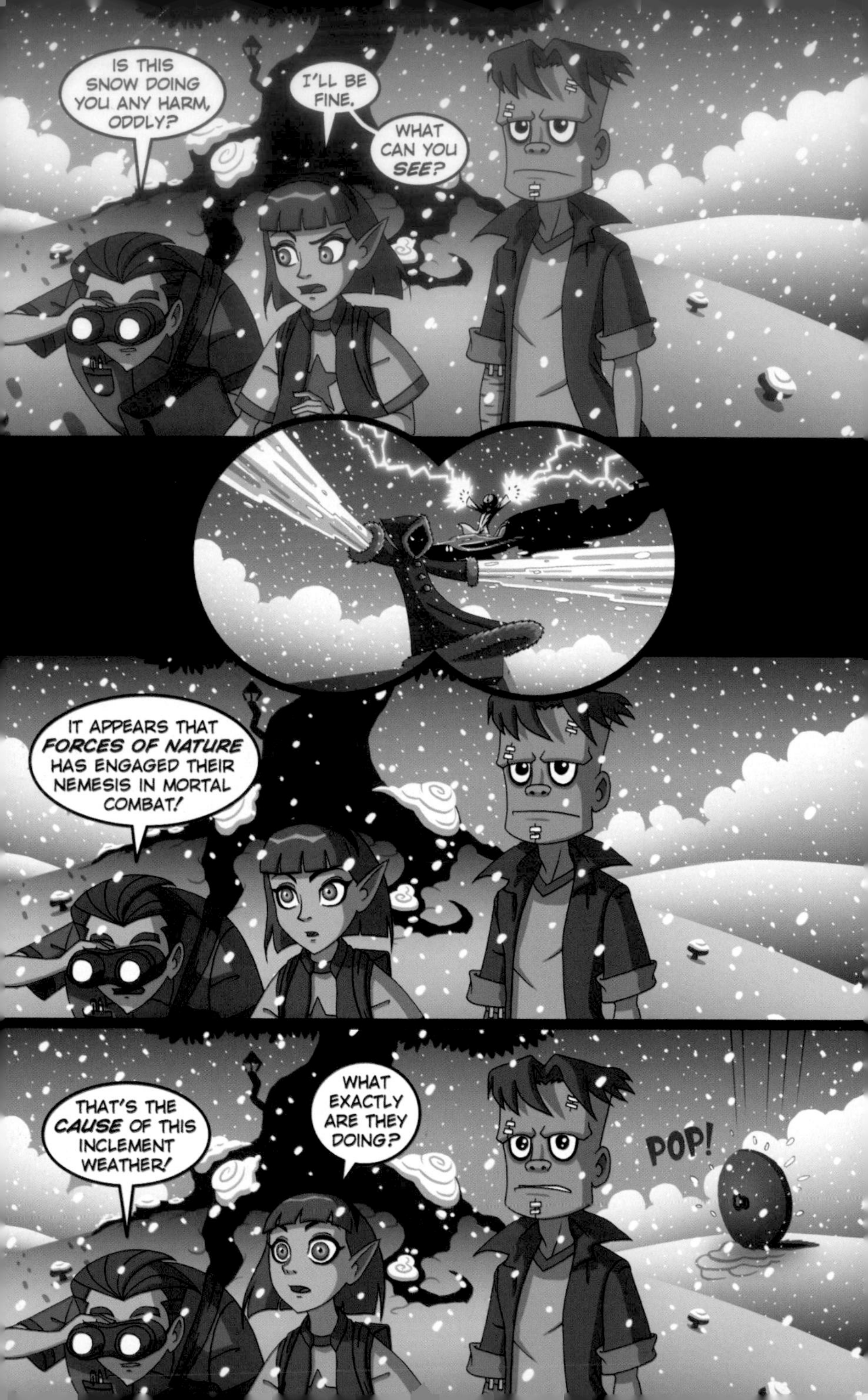
IS THIS SNOW DOING YOU ANY HARM, ODDLY?
I'LL BE FINE.
WHAT CAN YOU SEE?
IT APPEARS THAT FORCES OF NATURE HAS ENGAGED THEIR NEMESIS IN MORTAL COMBAT!
THAT'S THE CAUSE OF THIS INCLEMENT WEATHER!
WHAT EXACTLY ARE THEY DOING?
POP!

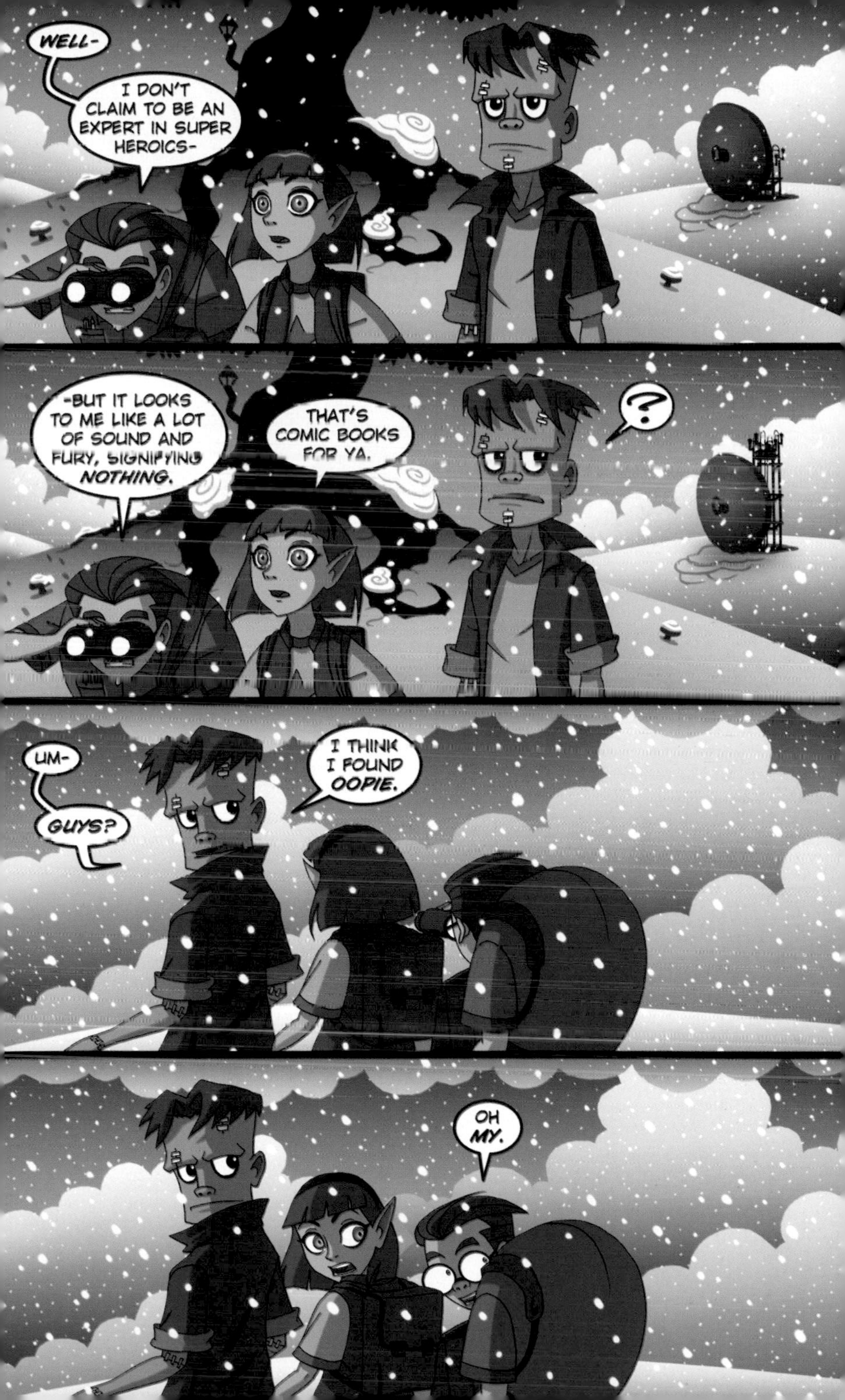
WELL-
I DON'T CLAIM TO BE AN EXPERT IN SUPER HEROICS-
-BUT IT LOOKS TO ME LIKE A LOT OF SOUND AND FURY, SIGNIFYING *NOTHING.*
THAT'S COMIC BOOKS FOR YA.
?
UM-
GUYS?
I THINK I FOUND *OOPIE.*
OH *MY.*

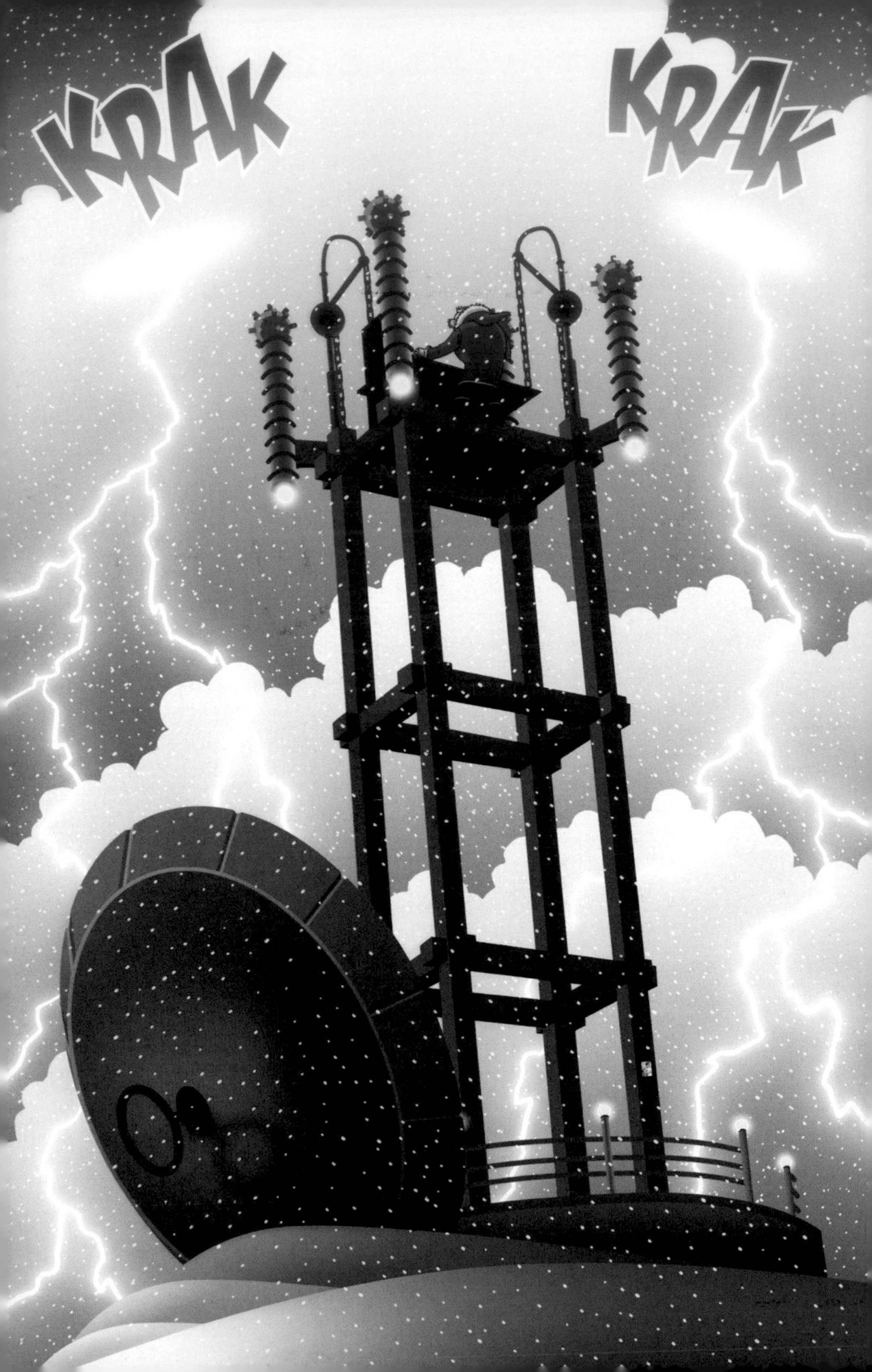
KRAK
KRAK

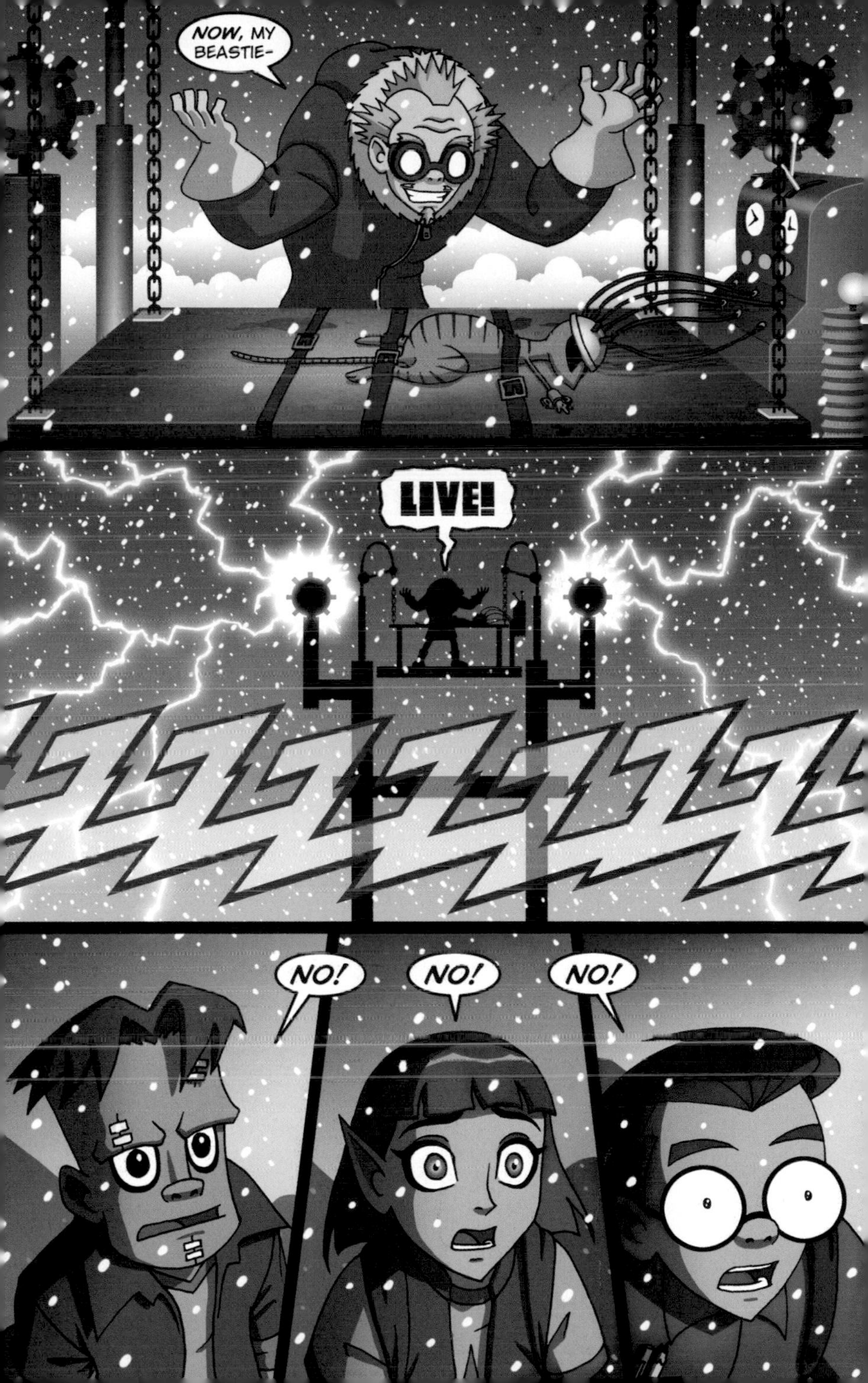
NOW, MY BEASTIE-
LIVE!
NO!
NO!
NO!

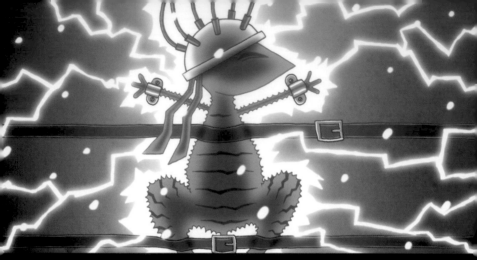

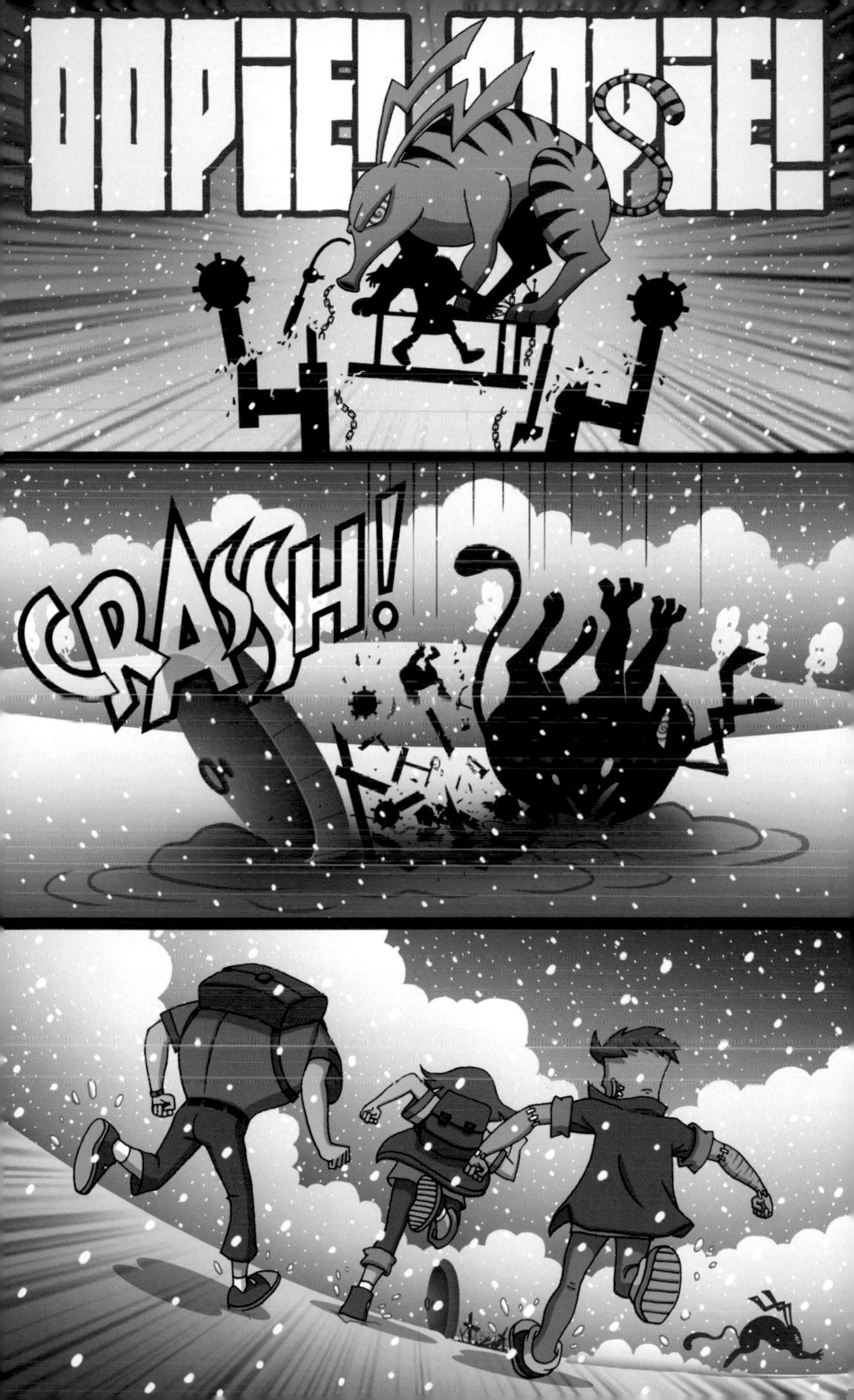
OOPiE!
CRASH!

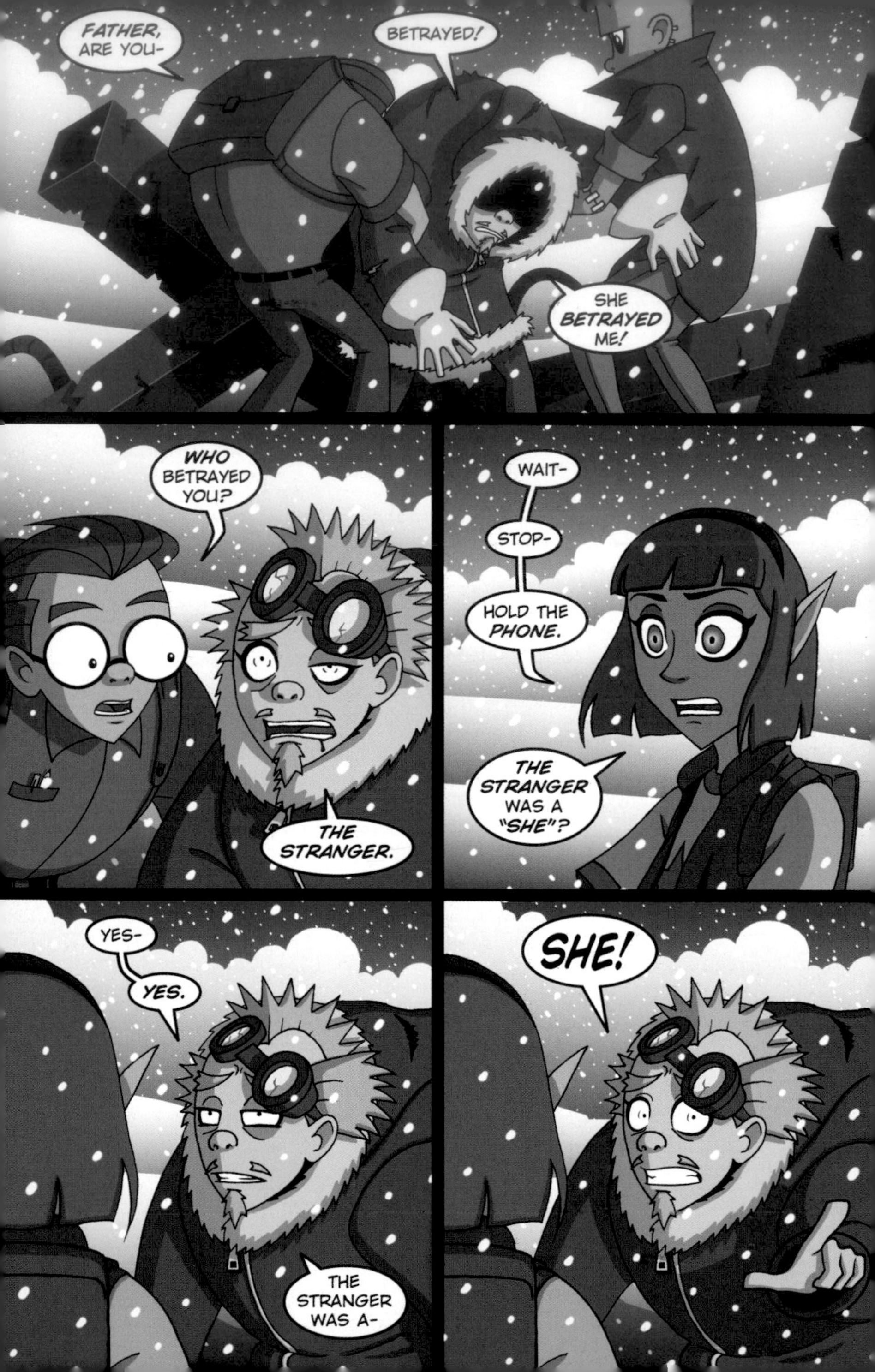
FATHER, ARE YOU-
BETRAYED!
SHE BETRAYED ME!
WHO BETRAYED YOU?
THE STRANGER.
WAIT-
STOP-
HOLD THE PHONE.
THE STRANGER WAS A "SHE"?
YES-
YES.
THE STRANGER WAS A-
SHE!

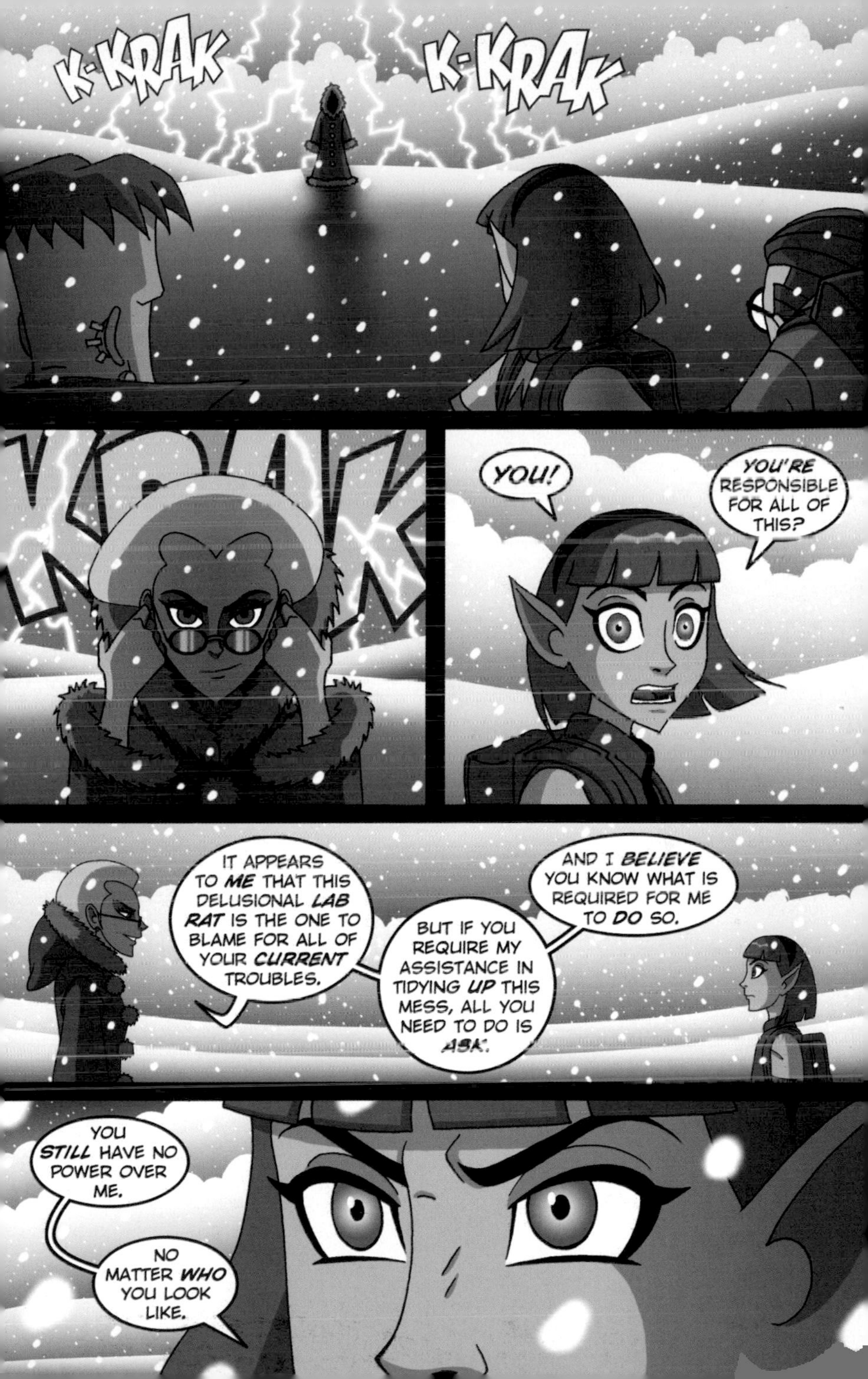
K-KRAK
K-KRAK
YOU!
YOU'RE RESPONSIBLE FOR ALL OF THIS?
IT APPEARS TO ME THAT THIS DELUSIONAL LAB RAT IS THE ONE TO BLAME FOR ALL OF YOUR CURRENT TROUBLES.
BUT IF YOU REQUIRE MY ASSISTANCE IN TIDYING UP THIS MESS, ALL YOU NEED TO DO IS ASK.
AND I BELIEVE YOU KNOW WHAT IS REQUIRED FOR ME TO DO SO.
YOU STILL HAVE NO POWER OVER ME.
NO MATTER WHO YOU LOOK LIKE.

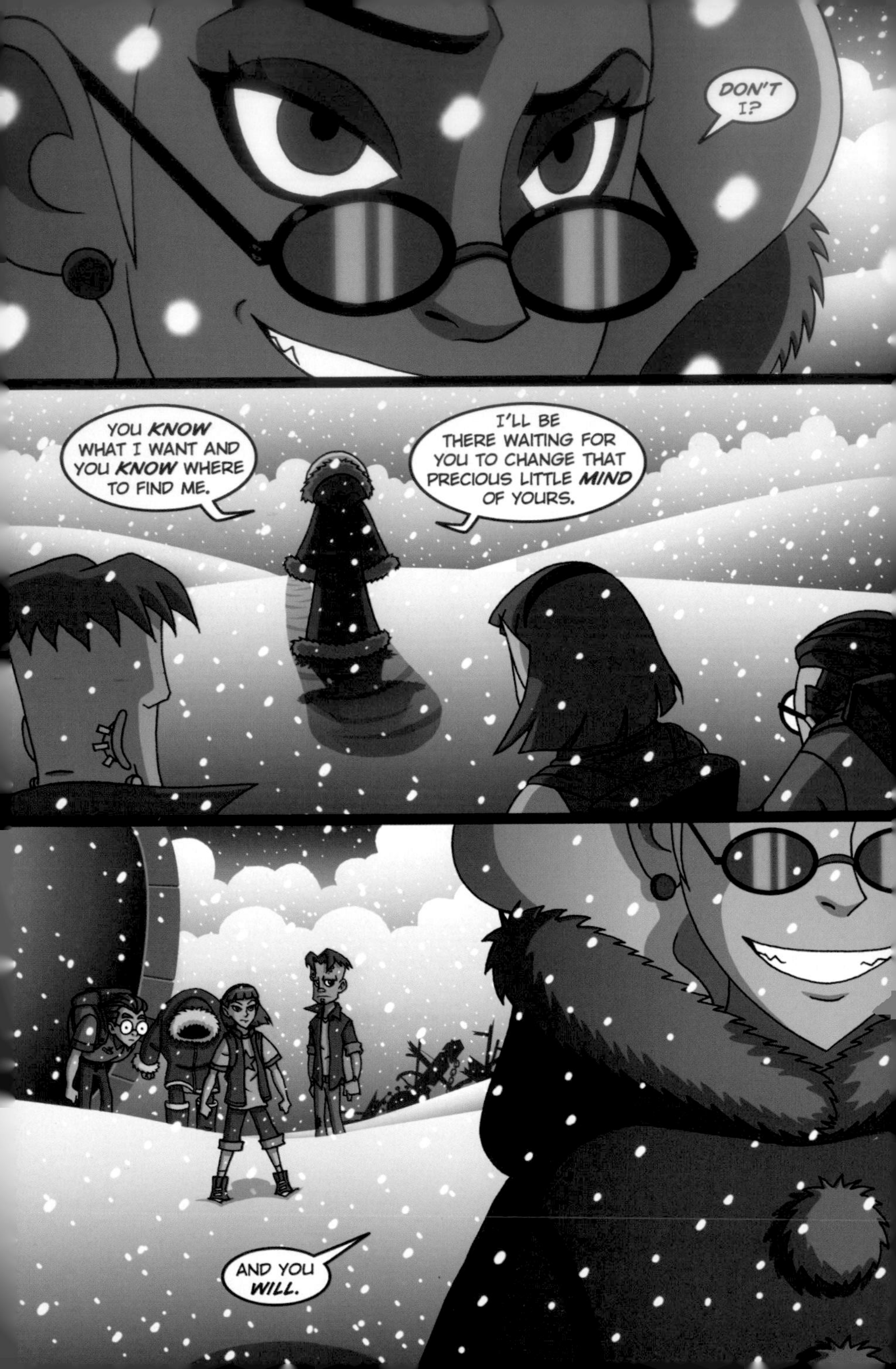
DON'T I?
YOU KNOW WHAT I WANT AND YOU KNOW WHERE TO FIND ME.
I'LL BE THERE WAITING FOR YOU TO CHANGE THAT PRECIOUS LITTLE MIND OF YOURS.
AND YOU WILL.

Chapter 6

Good Guys, Bad Guys, And Other Such Professions

OOPIE.
WHAT ARE YOU DOING?

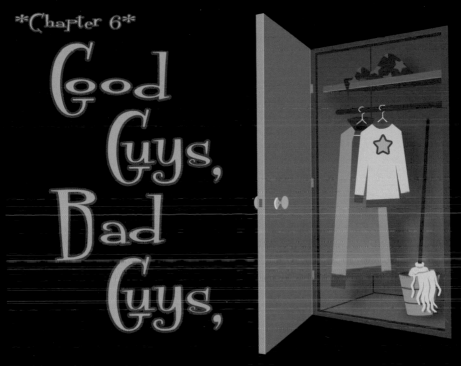

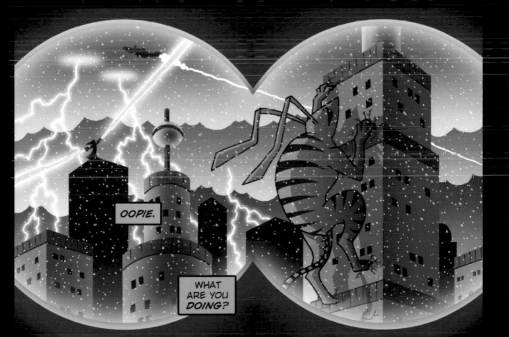

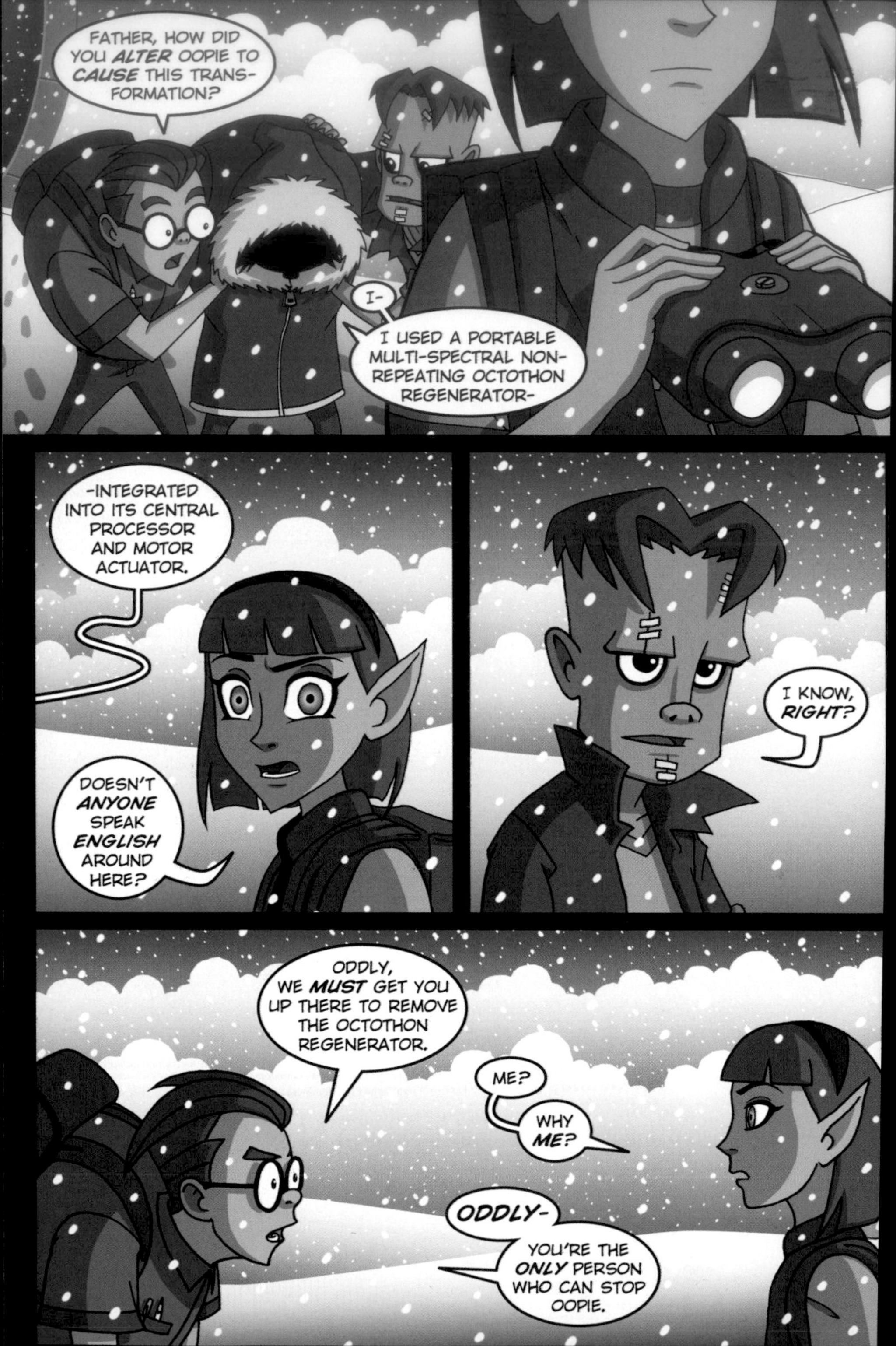
FATHER, HOW DID YOU ALTER OOPIE TO CAUSE THIS TRANS-FORMATION?
I-
I USED A PORTABLE MULTI-SPECTRAL NON-REPEATING OCTOTHON REGENERATOR-
-INTEGRATED INTO ITS CENTRAL PROCESSOR AND MOTOR ACTUATOR.
DOESN'T ANYONE SPEAK ENGLISH AROUND HERE?
I KNOW, RIGHT?
ODDLY, WE MUST GET YOU UP THERE TO REMOVE THE OCTOTHON REGENERATOR.
ME?
WHY ME?
ODDLY-
YOU'RE THE ONLY PERSON WHO CAN STOP OOPIE.

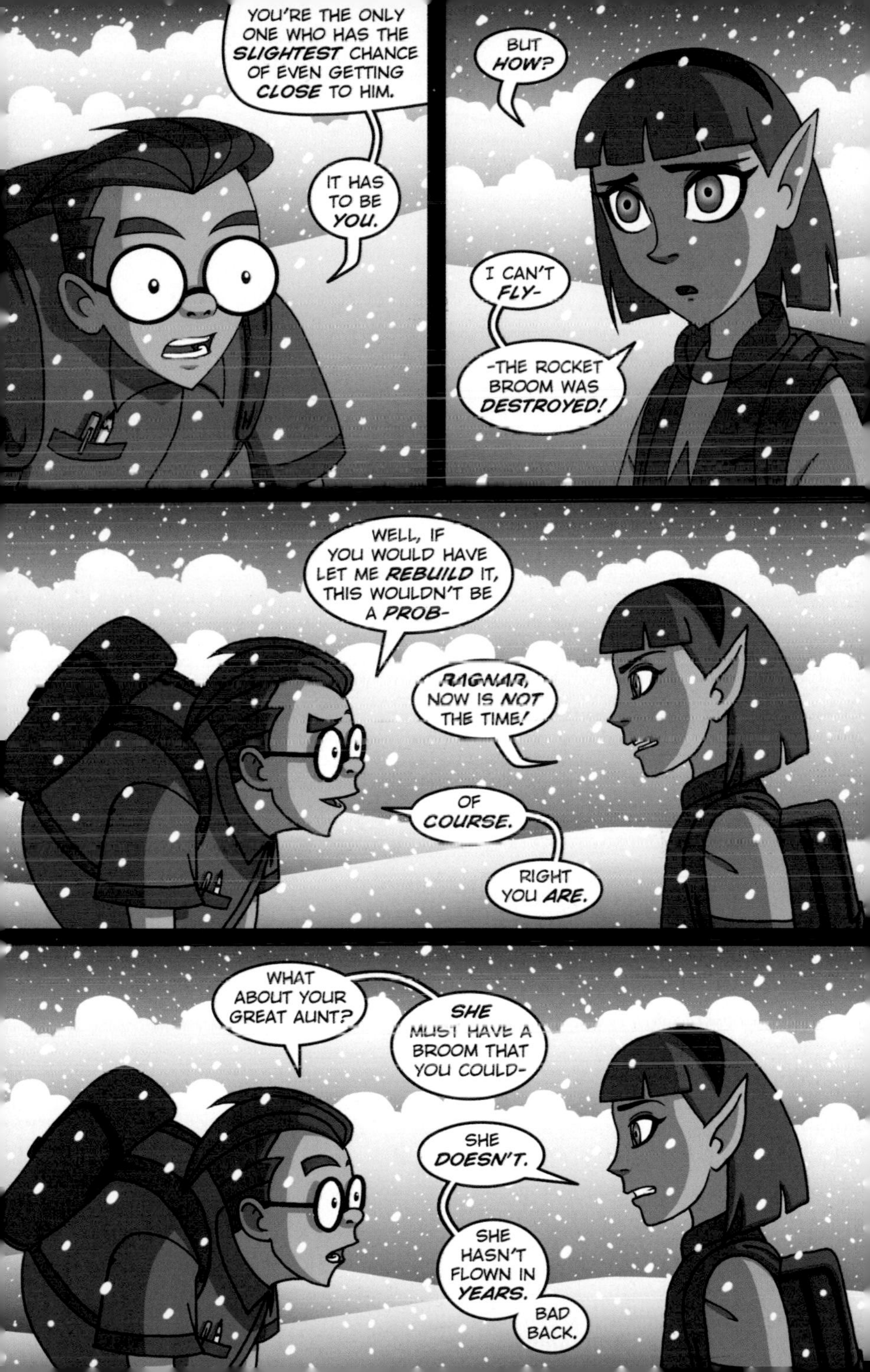
YOU'RE THE ONLY ONE WHO HAS THE SLIGHTEST CHANCE OF EVEN GETTING CLOSE TO HIM.
IT HAS TO BE YOU.
BUT HOW?
I CAN'T FLY-
-THE ROCKET BROOM WAS DESTROYED!
WELL, IF YOU WOULD HAVE LET ME REBUILD IT, THIS WOULDN'T BE A PROB-
RAGNAR, NOW IS NOT THE TIME!
OF COURSE.
RIGHT YOU ARE.
WHAT ABOUT YOUR GREAT AUNT?
SHE MUST HAVE A BROOM THAT YOU COULD-
SHE DOESN'T.
SHE HASN'T FLOWN IN YEARS.
BAD BACK.

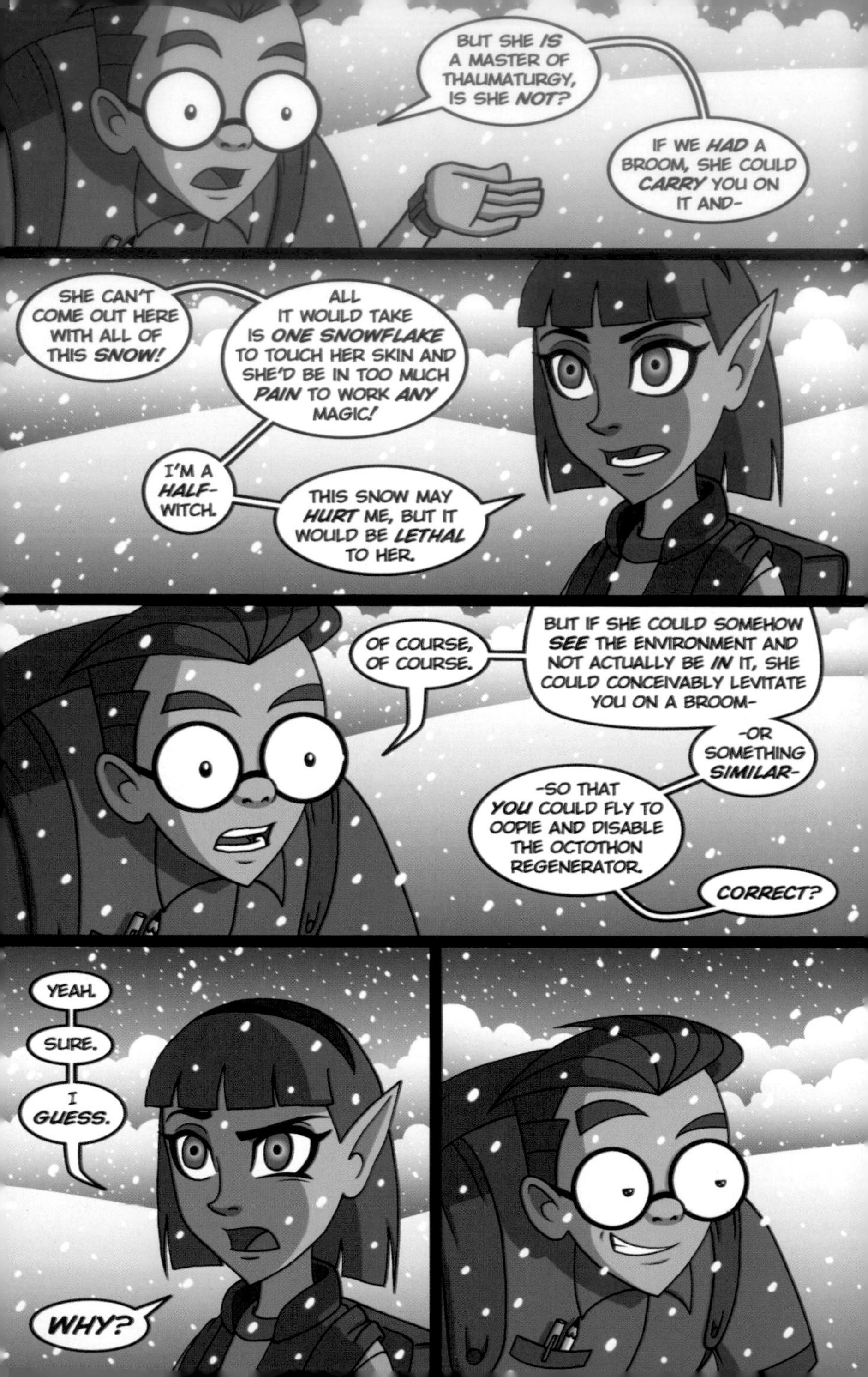
BUT SHE IS A MASTER OF THAUMATURGY, IS SHE NOT?
IF WE HAD A BROOM, SHE COULD CARRY YOU ON IT AND-
SHE CAN'T COME OUT HERE WITH ALL OF THIS SNOW!
ALL IT WOULD TAKE IS ONE SNOWFLAKE TO TOUCH HER SKIN AND SHE'D BE IN TOO MUCH PAIN TO WORK ANY MAGIC!
I'M A HALF-WITCH.
THIS SNOW MAY HURT ME, BUT IT WOULD BE LETHAL TO HER.
OF COURSE, OF COURSE.
BUT IF SHE COULD SOMEHOW SEE THE ENVIRONMENT AND NOT ACTUALLY BE IN IT, SHE COULD CONCEIVABLY LEVITATE YOU ON A BROOM-
-OR SOMETHING SIMILAR-
-SO THAT YOU COULD FLY TO OOPIE AND DISABLE THE OCTOTHON REGENERATOR.
CORRECT?
YEAH.
SURE.
I GUESS.
WHY?

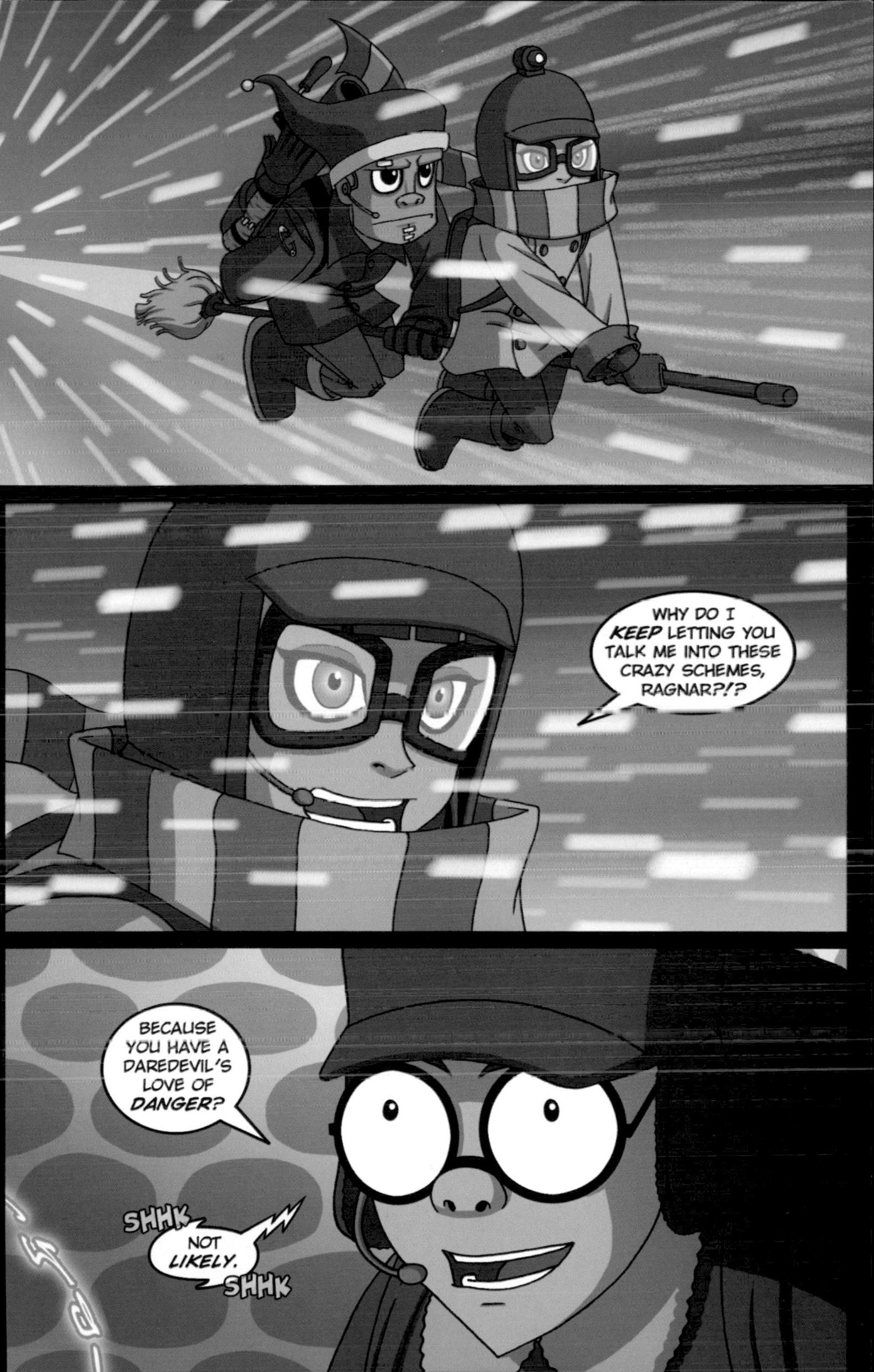
WHY DO I KEEP LETTING YOU TALK ME INTO THESE CRAZY SCHEMES, RAGNAR?!?
BECAUSE YOU HAVE A DAREDEVIL'S LOVE OF DANGER?
SHHK
NOT LIKELY.
SHHK

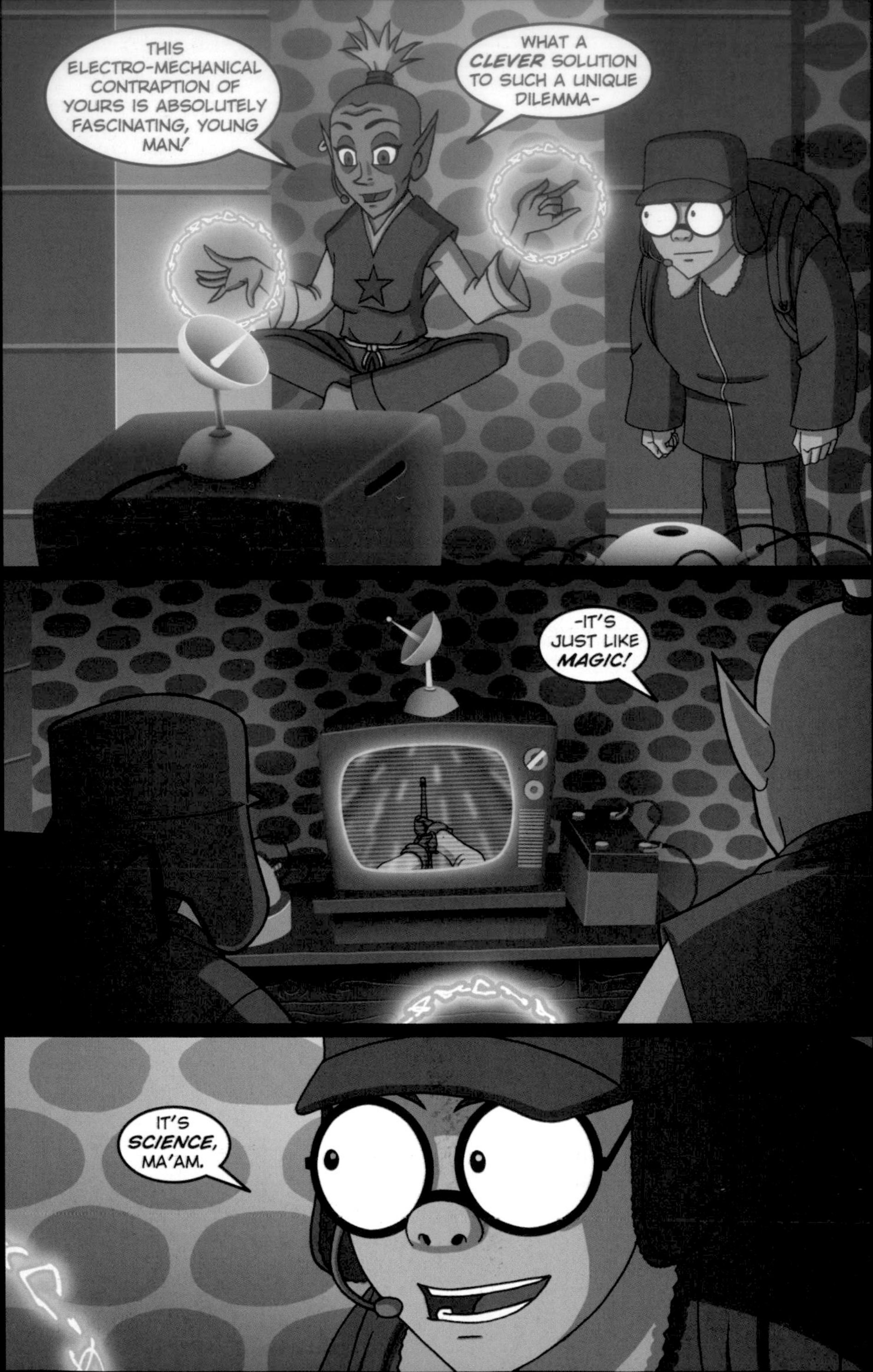
THIS ELECTRO-MECHANICAL CONTRAPTION OF YOURS IS ABSOLUTELY FASCINATING, YOUNG MAN!
WHAT A CLEVER SOLUTION TO SUCH A UNIQUE DILEMMA-
-IT'S JUST LIKE MAGIC!
IT'S SCIENCE, MA'AM.

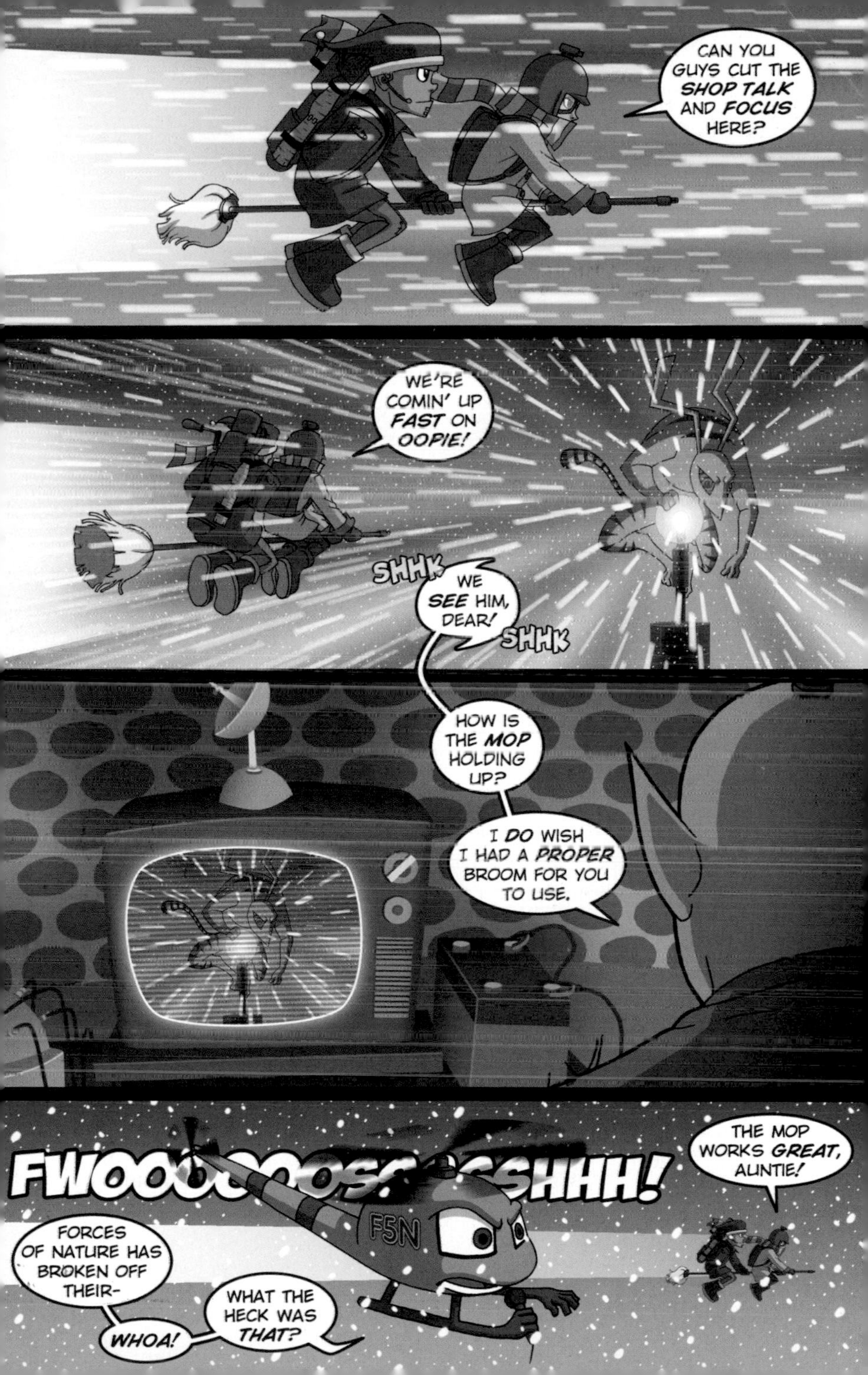
CAN YOU GUYS CUT THE SHOP TALK AND FOCUS HERE?
WE'RE COMIN' UP FAST ON OOPIE!
SHHK
WE SEE HIM, DEAR!
SHHK
HOW IS THE MOP HOLDING UP?
I DO WISH I HAD A PROPER BROOM FOR YOU TO USE.
FWOOOOOOOSSSSHHH!
THE MOP WORKS GREAT, AUNTIE!
F5N
FORCES OF NATURE HAS BROKEN OFF THEIR-
WHOA!
WHAT THE HECK WAS THAT?

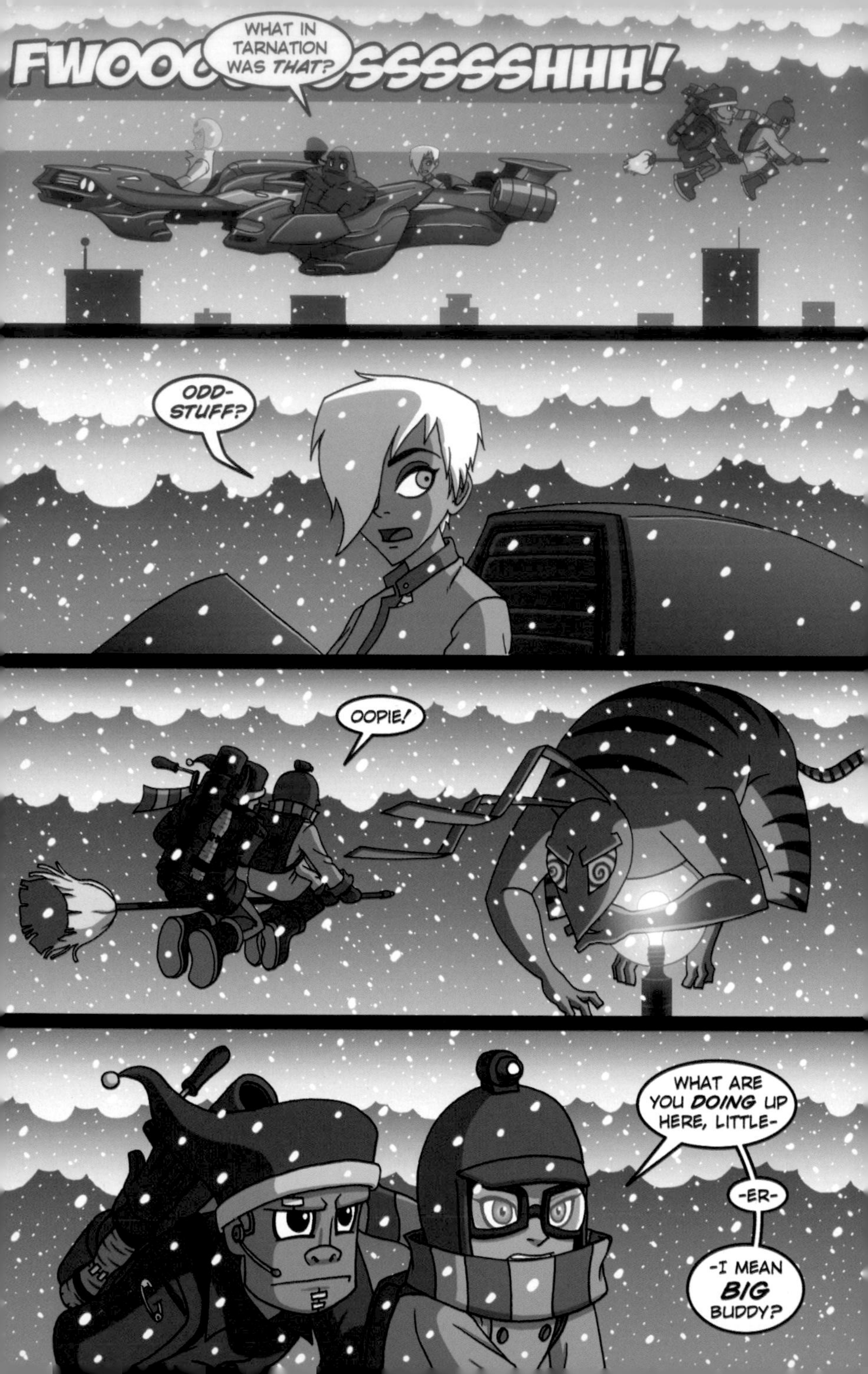

FWOOO
WHAT IN TARNATION WAS THAT?
SSSSSSHHH!
ODD-STUFF?
OOPIE!
WHAT ARE YOU DOING UP HERE, LITTLE-
-ER-
-I MEAN BIG BUDDY?

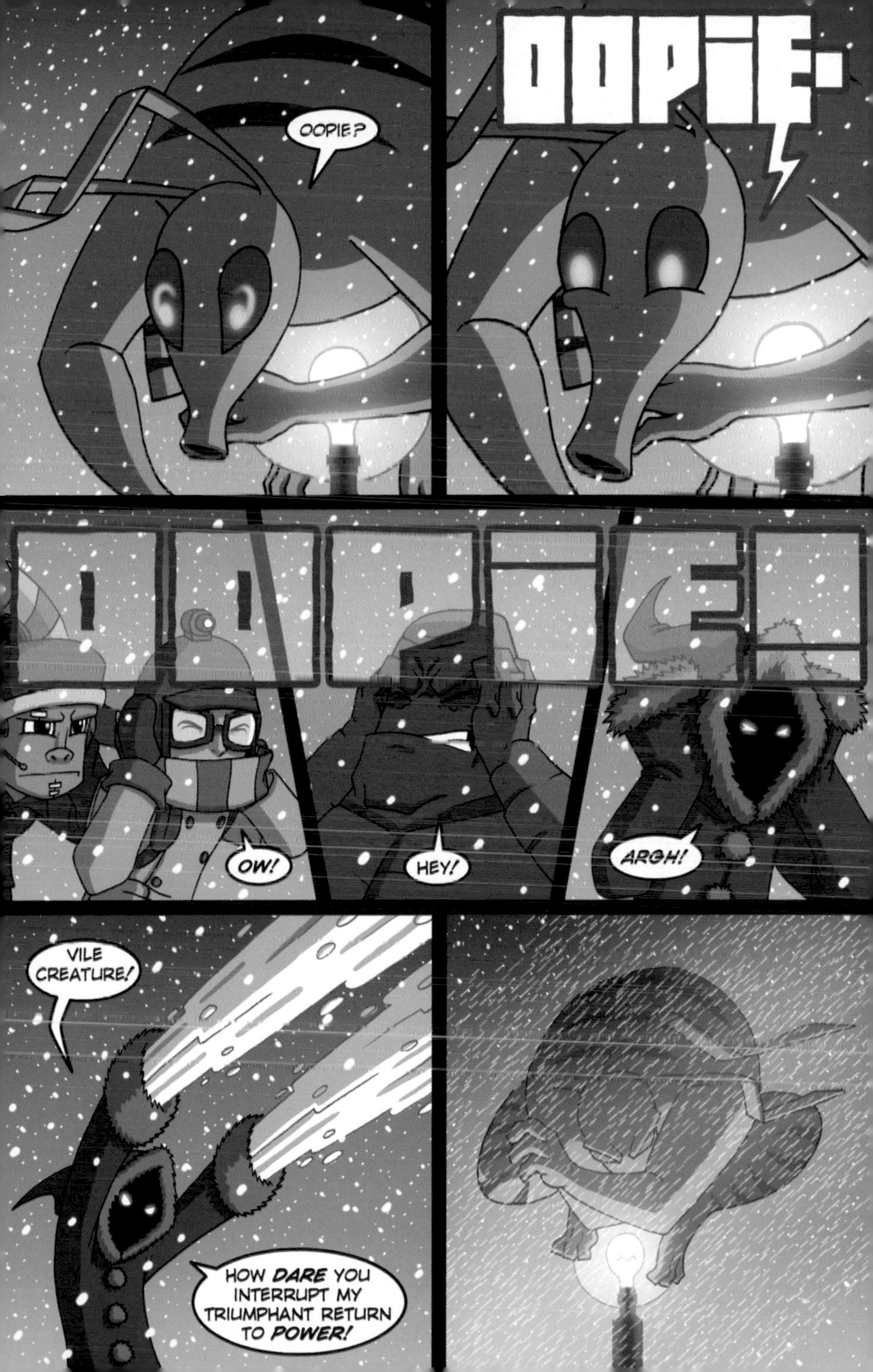
OOPIE?
OOPIE-
OOPIE!
OW!
HEY!
ARGH!
VILE CREATURE!
HOW DARE YOU INTERRUPT MY TRIUMPHANT RETURN TO POWER!

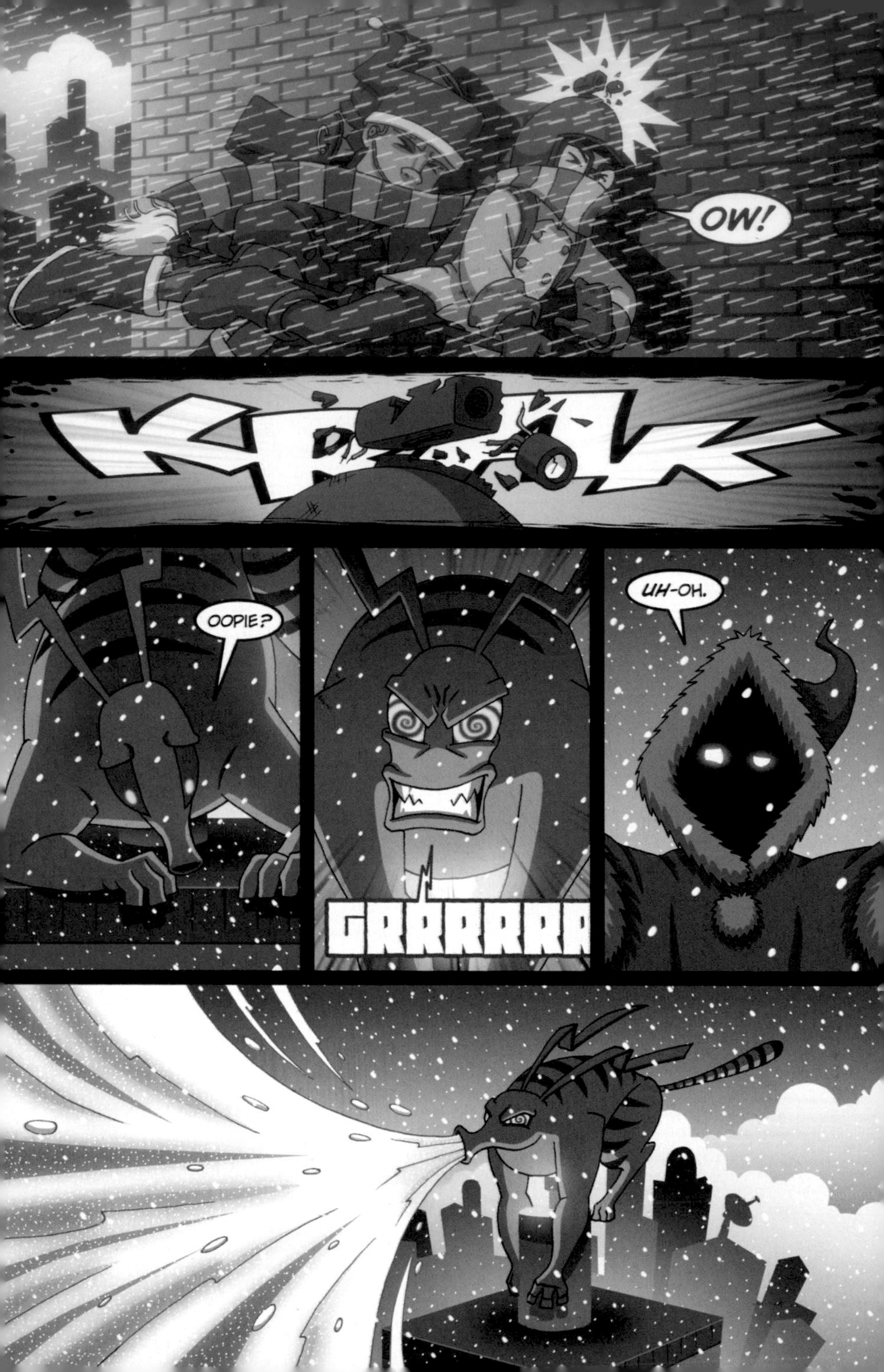
OW!
KRAK
OOPIE?
GRRRRRR
UH-OH.

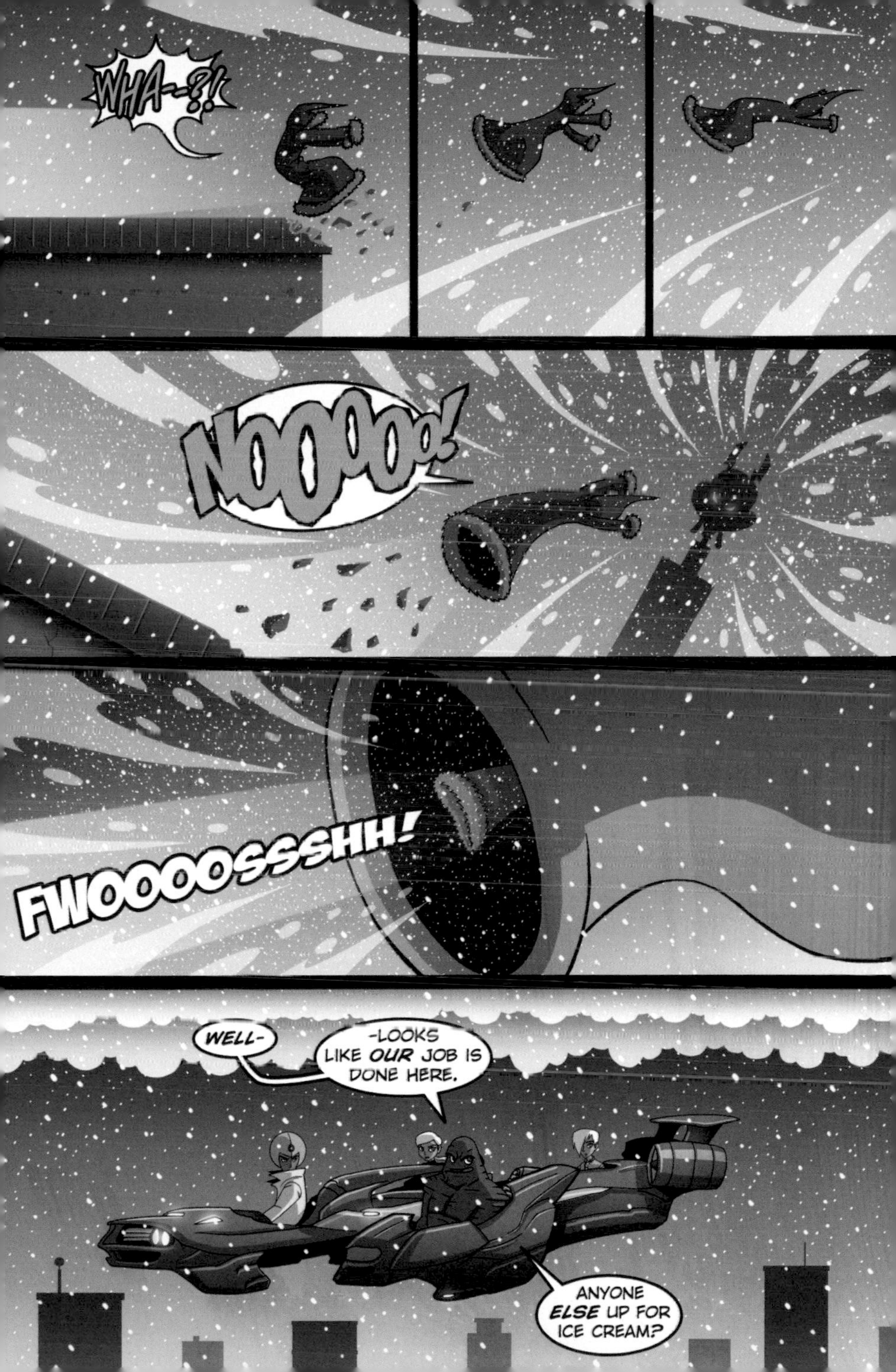
WHA--?!
NOOOOO!
FWOOOOOSSSHH!
WELL-
-LOOKS LIKE OUR JOB IS DONE HERE.
ANYONE ELSE UP FOR ICE CREAM?

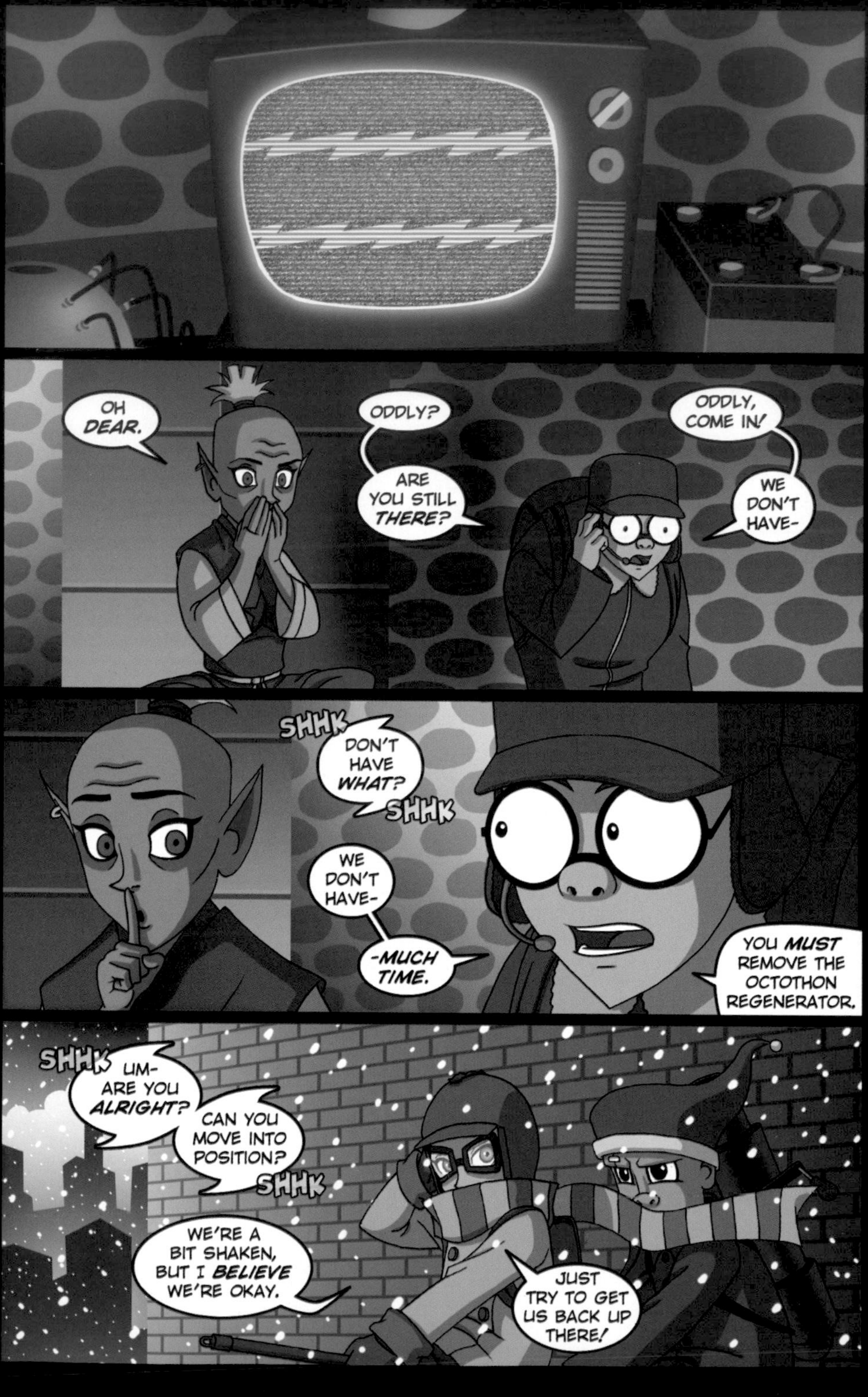
OH DEAR.
ODDLY?
ARE YOU STILL THERE?
ODDLY, COME IN!
WE DON'T HAVE-
SHHK
DON'T HAVE WHAT?
SHHK
WE DON'T HAVE-
-MUCH TIME.
YOU MUST REMOVE THE OCTOTHON REGENERATOR.
SHHK
UM- ARE YOU ALRIGHT?
CAN YOU MOVE INTO POSITION?
SHHK
WE'RE A BIT SHAKEN, BUT I BELIEVE WE'RE OKAY.
JUST TRY TO GET US BACK UP THERE!

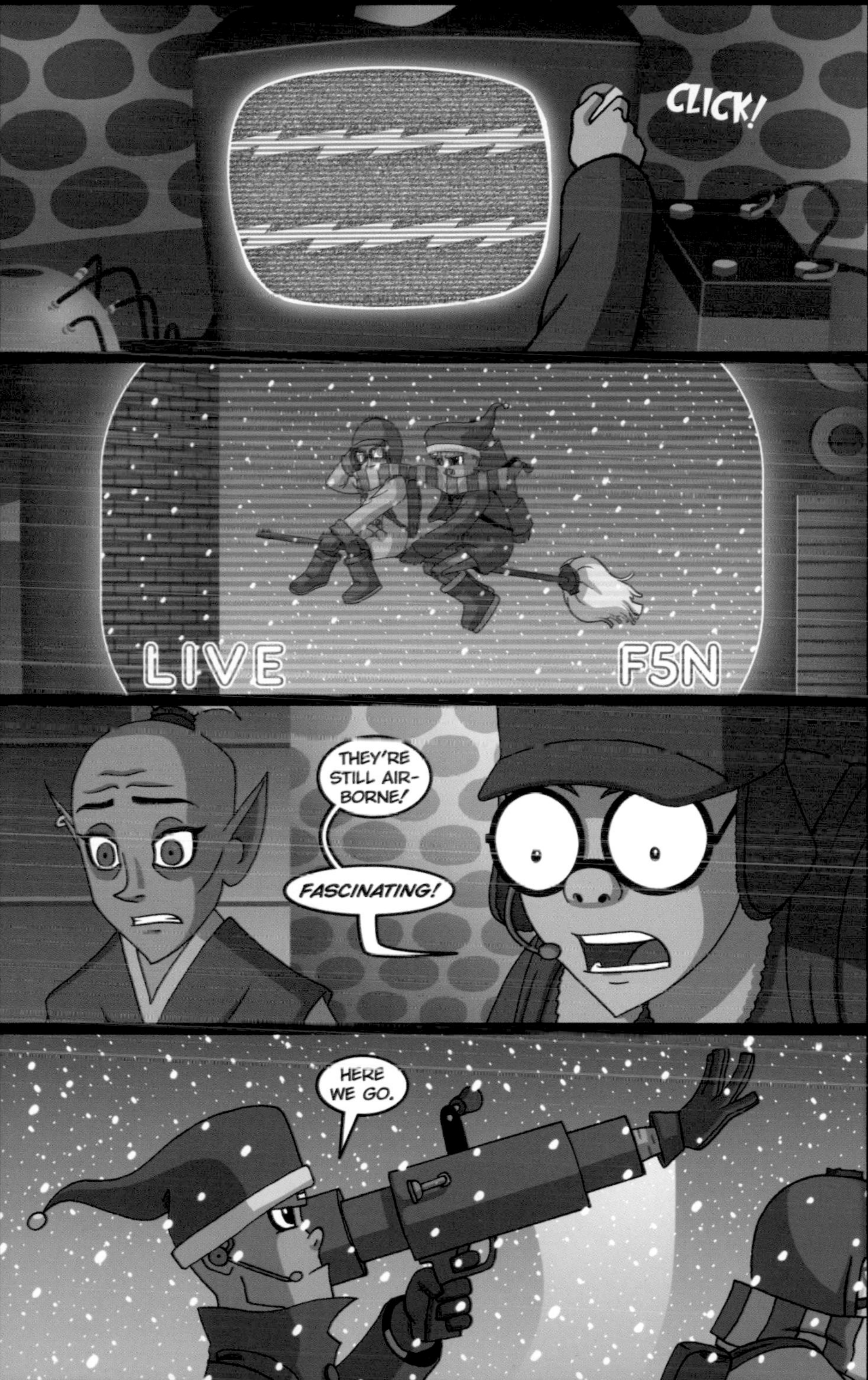
CLICK!
LIVE
F5N
THEY'RE STILL AIR-BORNE!
FASCINATING!
HERE WE GO.

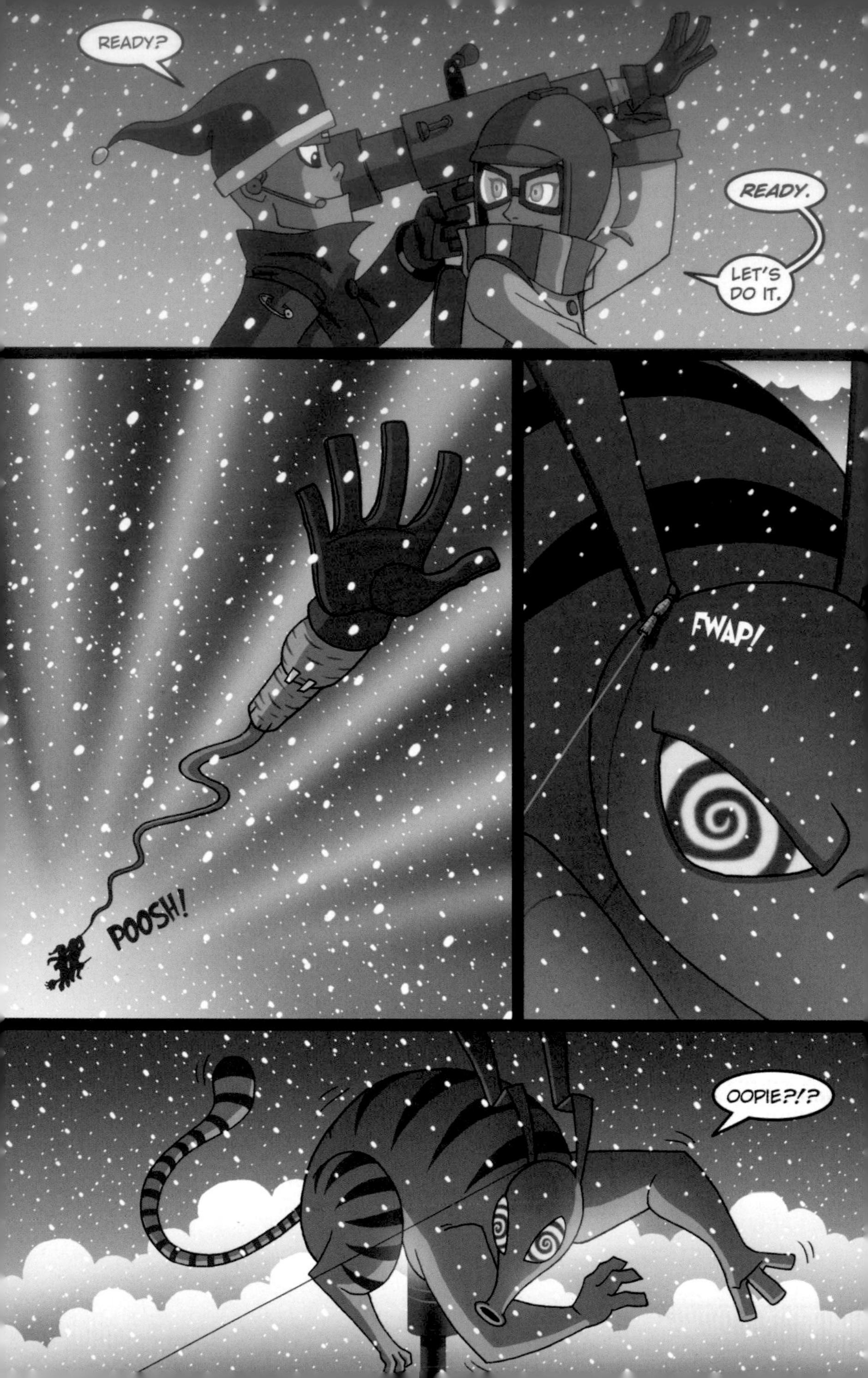
READY?
READY.
LET'S DO IT.
POOSH!
FWAP!
OOPIE?!?

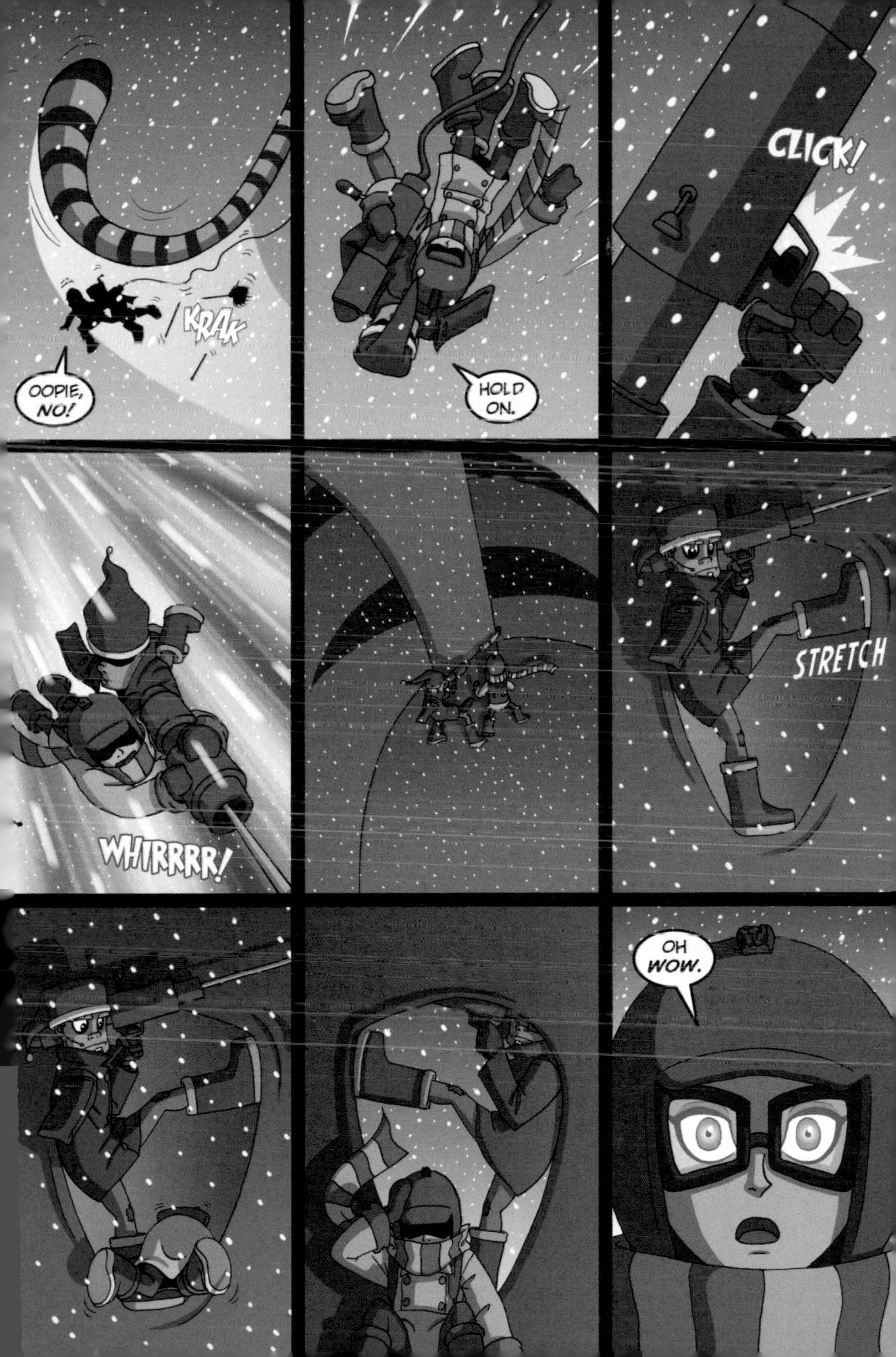
KRAK
OOPIE, NO!
HOLD ON.
CLICK!
WHIRRRR!
STRETCH
OH WOW.

Chapter 7

Snowfall

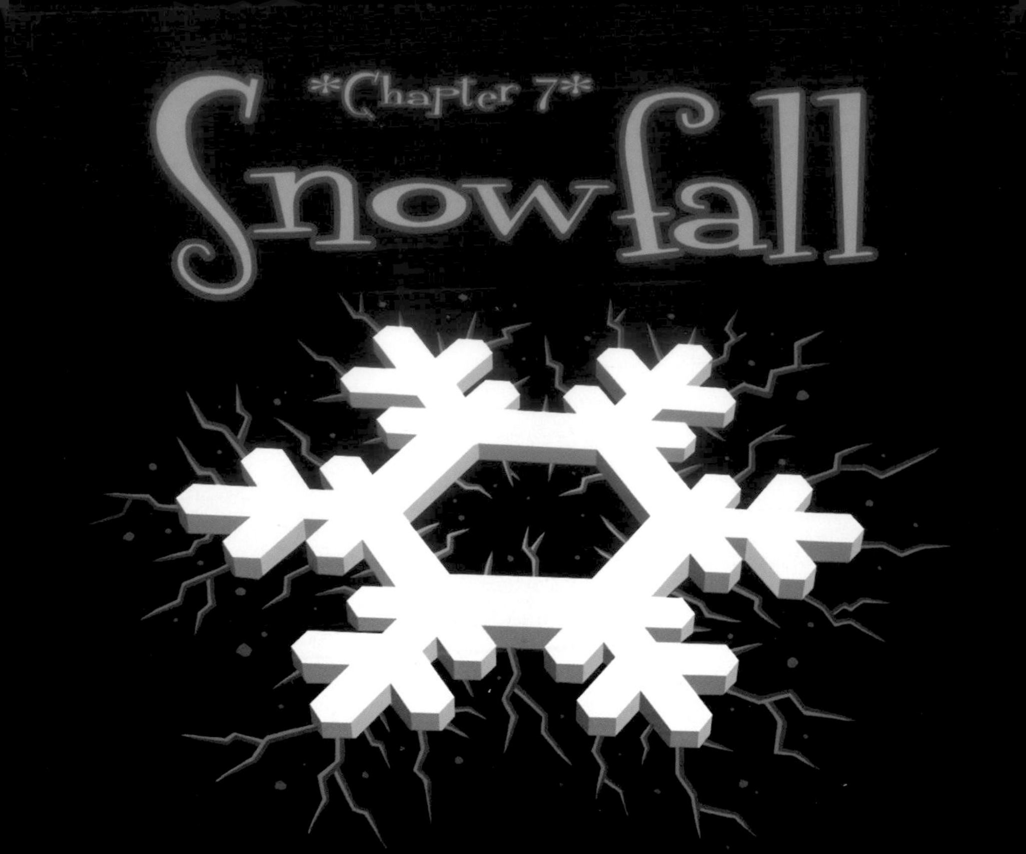

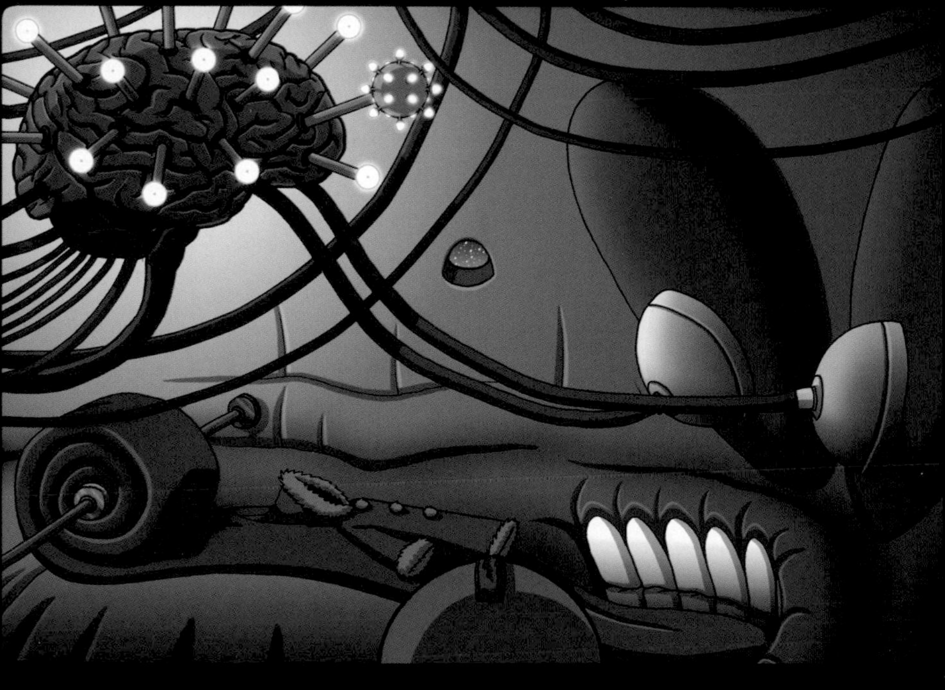

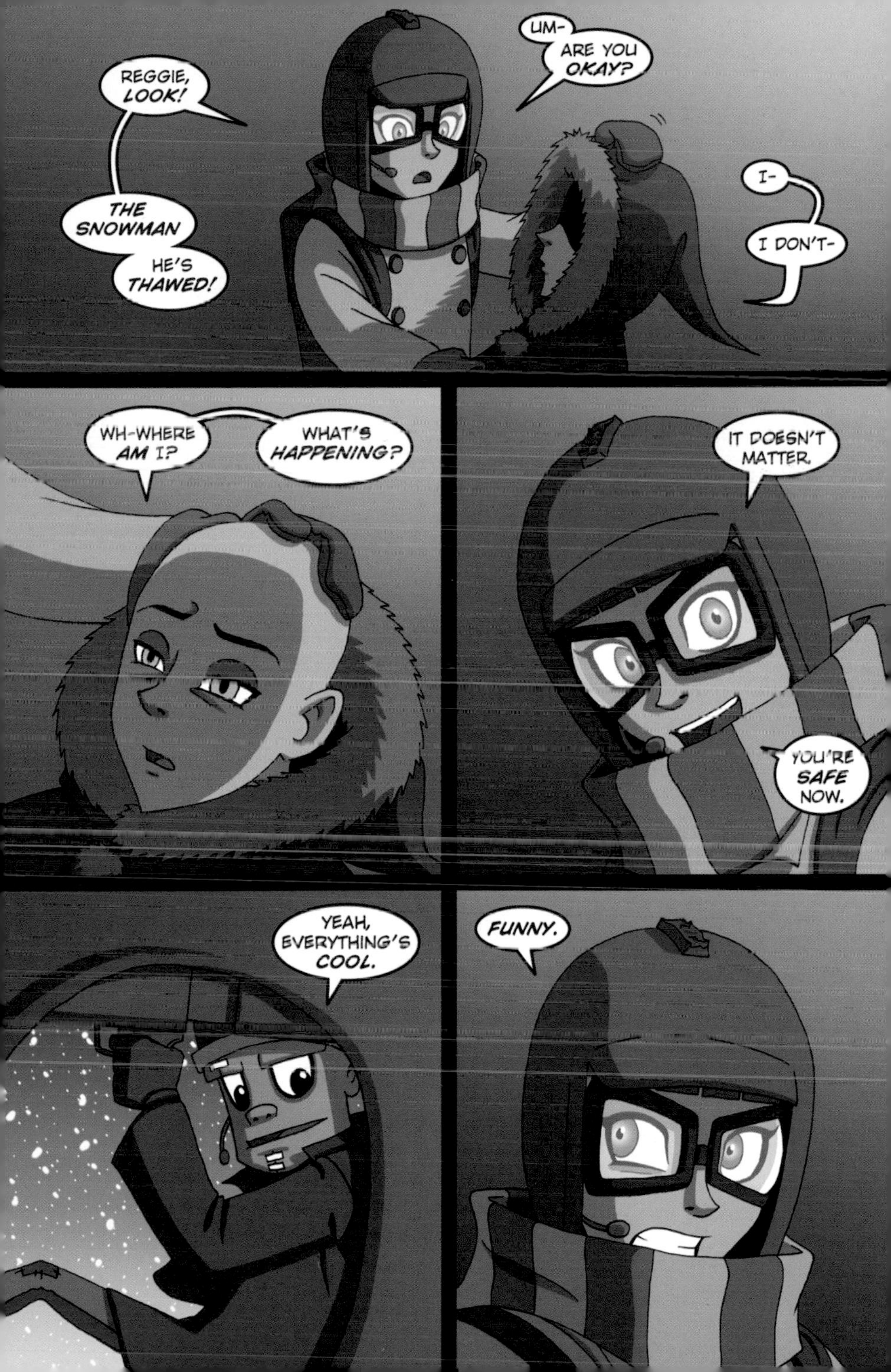
REGGIE, LOOK!
THE SNOWMAN
HE'S THAWED!
UM-
ARE YOU OKAY?
I-
I DON'T-
WH-WHERE AM I?
WHAT'S HAPPENING?
IT DOESN'T MATTER.
YOU'RE SAFE NOW.
YEAH, EVERYTHING'S COOL.
FUNNY.

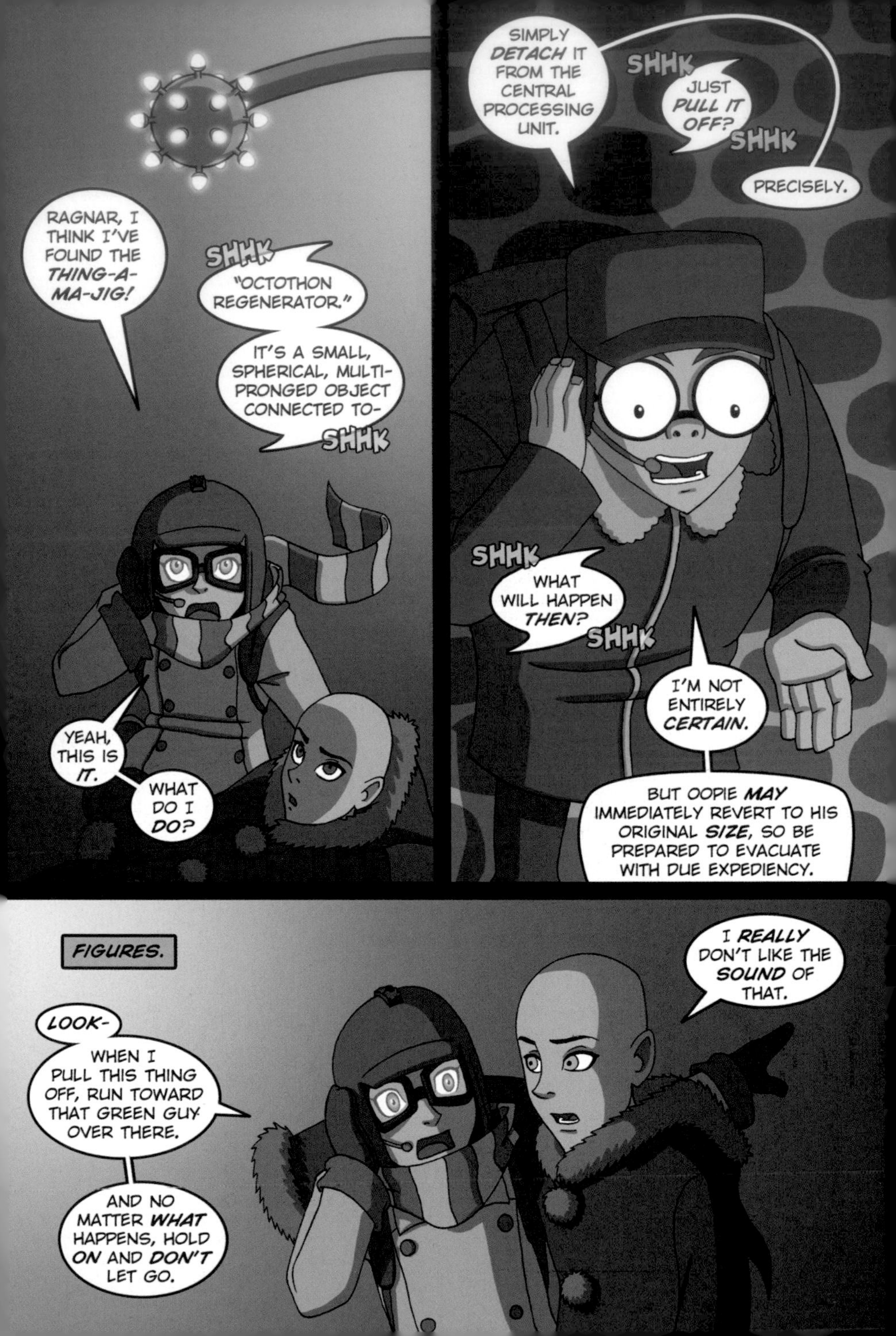
RAGNAR, I THINK I'VE FOUND THE *THING-A-MA-JIG!*
SHHK
"OCTOTHON REGENERATOR."
IT'S A SMALL, SPHERICAL, MULTI-PRONGED OBJECT CONNECTED TO-
SHHK
YEAH, THIS IS *IT.*
WHAT DO I *DO?*
SIMPLY *DETACH* IT FROM THE CENTRAL PROCESSING UNIT.
SHHK
JUST *PULL IT OFF?*
SHHK
PRECISELY.
SHHK
WHAT WILL HAPPEN *THEN?*
SHHK
I'M NOT ENTIRELY *CERTAIN.*
BUT OOPIE *MAY* IMMEDIATELY REVERT TO HIS ORIGINAL *SIZE,* SO BE PREPARED TO EVACUATE WITH DUE EXPEDIENCY.
FIGURES.
I *REALLY* DON'T LIKE THE *SOUND* OF THAT.
LOOK-
WHEN I PULL THIS THING OFF, RUN TOWARD THAT GREEN GUY OVER THERE.
AND NO MATTER *WHAT* HAPPENS, HOLD *ON* AND *DON'T* LET GO.

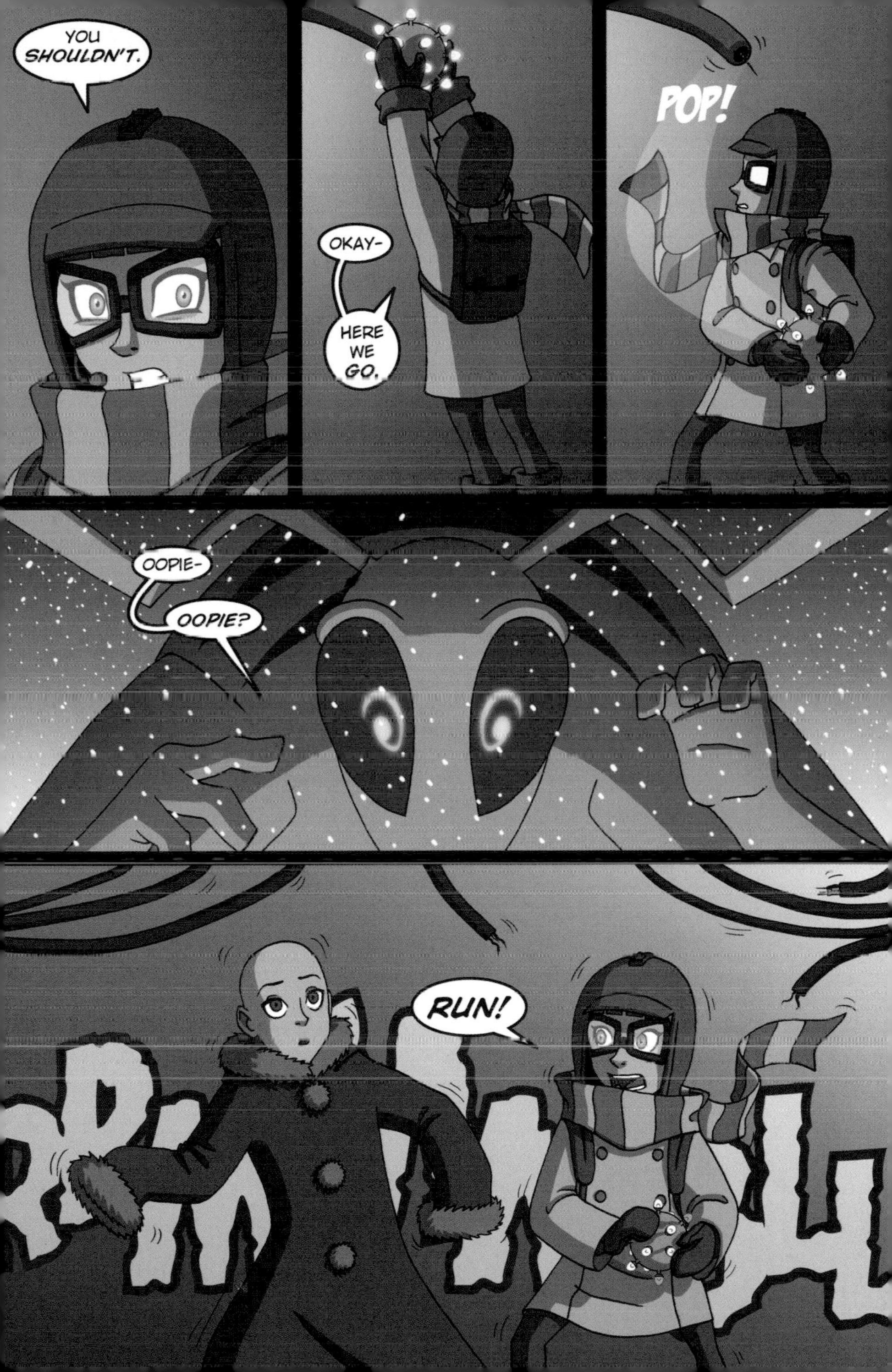
YOU SHOULDN'T.
OKAY-
HERE WE GO.
POP!
OOPIE-
OOPIE?
RUN!

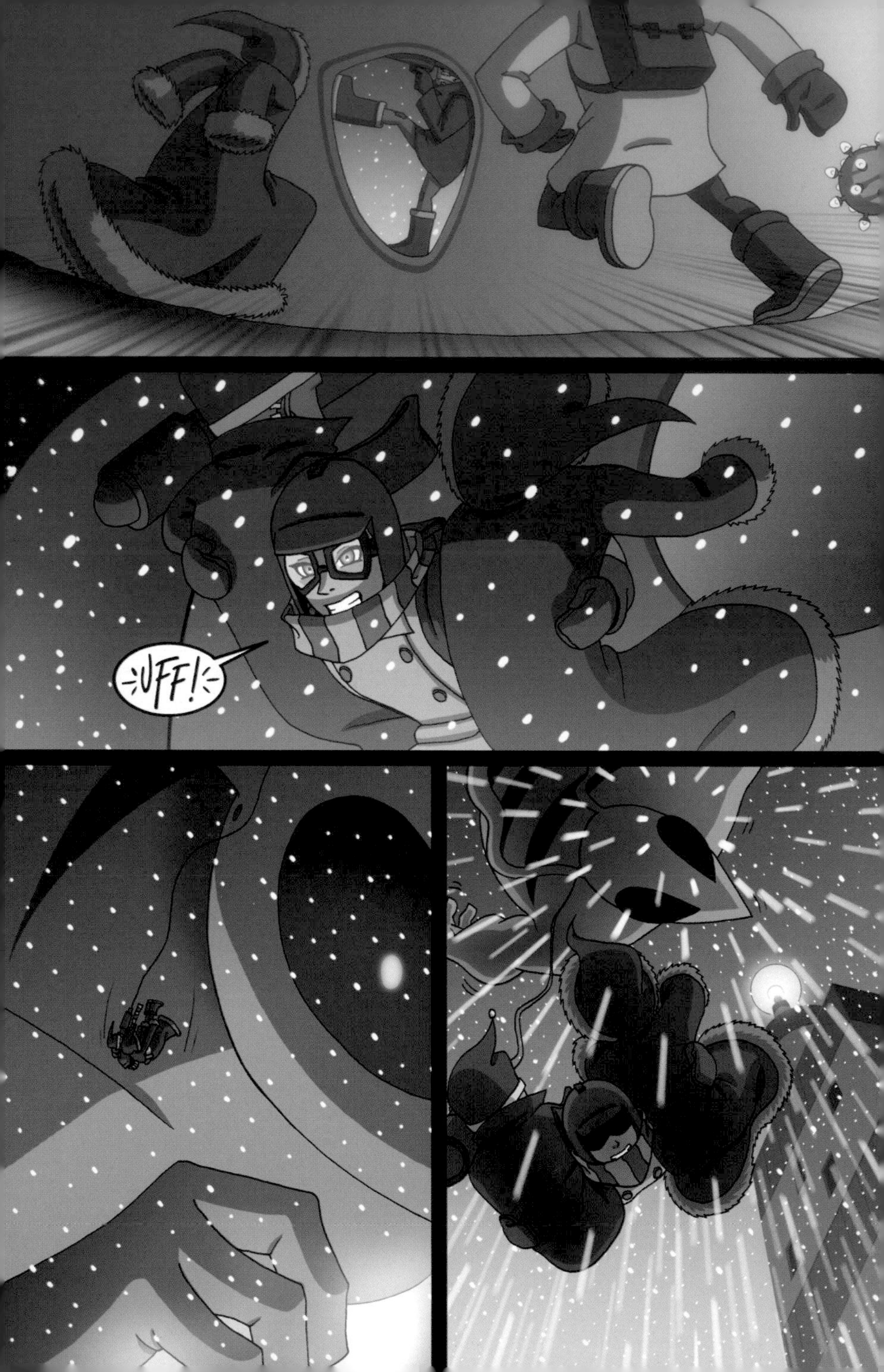
UFF!

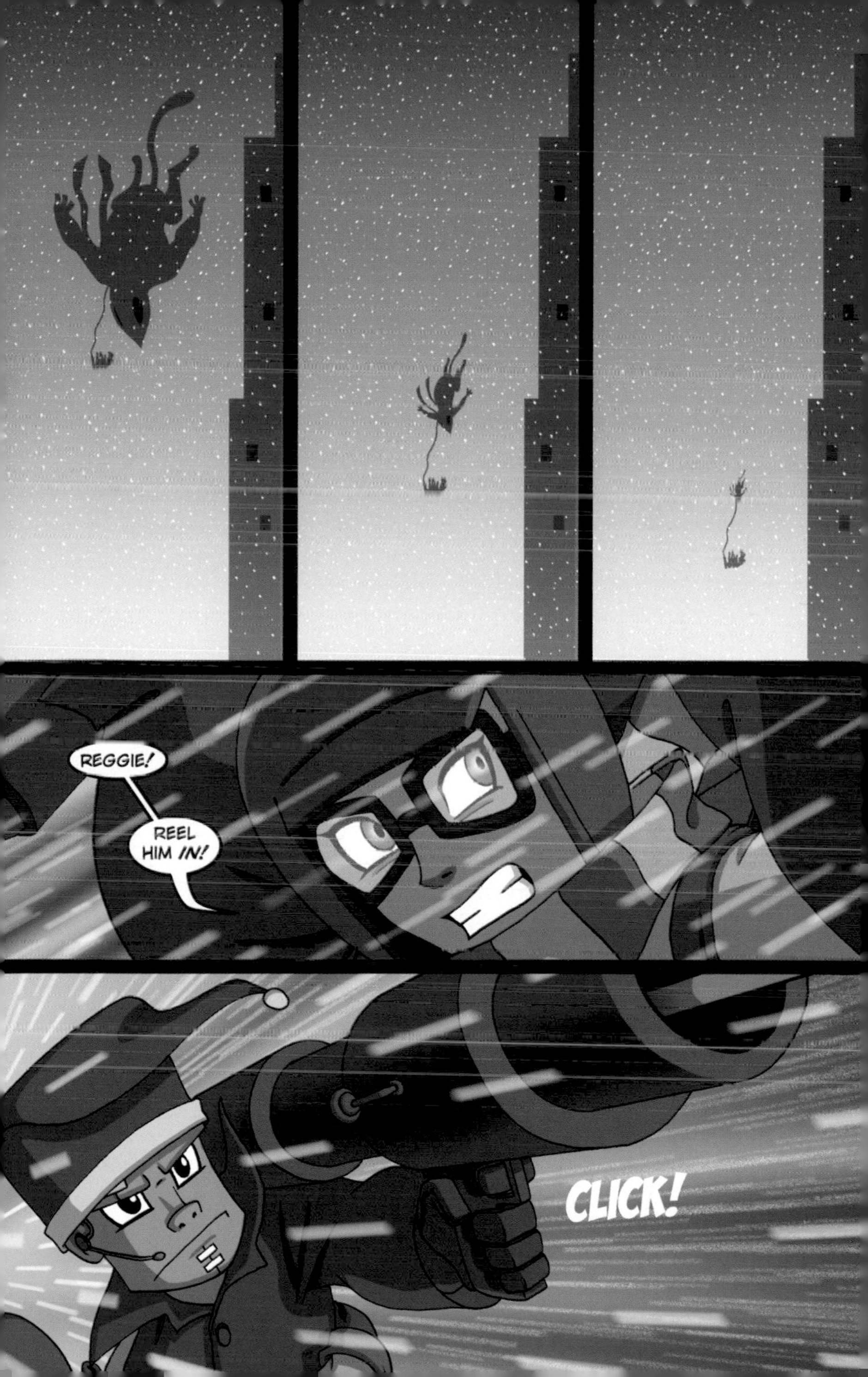
REGGIE!
REEL HIM IN!
CLICK!

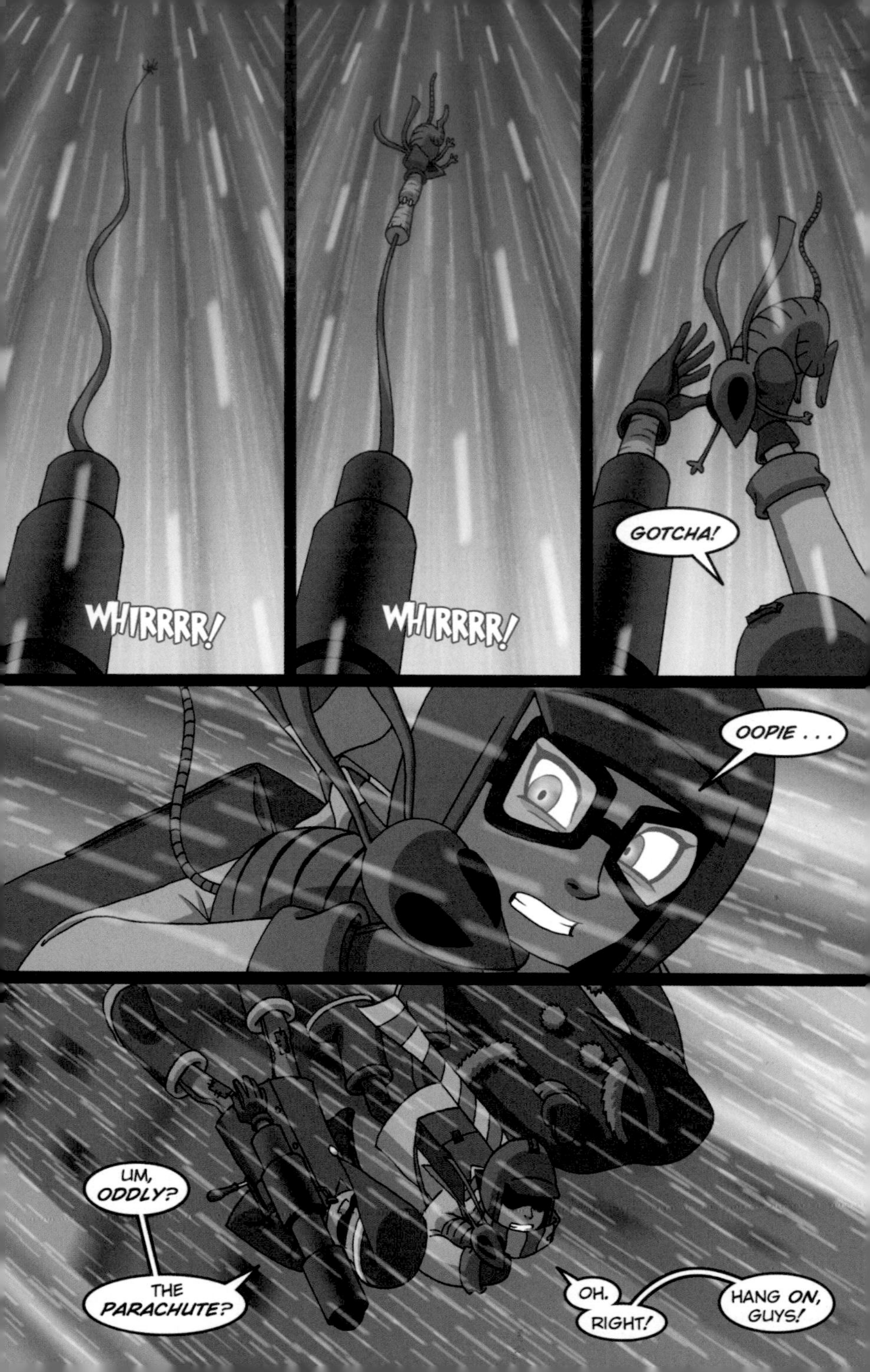
WHIRRRR!
WHIRRRR!
GOTCHA!
OOPIE . . .
UM, ODDLY?
THE PARACHUTE?
OH. RIGHT!
HANG ON, GUYS!

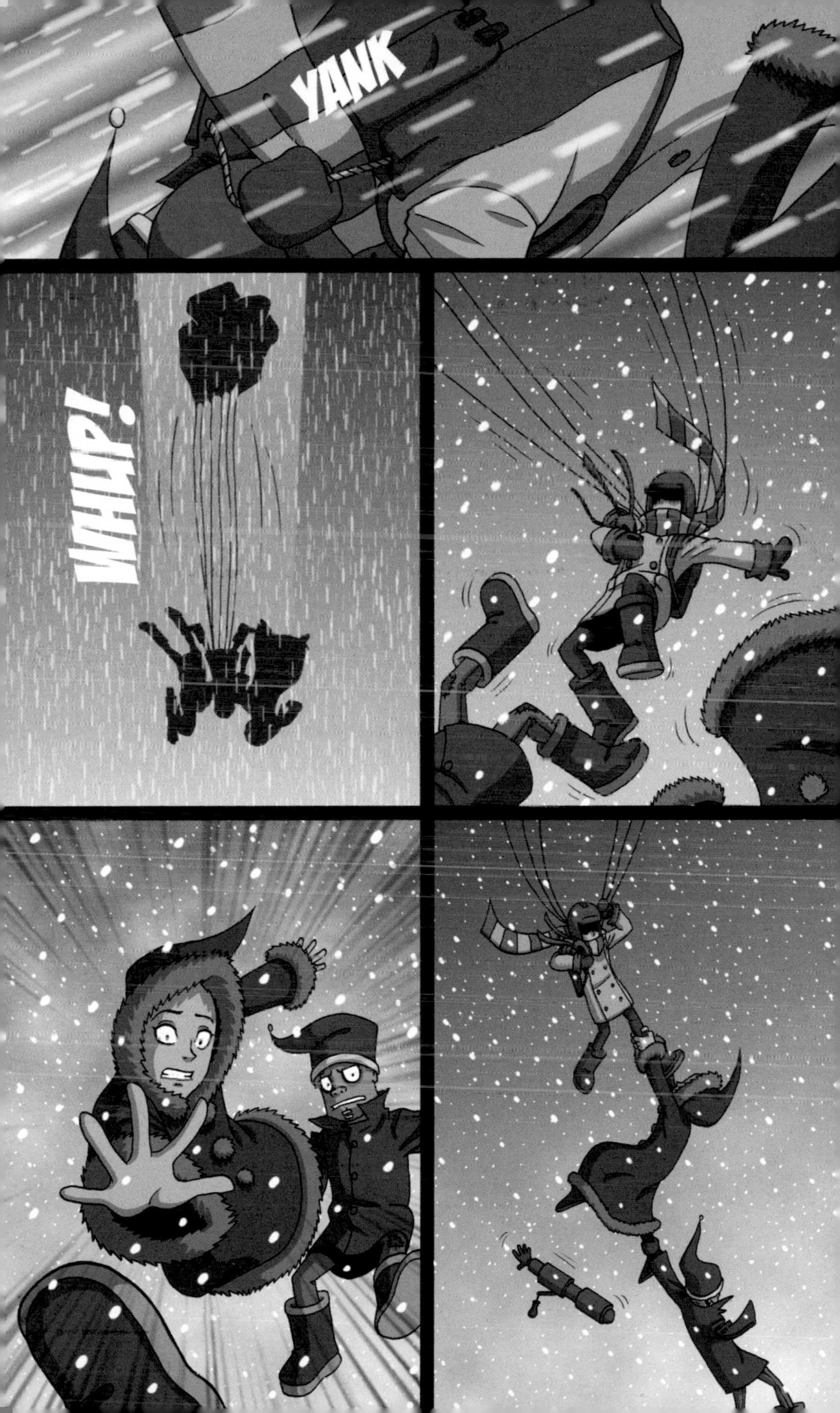
YANK
WHUP!

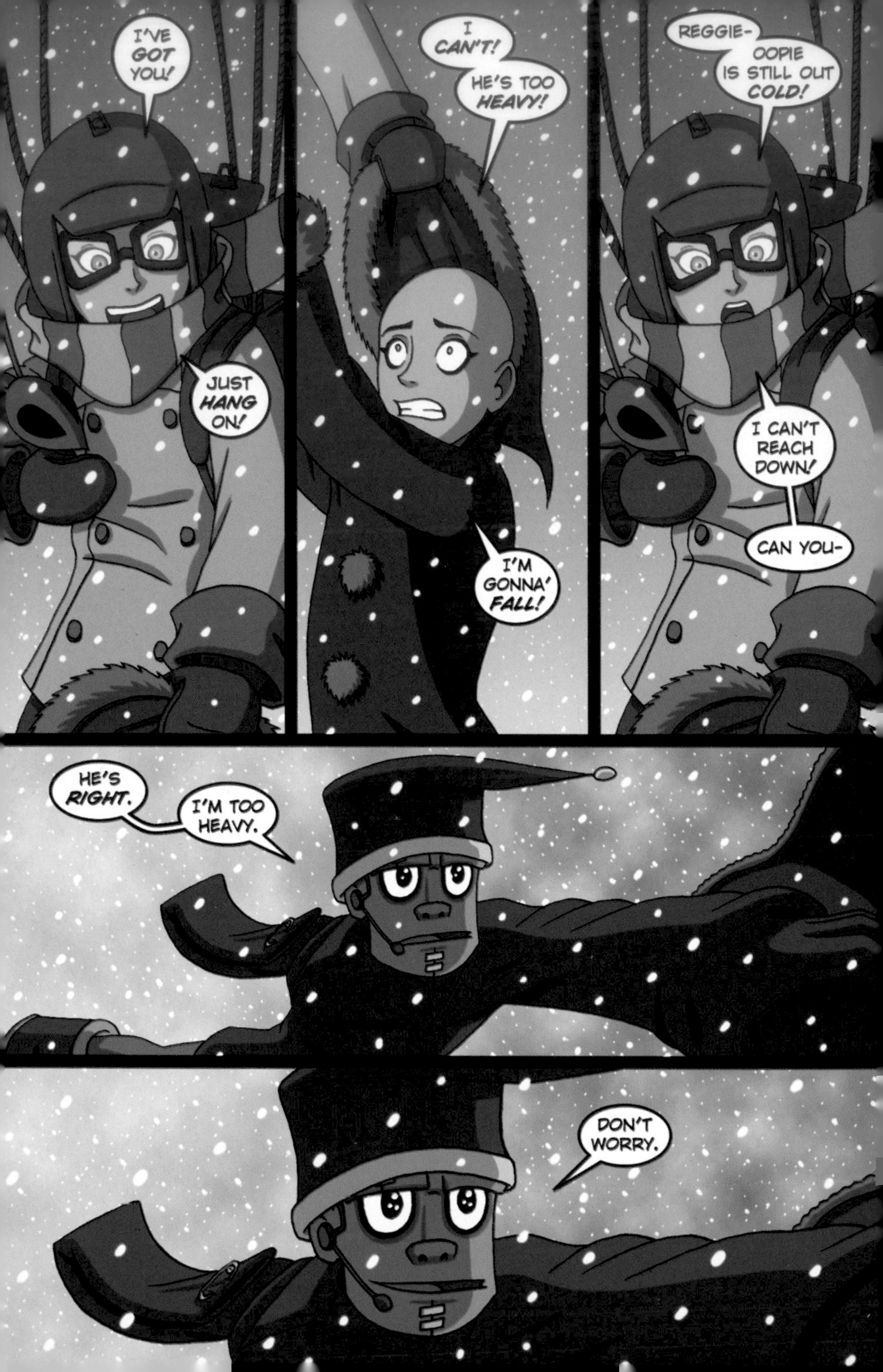
I'VE GOT YOU!
JUST HANG ON!
I CAN'T!
HE'S TOO HEAVY!
I'M GONNA' FALL!
REGGIE-
OOPIE IS STILL OUT COLD!
I CAN'T REACH DOWN!
CAN YOU-
HE'S RIGHT.
I'M TOO HEAVY.
DON'T WORRY.

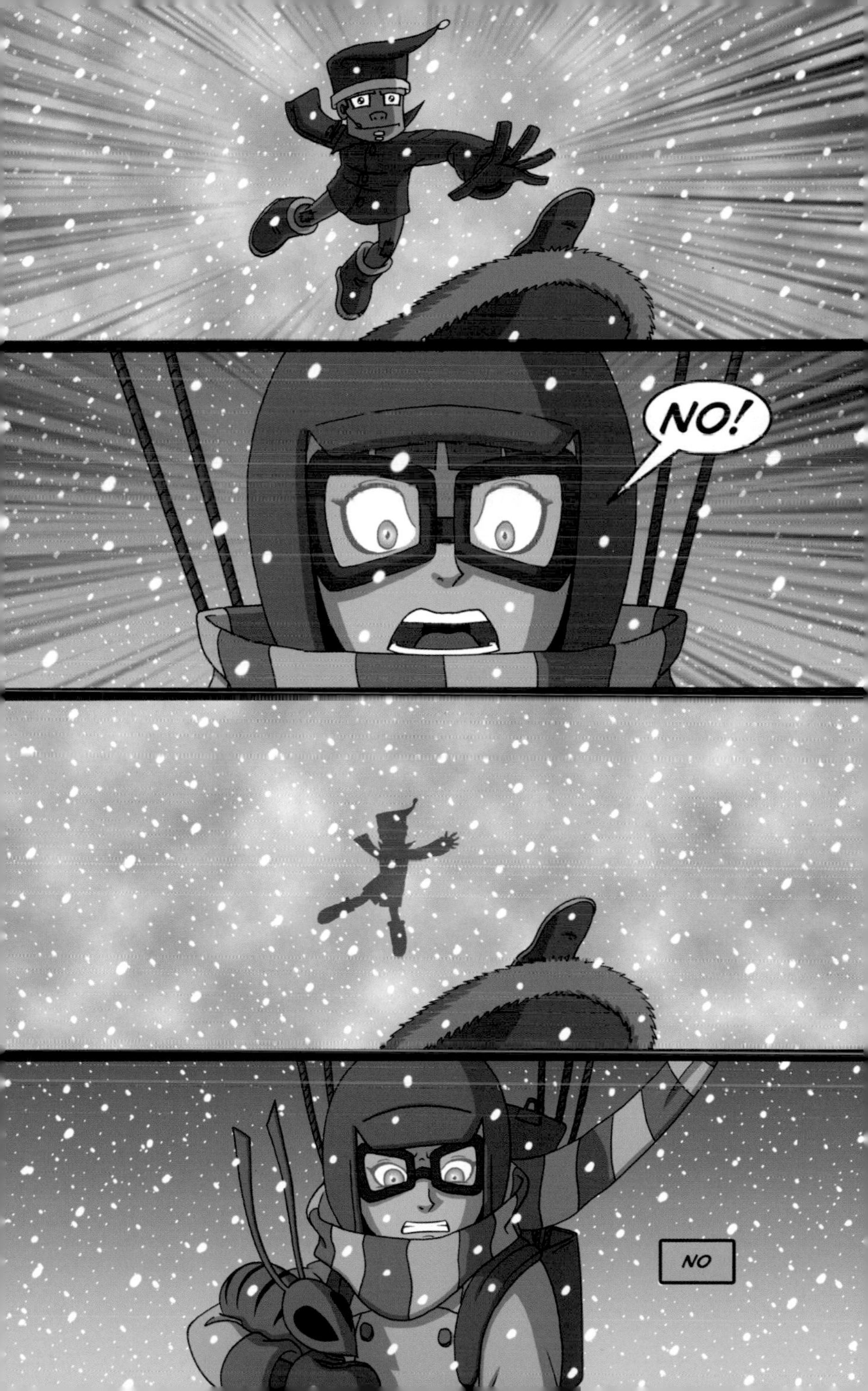
NO!
NO

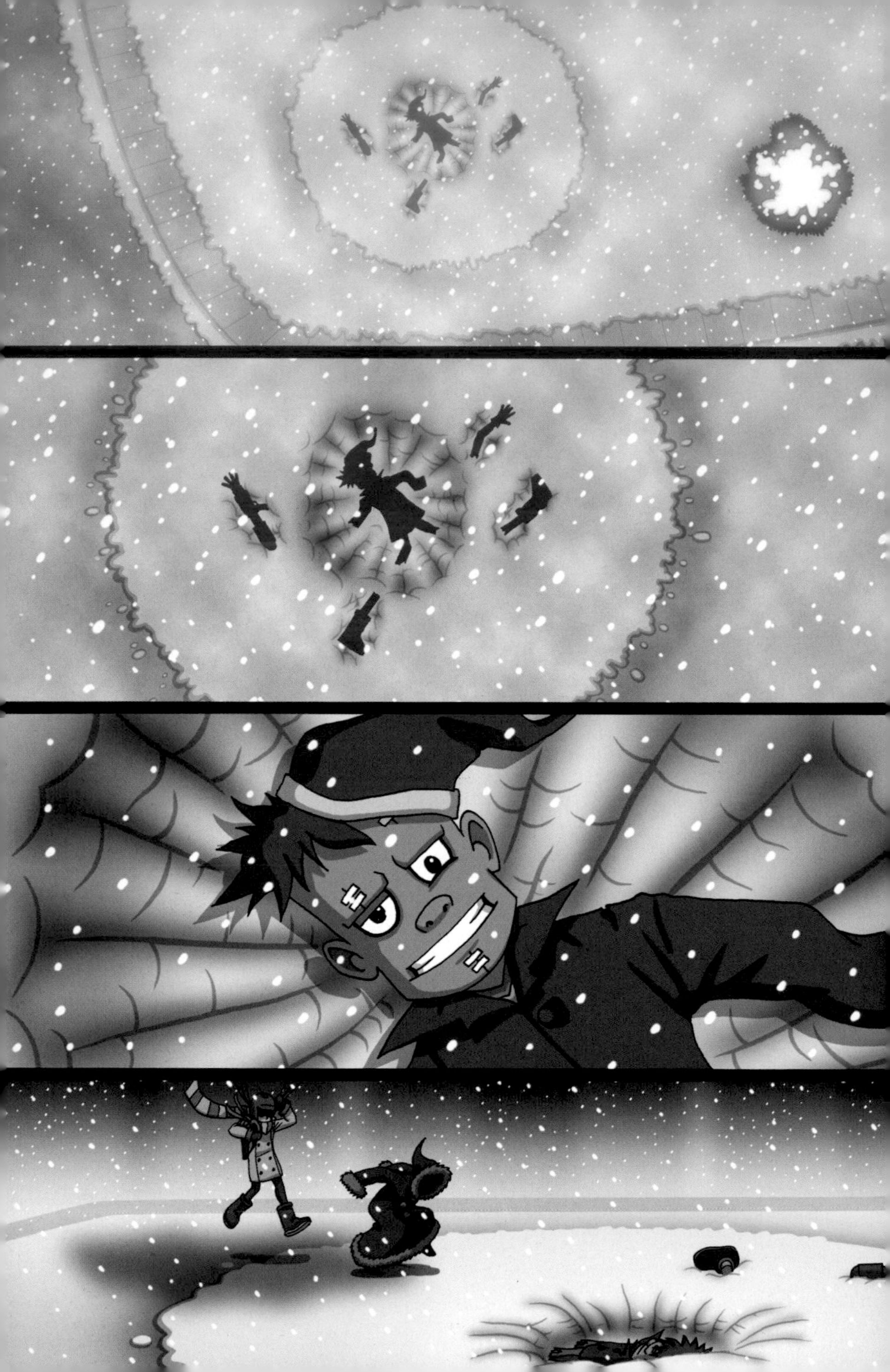

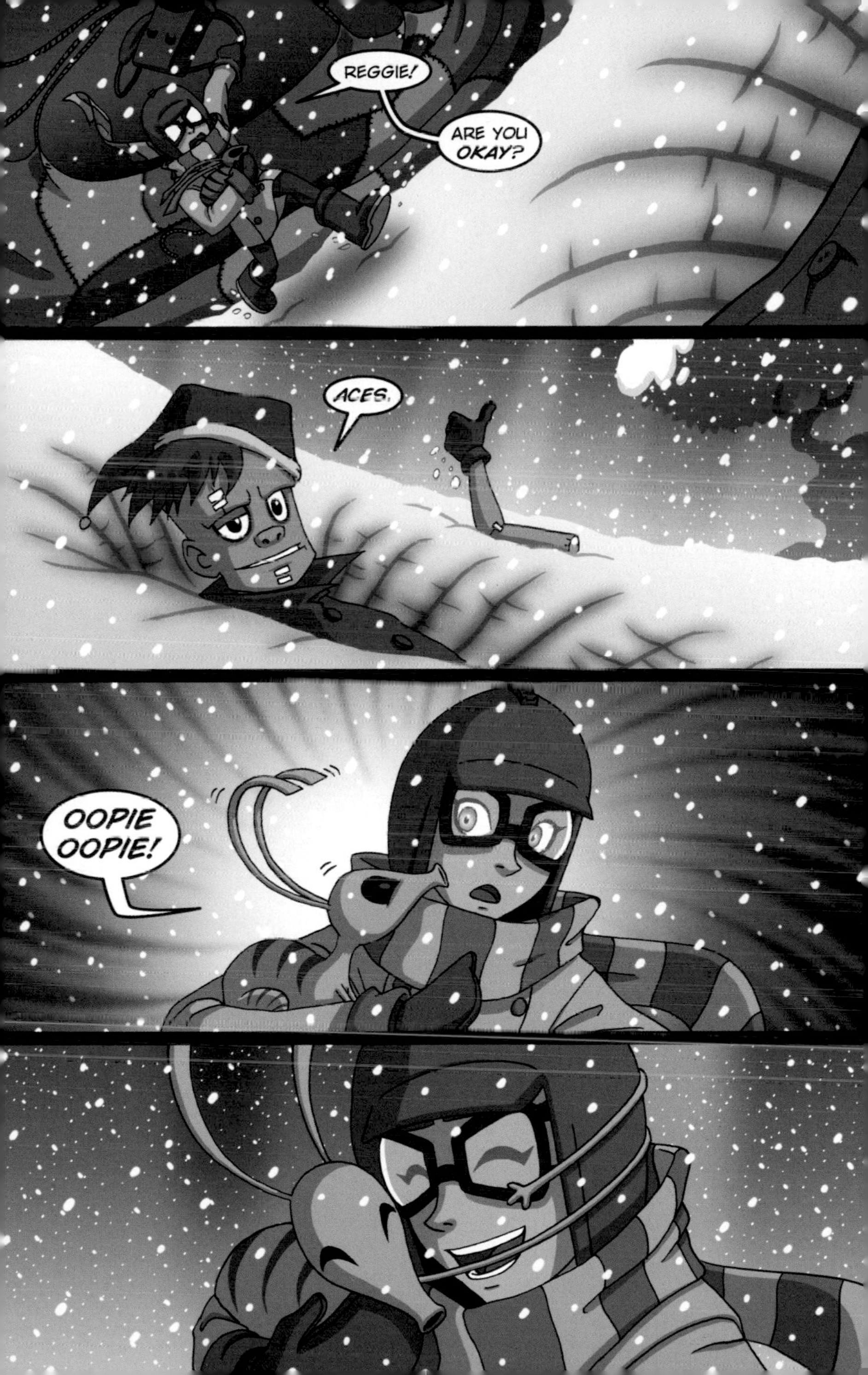
REGGIE!
ARE YOU OKAY?
ACES.
OOPIE OOPIE!

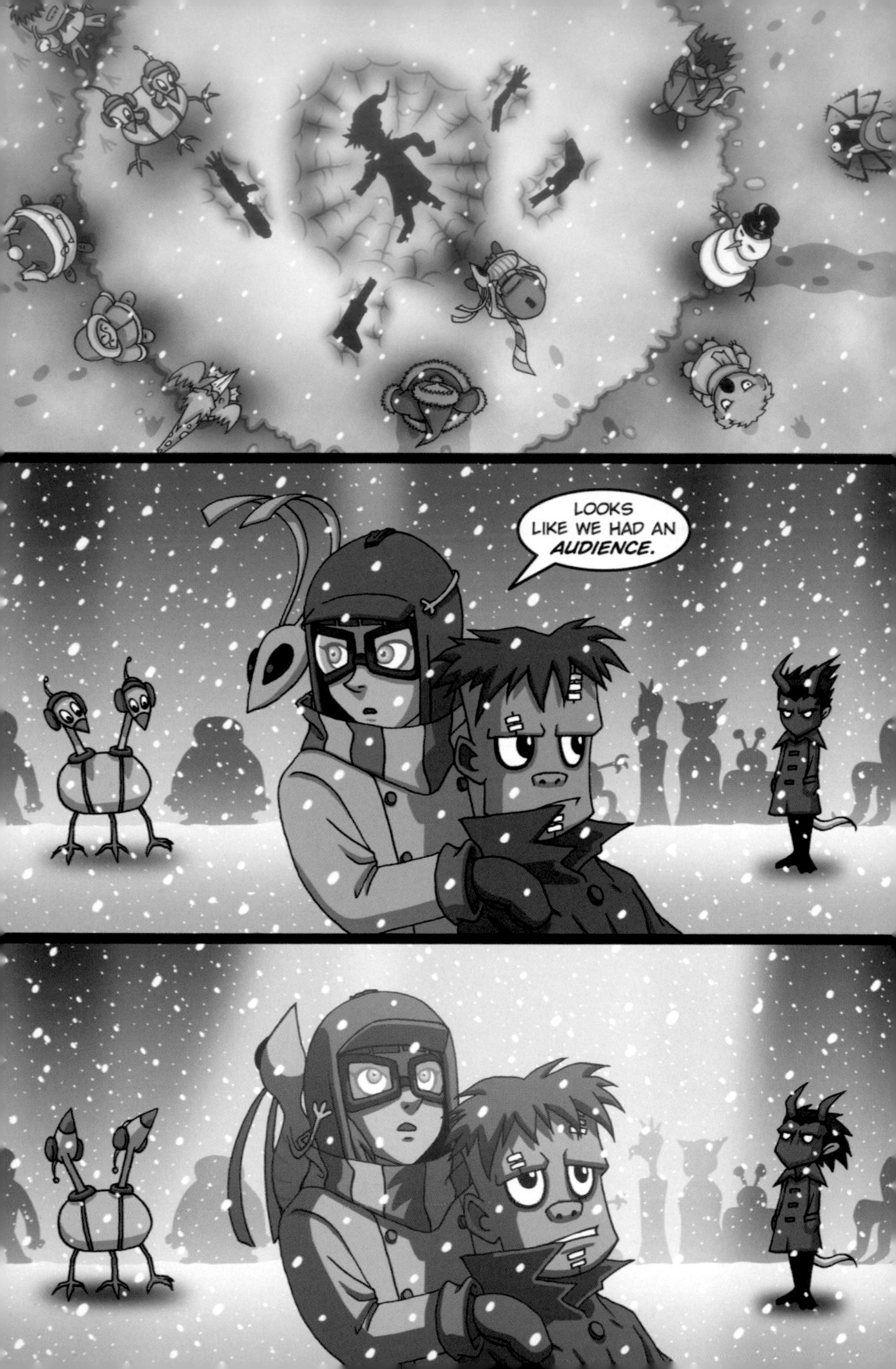
LOOKS LIKE WE HAD AN *AUDIENCE.*

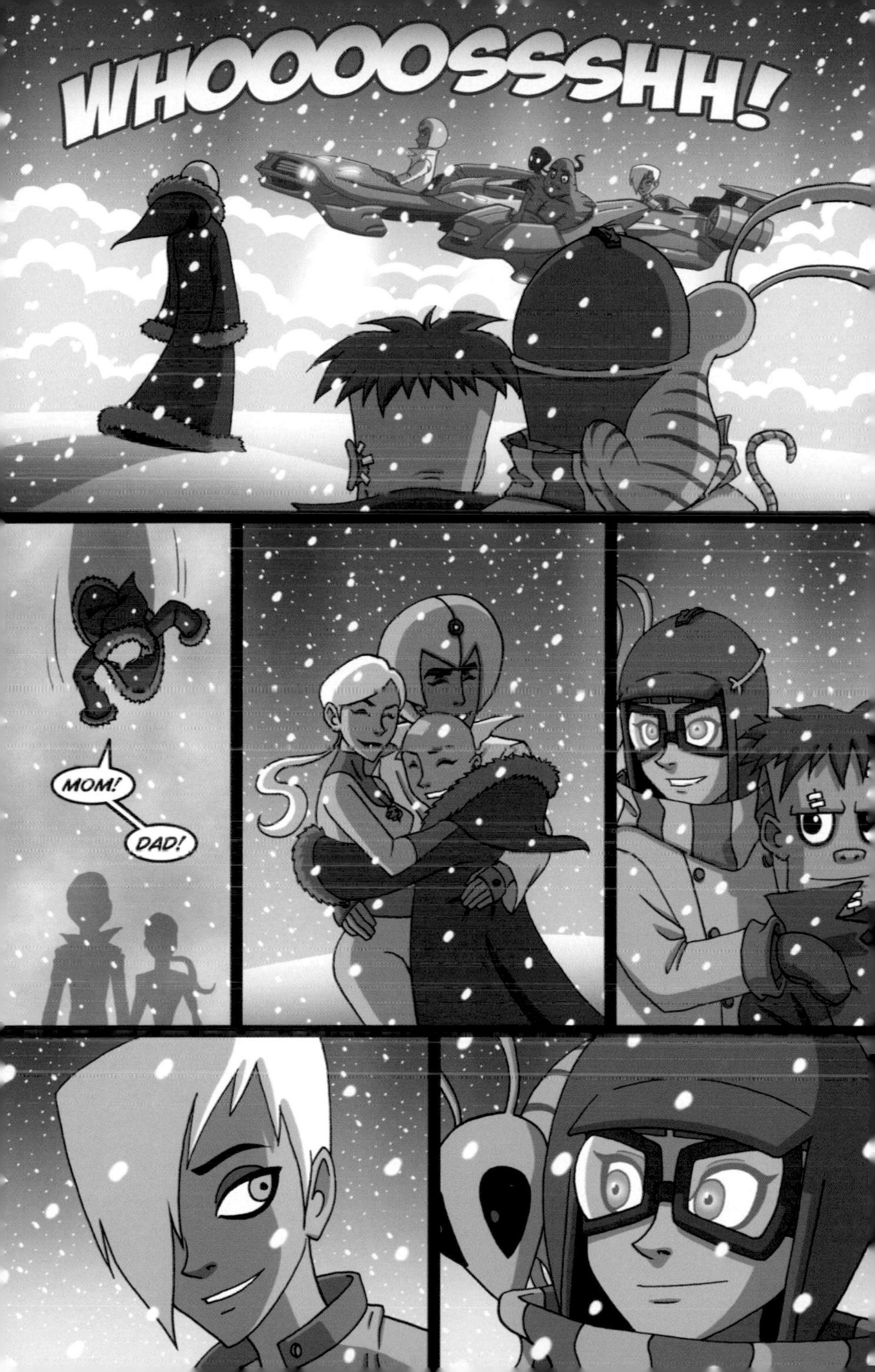
WHOOOOOSSSHH!
MOM!
DAD!

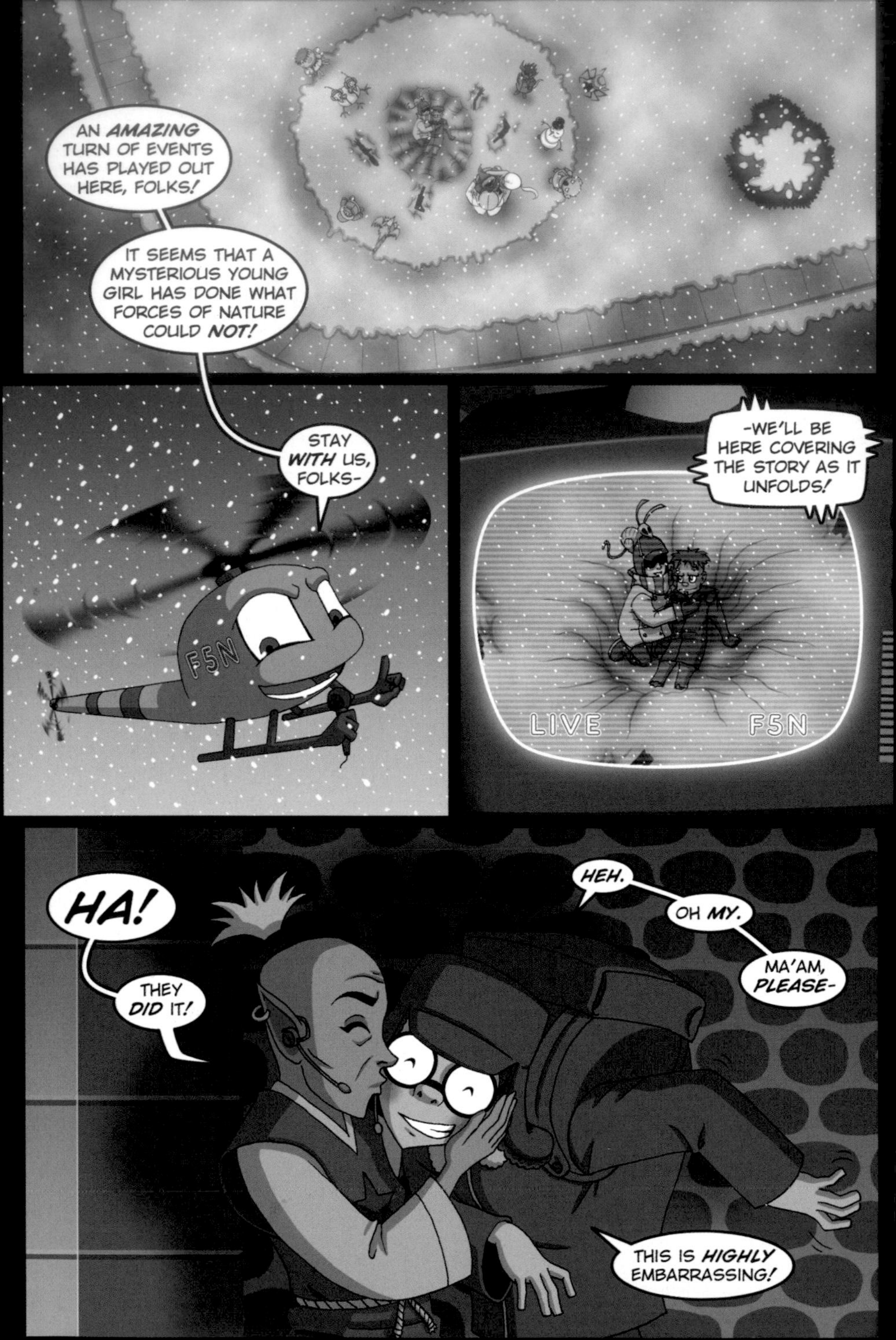
AN *AMAZING* TURN OF EVENTS HAS PLAYED OUT HERE, FOLKS!
IT SEEMS THAT A MYSTERIOUS YOUNG GIRL HAS DONE WHAT FORCES OF NATURE COULD *NOT!*
STAY *WITH* US, FOLKS-
F5N
-WE'LL BE HERE COVERING THE STORY AS IT UNFOLDS!
LIVE
F5N
HA!
THEY *DID* IT!
HEH.
OH *MY.*
MA'AM, *PLEASE-*
THIS IS *HIGHLY* EMBARRASSING!

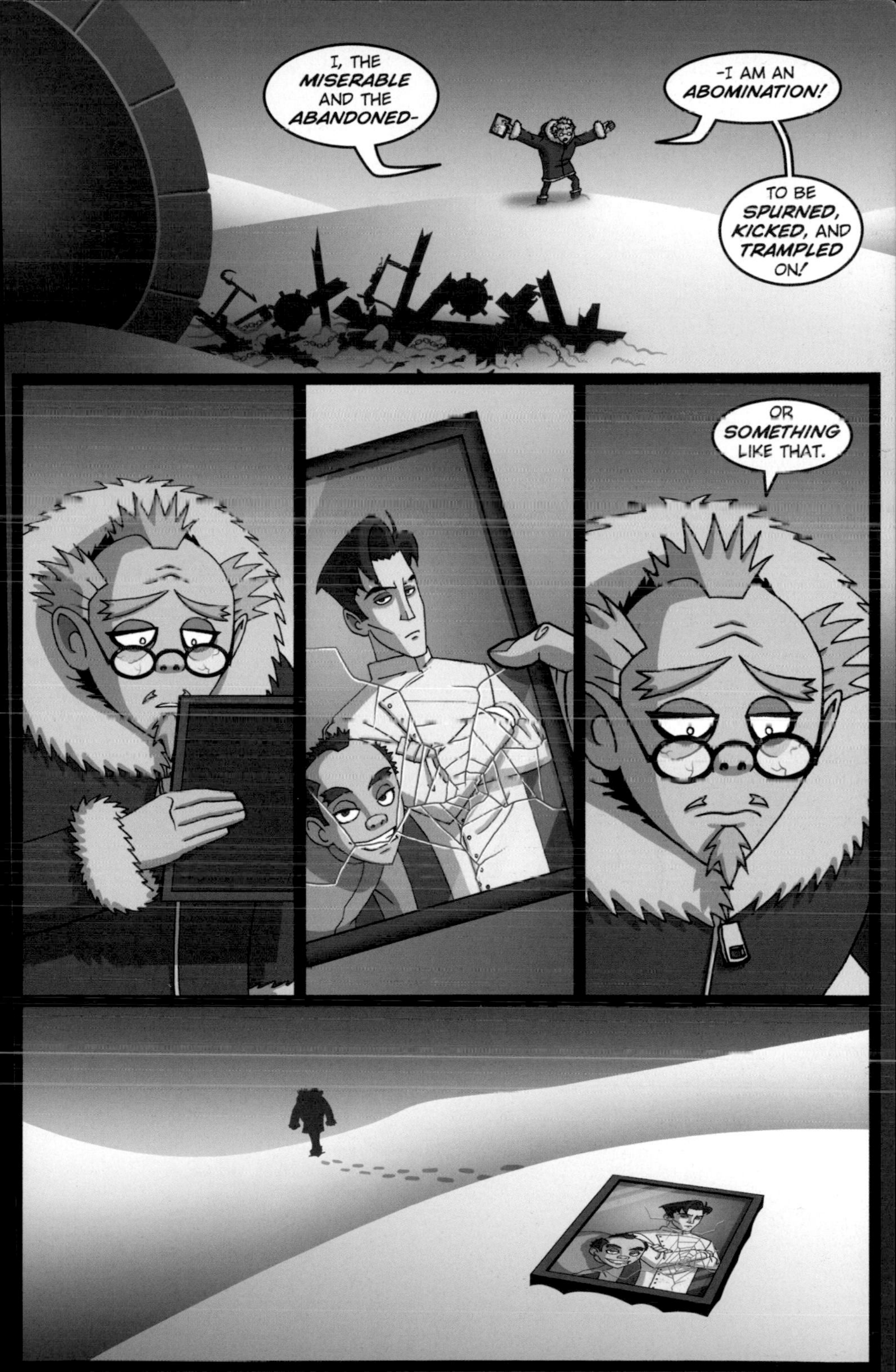
I, THE MISERABLE AND THE ABANDONED-
-I AM AN ABOMINATION!
TO BE SPURNED, KICKED, AND TRAMPLED ON!
OR SOMETHING LIKE THAT.

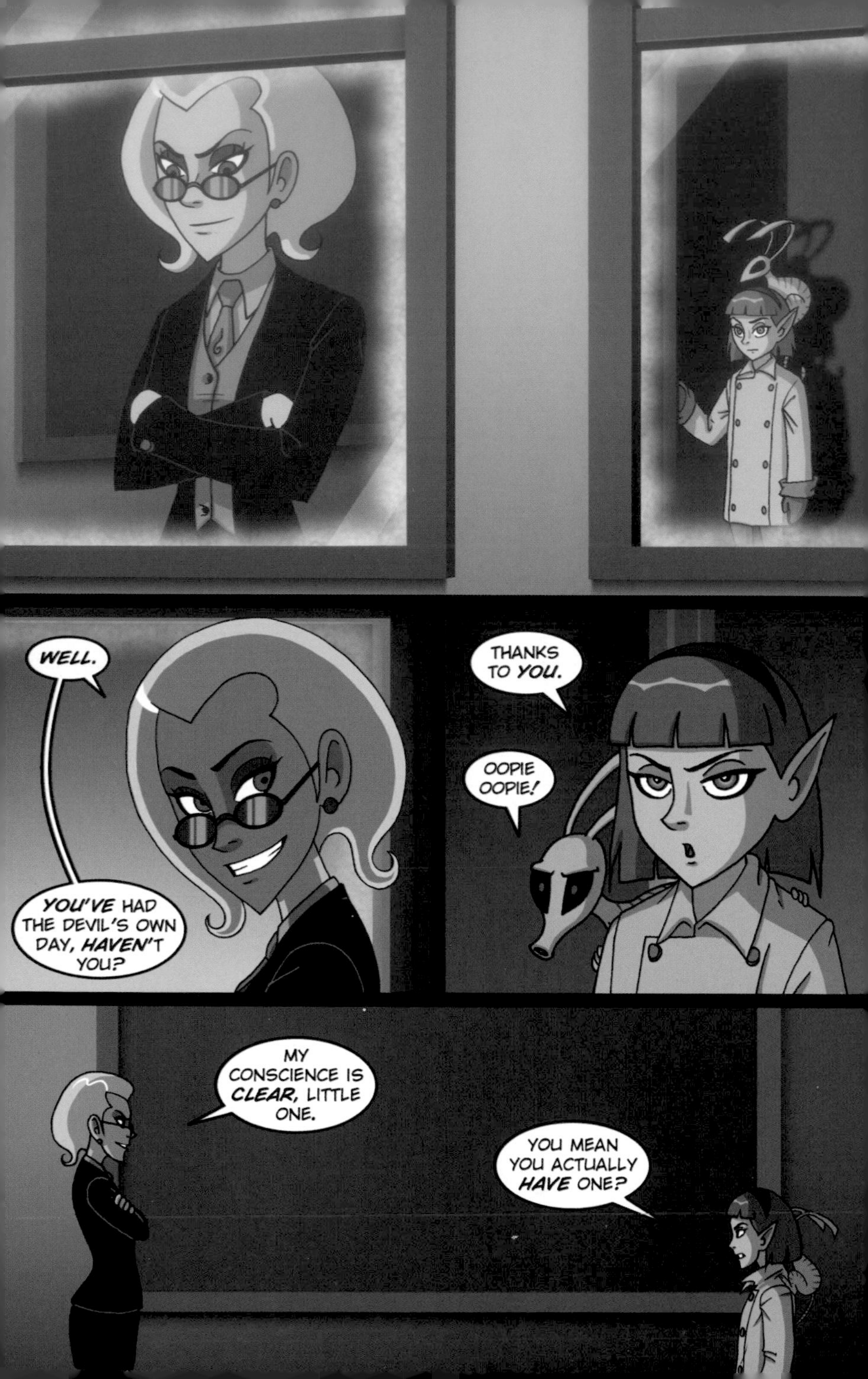
WELL.
YOU'VE HAD THE DEVIL'S OWN DAY, HAVEN'T YOU?
THANKS TO YOU.
OOPIE OOPIE!
MY CONSCIENCE IS CLEAR, LITTLE ONE.
YOU MEAN YOU ACTUALLY HAVE ONE?

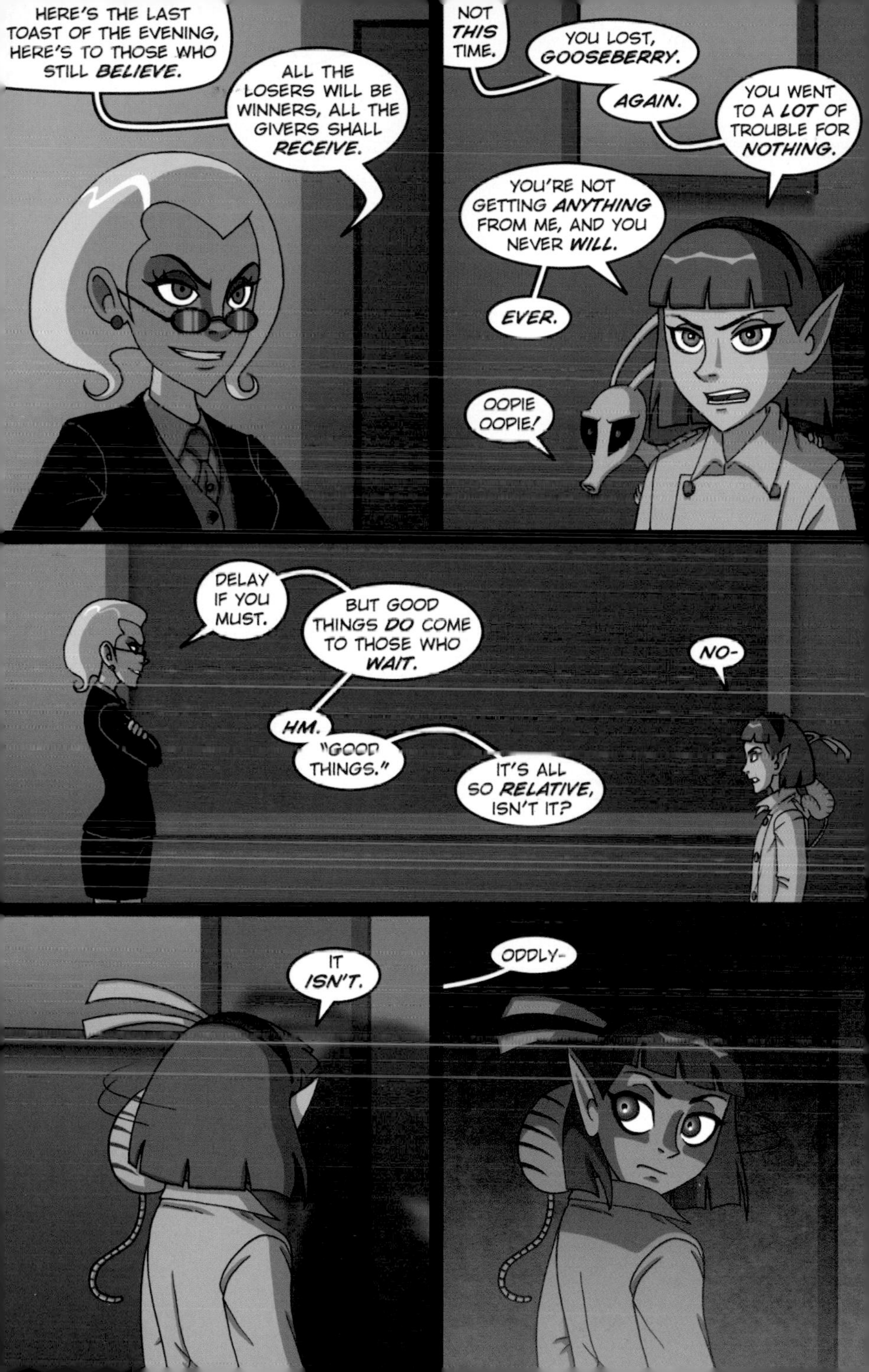
HERE'S THE LAST TOAST OF THE EVENING, HERE'S TO THOSE WHO STILL ***BELIEVE.***
ALL THE LOSERS WILL BE WINNERS, ALL THE GIVERS SHALL ***RECEIVE.***
NOT ***THIS*** TIME.
YOU LOST, ***GOOSEBERRY.***
AGAIN.
YOU WENT TO A ***LOT*** OF TROUBLE FOR ***NOTHING.***
YOU'RE NOT GETTING ***ANYTHING*** FROM ME, AND YOU NEVER ***WILL.***
EVER.
OOPIE OOPIE!
DELAY IF YOU MUST.
BUT GOOD THINGS ***DO*** COME TO THOSE WHO ***WAIT.***
NO-
HM.
"GOOD THINGS."
IT'S ALL SO ***RELATIVE,*** ISN'T IT?
IT ***ISN'T.***
ODDLY-

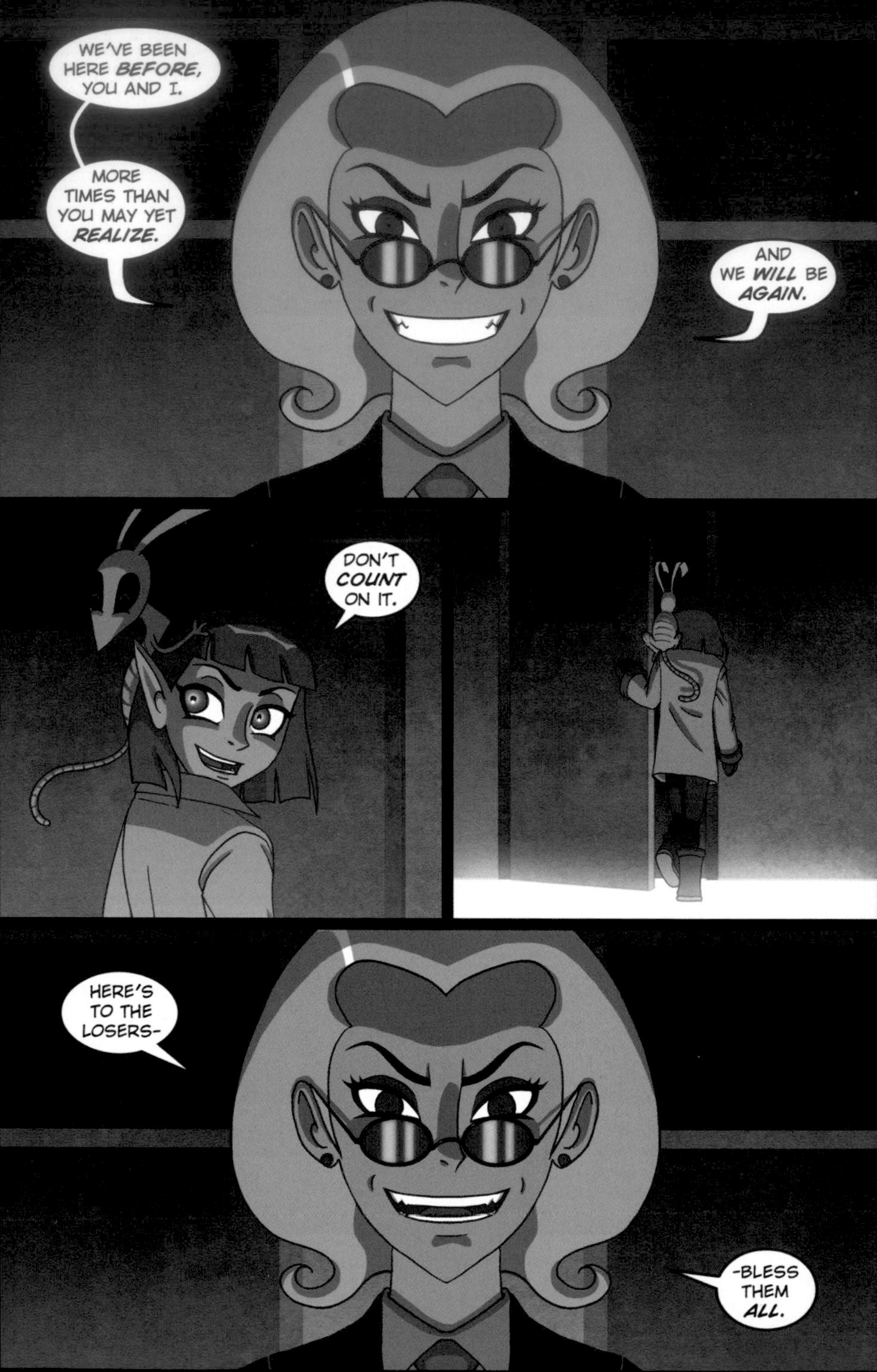
WE'VE BEEN HERE *BEFORE*, YOU AND I.
MORE TIMES THAN YOU MAY YET *REALIZE*.
AND WE *WILL* BE *AGAIN*.
DON'T *COUNT* ON IT.
HERE'S TO THE LOSERS-
-BLESS THEM *ALL*.

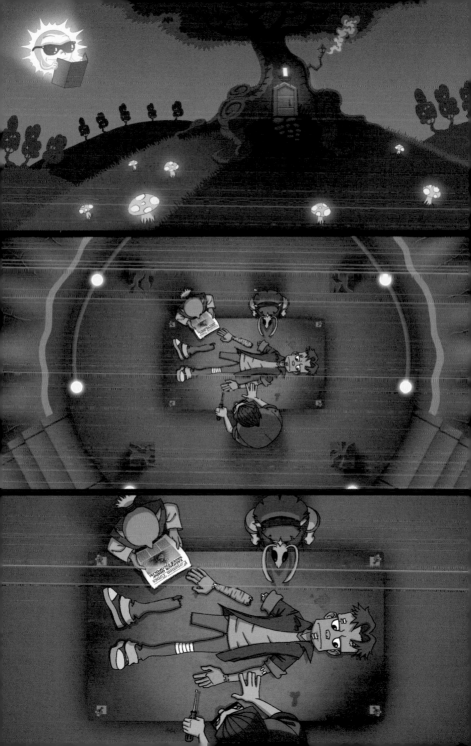

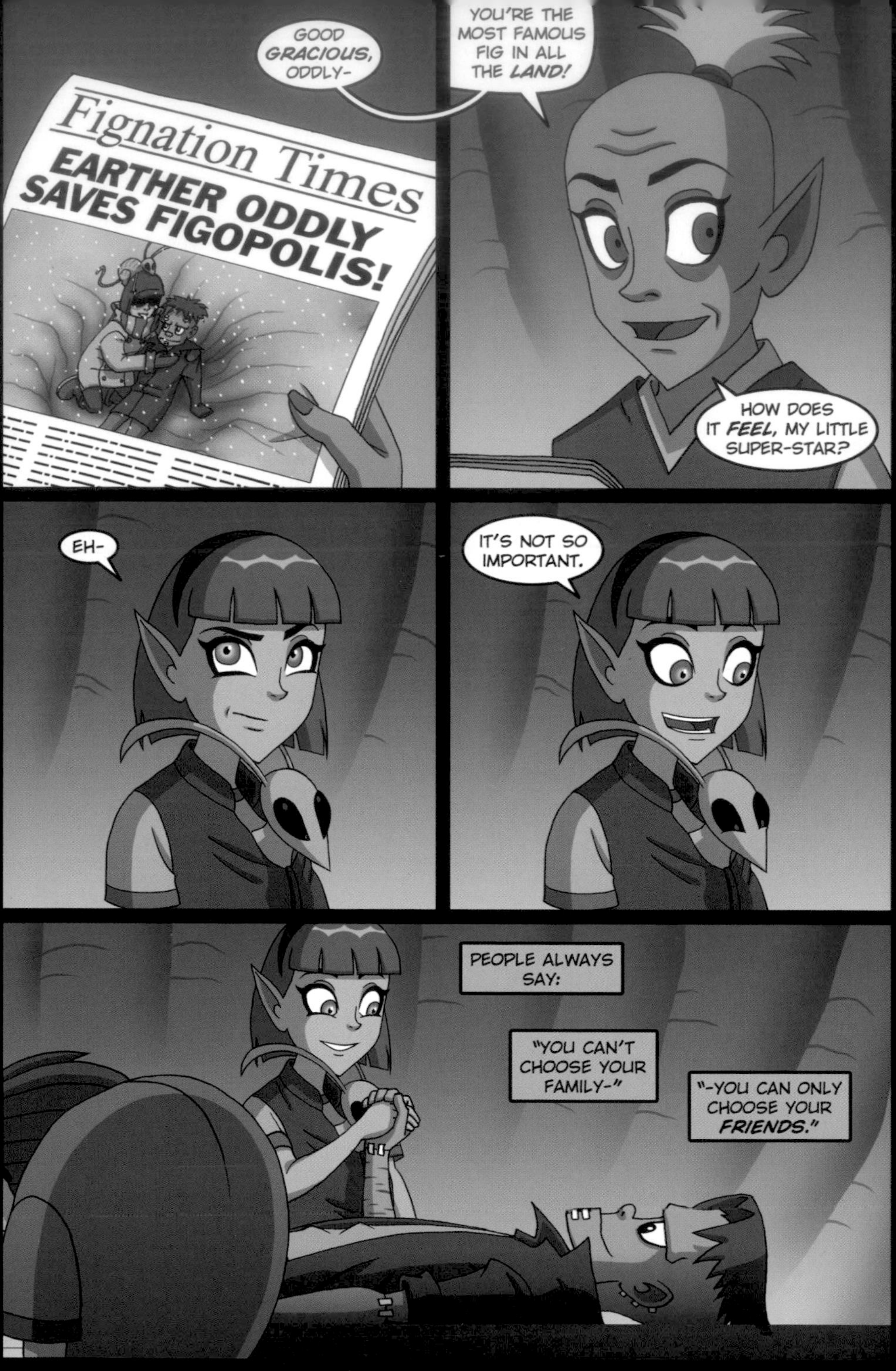
Fignation Times
EARTHER ODDLY SAVES FIGOPOLIS!
GOOD GRACIOUS, ODDLY-
YOU'RE THE MOST FAMOUS FIG IN ALL THE LAND!
HOW DOES IT FEEL, MY LITTLE SUPER-STAR?
EH-
IT'S NOT SO IMPORTANT.
PEOPLE ALWAYS SAY:
"YOU CAN'T CHOOSE YOUR FAMILY-"
"-YOU CAN ONLY CHOOSE YOUR FRIENDS."

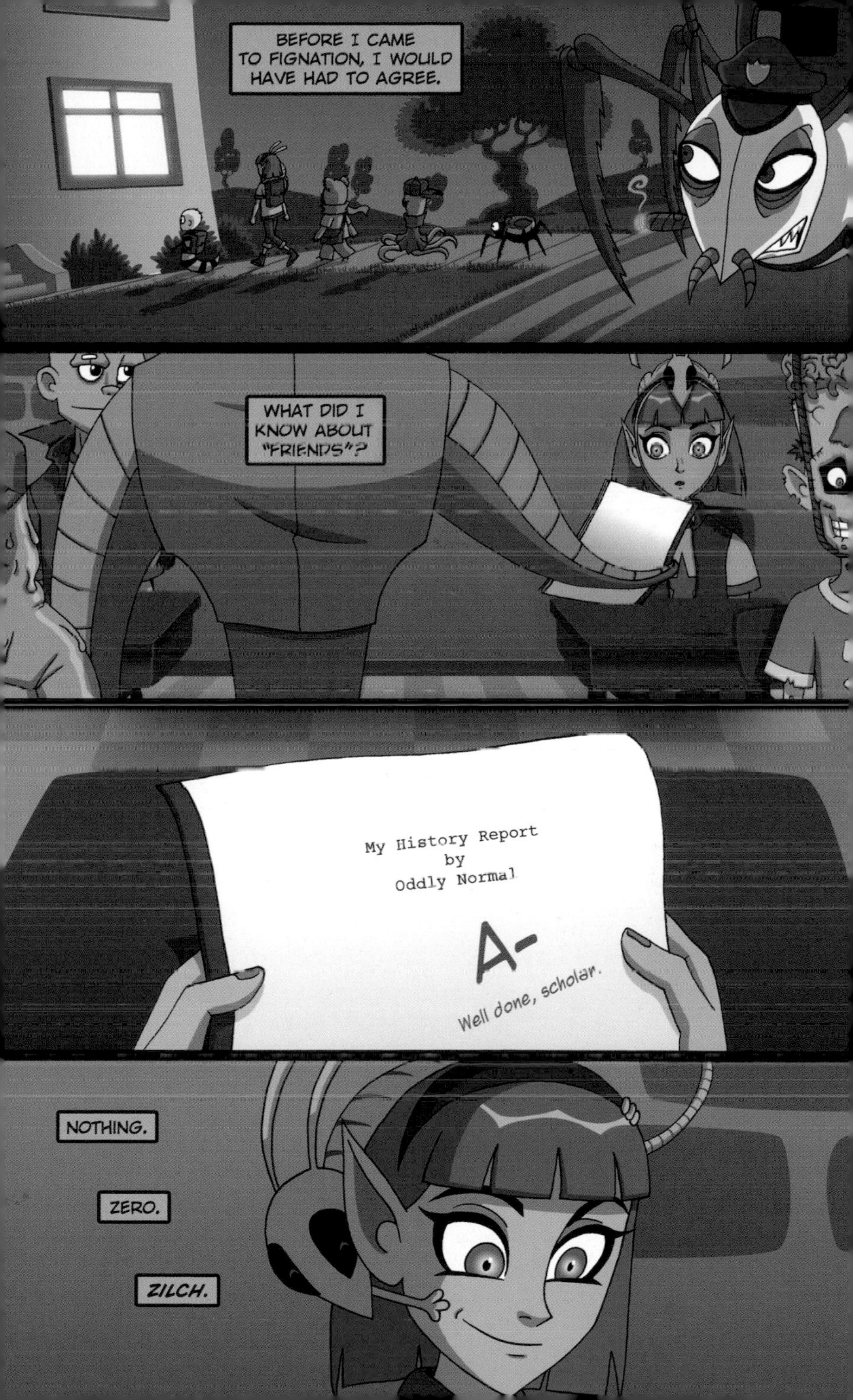
BEFORE I CAME TO FIGNATION, I WOULD HAVE HAD TO AGREE.
WHAT DID I KNOW ABOUT "FRIENDS"?
My History Report
by
Oddly Normal
A-
Well done, scholar.
NOTHING.
ZERO.
ZILCH.

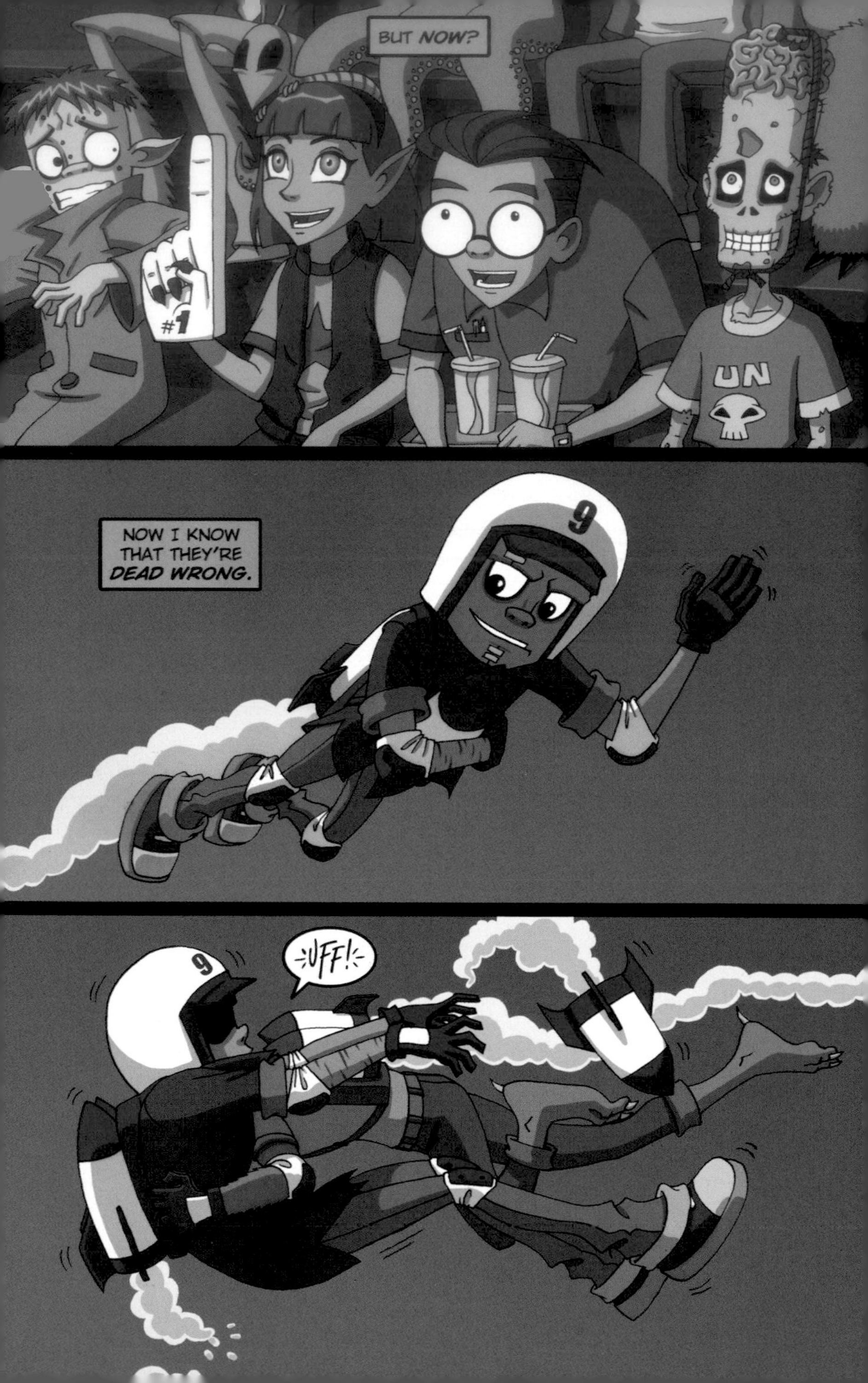
BUT NOW?
#1
UN
NOW I KNOW THAT THEY'RE DEAD WRONG.
9
9
UFF!

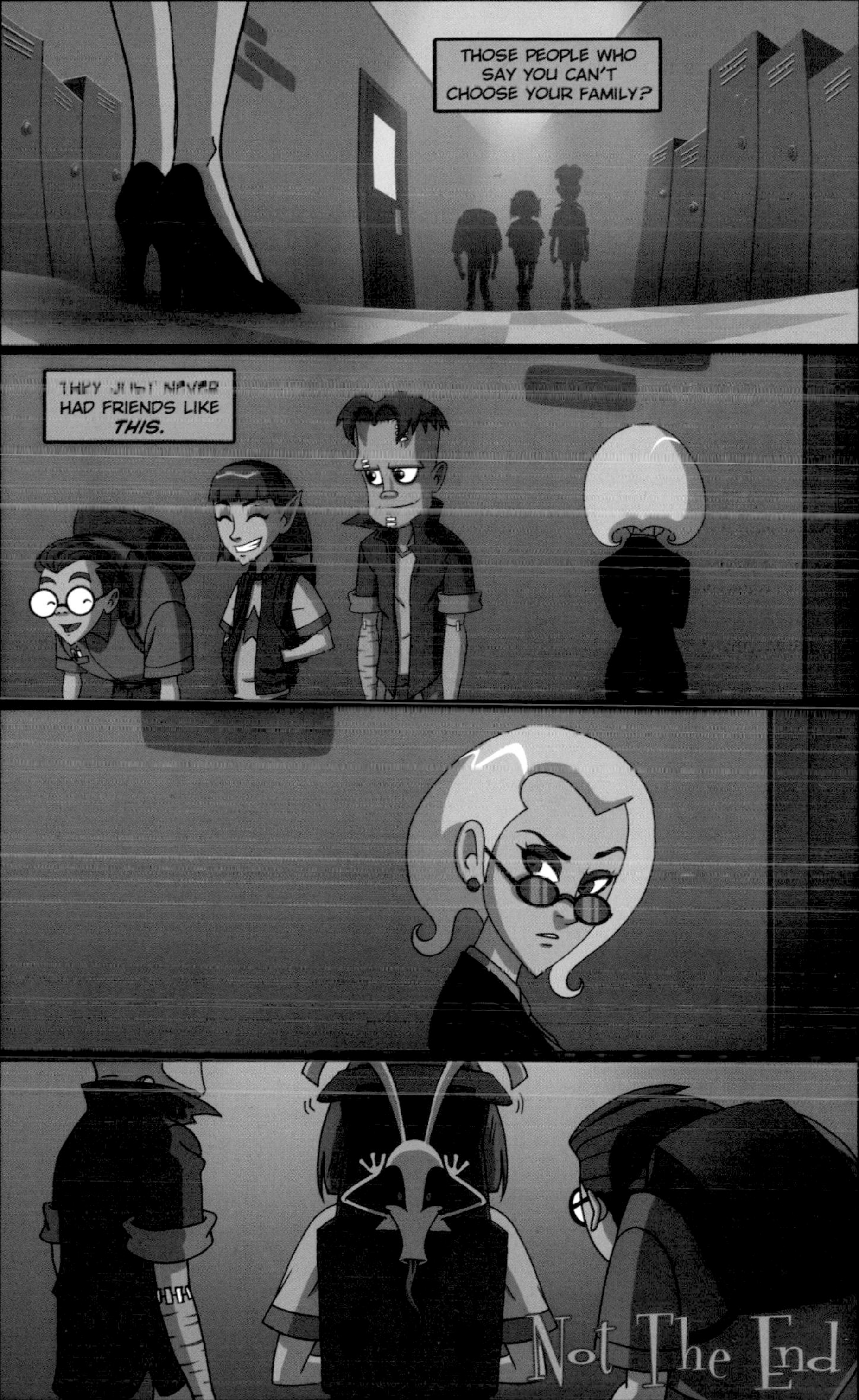
THOSE PEOPLE WHO SAY YOU CAN'T CHOOSE YOUR FAMILY?
THEY JUST NEVER HAD FRIENDS LIKE *THIS.*
Not The End

ACKNOWLEDGEMENTS

First and foremost, I want to thank the amazing artist who provided me with the pictures to match my words . . . Sergio Quijada. It was a pleasure and an honor to collaborate with Sergio on this book. Coloring his line work was a joy and I'm very proud of the work that we've done together.

I also owe a big "thank you" to my coloring assistant . . . my wife, Leigh. She denied me my desire to give her some kind of official credit for her work on the book, so I'm forced to mention her contribution here at the end. Leigh came to my rescue about halfway through production and helped out with color flats, which sped up the coloring process for me considerably. She called it "menial labor". I call it "invaluable assistance".

Thanks also go out to . . .

James Powell , Jessica Hickman, Katie Cook, Mike Sims & Jenny Seay for proofing this book, Crystal for her "babysitting" duties, the guys and gals of SAIC and the 480th for their support and for putting up with me, Sandy and Sam for their continued support for local creators and lastly to all of the amazing artists who contributed to the Oddly Gallery in the back of this book.

Thanks also to the readers. Once again, I hope those of you who have read this book have enjoyed it and have found something in the tale that resonates. And thanks for staying with Oddly and her friends for yet another story . . . there IS more to come. Watch for "Oddly Normal: Fignation Times" in 2008!

And as always, many thanks to Jim Resnowski and Jessie Garza for making this series of books a reality.

-Otis Frampton

First I would like to express my sincerest gratitude and thanks to Otis Frampton who gave me this great opportunity to draw a wonderful comic. And to Viper Comics, of course.

Also, I want to say thanks to everyone who gave me a hand when I needed it, especially my friends Rex Ricaldi and Guillermo Ahumada. Finally, thanks to my family for all of their support.

-Sergio Quijada

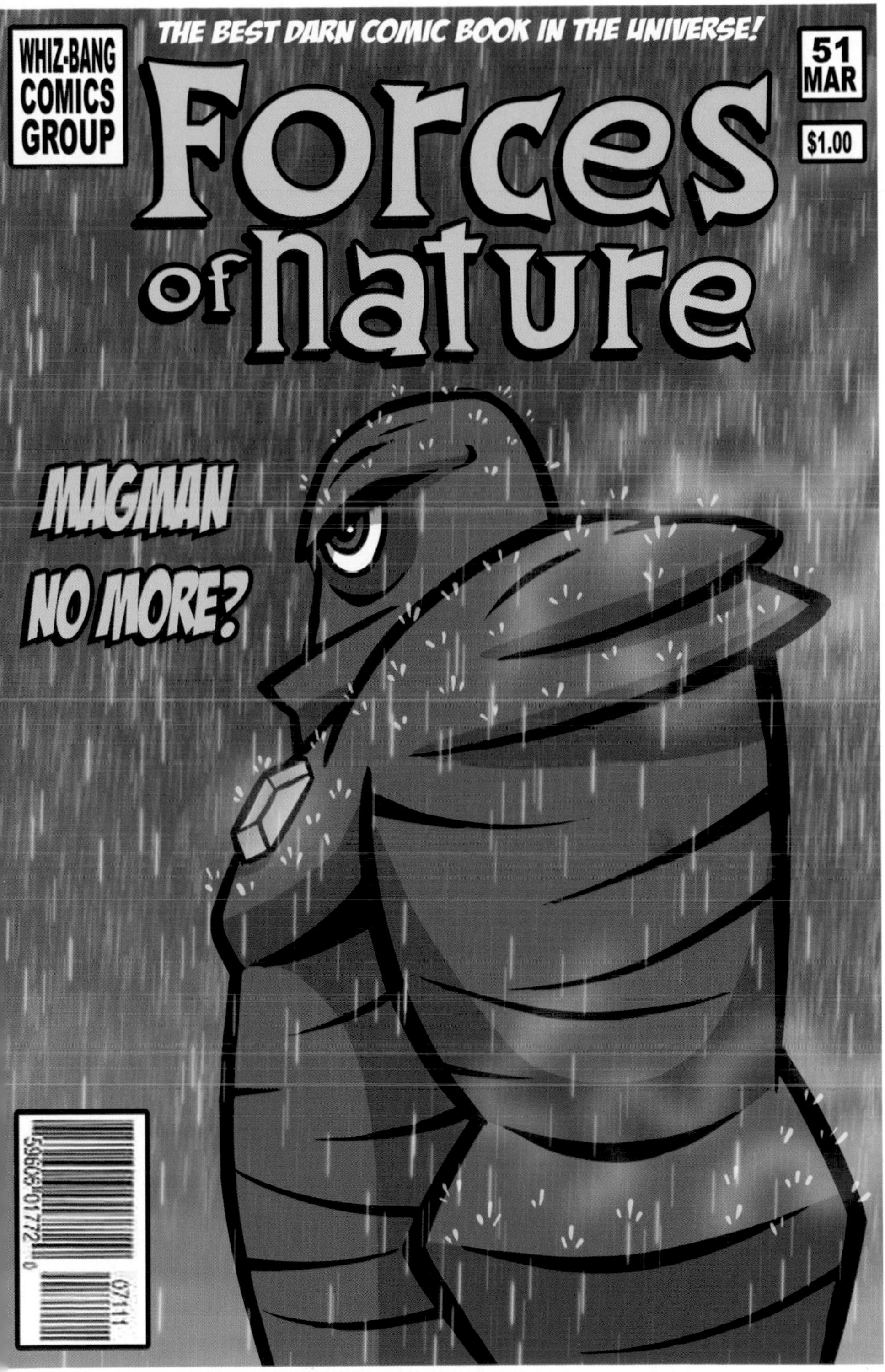
THE BEST DARN COMIC BOOK IN THE UNIVERSE!
WHIZ-BANG COMICS GROUP
51 MAR
$1.00
Forces of Nature
MAGMAN NO MORE?

Oddly ★ Gallery

Rex'07

CRISTIAN RICALDI

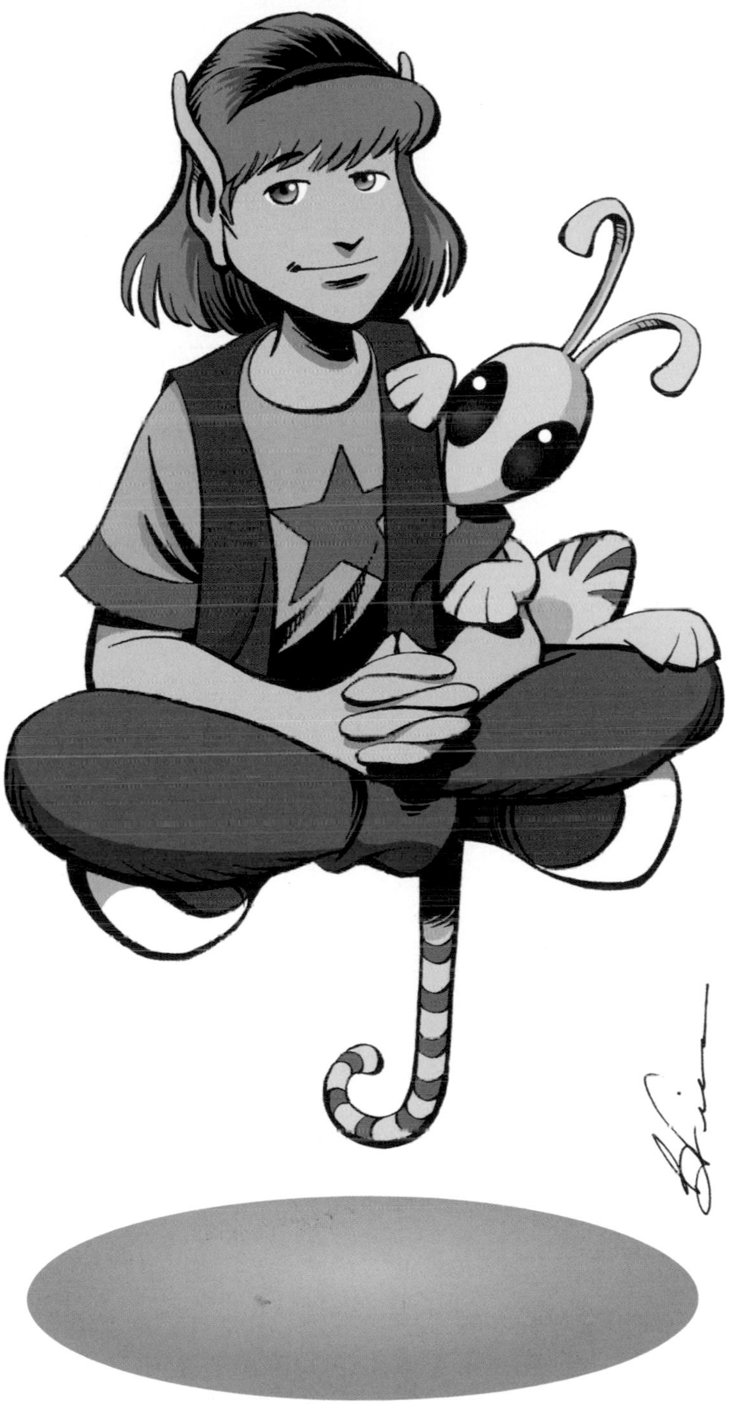

RIAN FIES

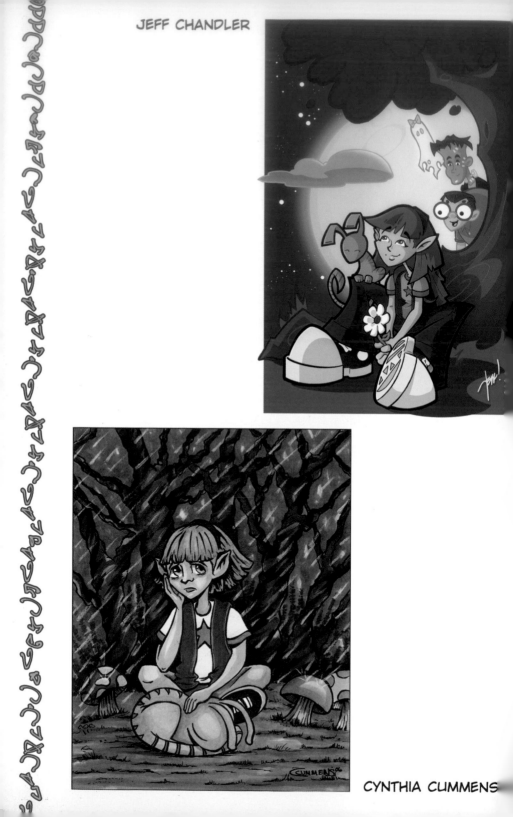

JEFF CHANDLER

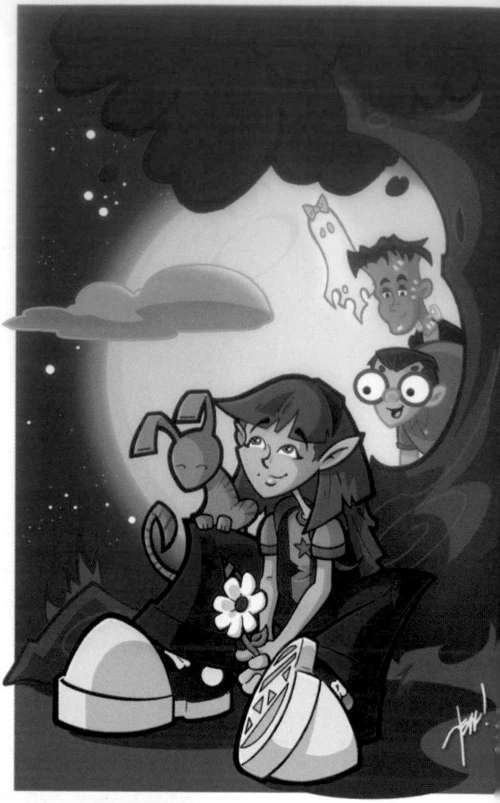

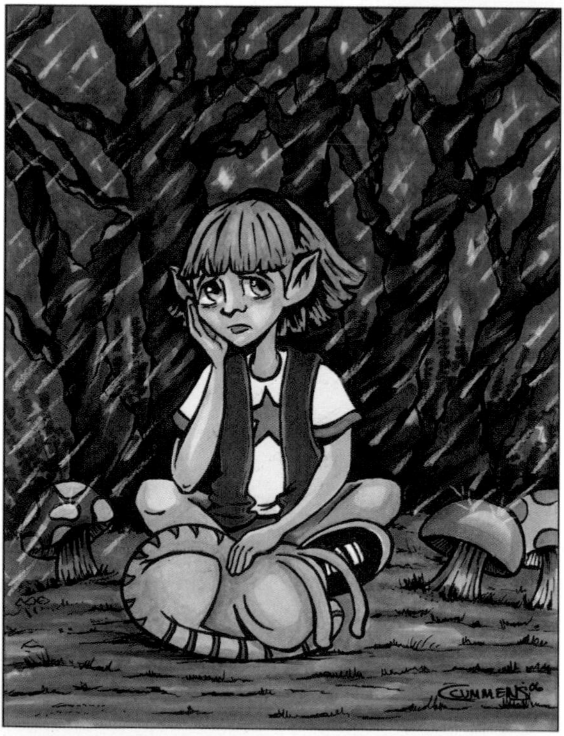

CYNTHIA CUMMENS

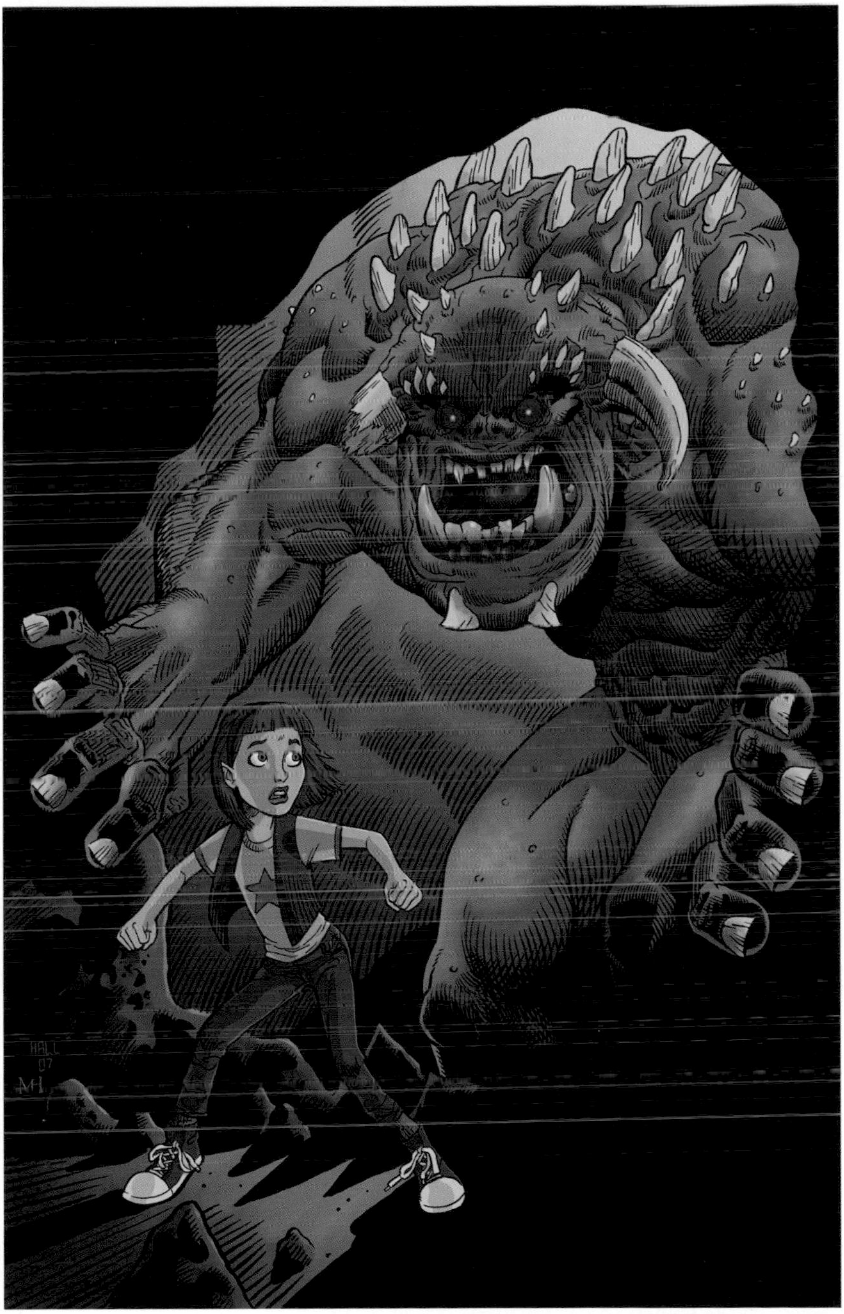

BENJAMIN & MARLENA HALL

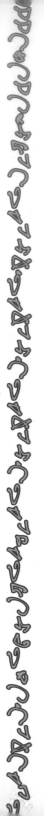

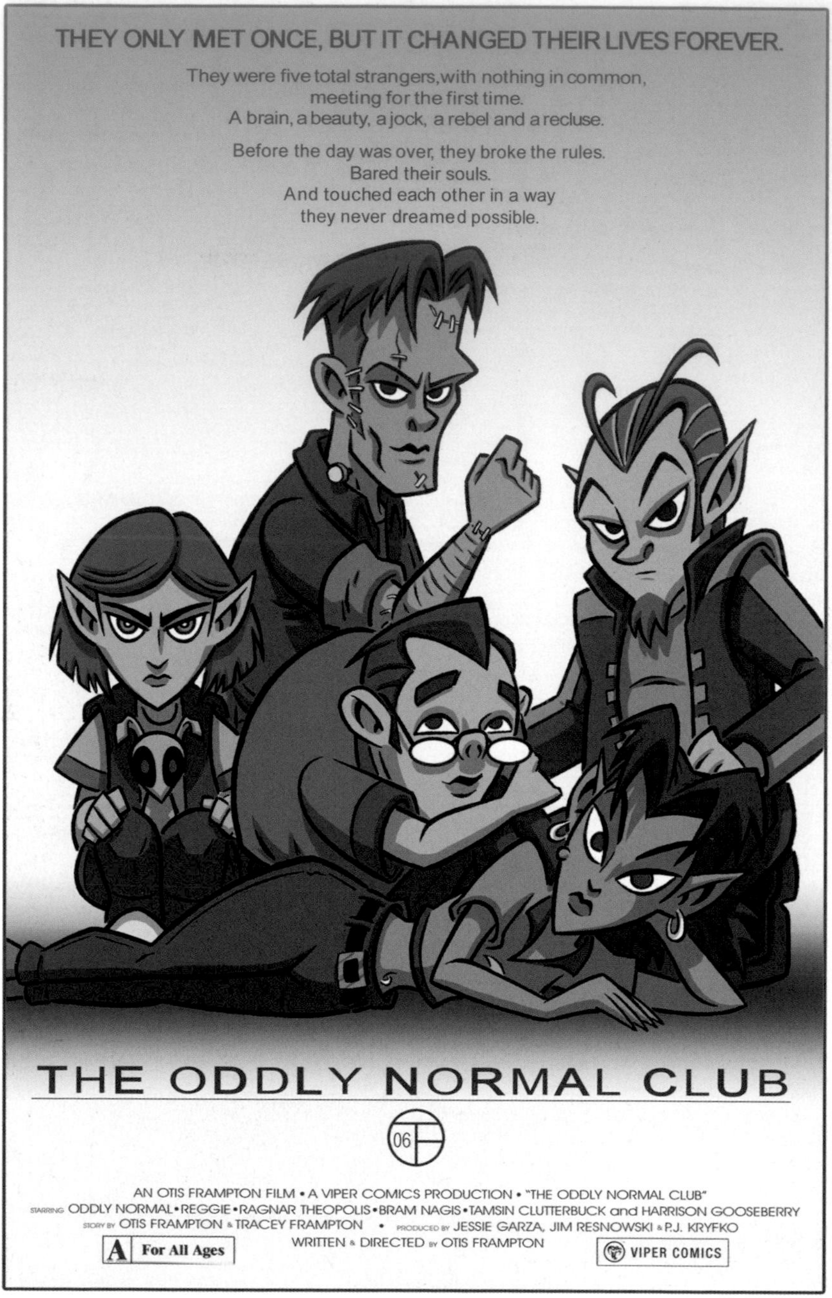
THEY ONLY MET ONCE, BUT IT CHANGED THEIR LIVES FOREVER.
They were five total strangers, with nothing in common, meeting for the first time. A brain, a beauty, a jock, a rebel and a recluse.
Before the day was over, they broke the rules. Bared their souls. And touched each other in a way they never dreamed possible.
THE ODDLY NORMAL CLUB
06
AN OTIS FRAMPTON FILM • A VIPER COMICS PRODUCTION • "THE ODDLY NORMAL CLUB"
STARRING ODDLY NORMAL • REGGIE • RAGNAR THEOPOLIS • BRAM NAGIS • TAMSIN CLUTTERBUCK and HARRISON GOOSEBERRY
STORY BY OTIS FRAMPTON & TRACEY FRAMPTON • PRODUCED BY JESSIE GARZA, JIM RESNOWSKI & P.J. KRYFKO
WRITTEN & DIRECTED BY OTIS FRAMPTON
A For All Ages
VIPER COMICS
OTIS FRAMPTON

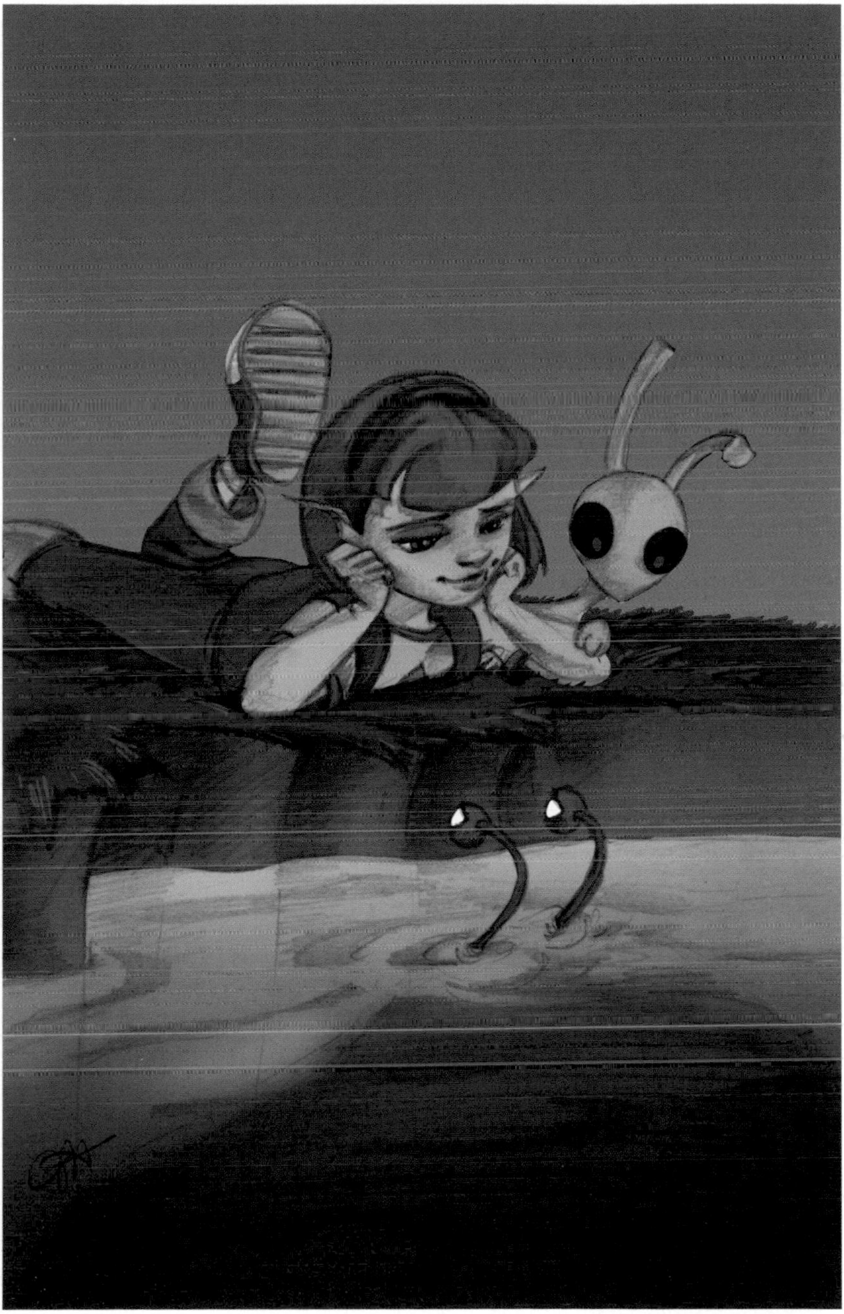

JESSICA HICKMAN

Otis Frampton is a writer and illustrator best known for creating the Viper Comics series "Oddly Normal." His illustration credits include work for such clients as Lucasfilm, Marvel Comics, Topps Trading Card Company, New Line Cinema and DC Comics. He is currently working on a new graphic novel as well as the next book in the "Oddly Normal" series.

Otis lives in Virginia with his wife Leigh and their two furry kids.

You can learn more about Otis and his work by visiting otisframpton.com!

Sergio Quijada is a graphic designer and illustrator living in Santiago, Chile. He studied at the University of Bío-Bío and has worked on such projects as "Diablo," "Humankind" and "Hero Hooks."

You can learn more about Sergio and his work by visiting sergioquijada.cl!